TREVOR HOWARD

A PERSONAL BIOGRAPHY

By the same author

Bogart

British Film Character Actors

Raising Hell

TREVOR HOWARD

A PERSONAL BIOGRAPHY

TERENCE PETTIGREW

PETER OWEN
London and Chester Springs

PETER OWEN PUBLISHERS
73 Kenway Road, London SW5 0RE

Peter Owen books are distributed in the USA by
Dufour Editions Inc., Chester Springs, PA 19425-0007

First published in Great Britain 2001

ISBN 0 7206 1124 5

A catalogue record for this book is available from
the British Library.

Printed and bound in Great Britain by
MPG Books Ltd, Bodmin, Cornwall

For Sheila
1943–1996

ACKNOWLEDGEMENTS

WHILE the writing of a book is essentially a solitary experience, in biographical writing the need for individuals to join you in the enterprise is overwhelming. Walkers attempting marathon distances value the company of helpers who join them, if only for a few miles. Writing a biography and doing a marathon walk have some obvious parallels. I, too, have had numerous helpers to join me, striding beside me for a few miles at a time, some a little further than others, whose reminiscences, friendship and encouragement have helped me reach the end of my journey without even thinking about my blisters.

To those who have been of help, whose names for whatever reason do not appear here, I thank them now, most profoundly. I am particularly indebted to Helen Howard, who, though now a lady of advanced years, found time to welcome me to her home in Arkley on many occasions, as, indeed, her late husband had done many years previously. Her warmth and readiness to answer my questions were much appreciated. Two other names stand out among those who have shared with me some parts of the journey. David Williams, who was a friend and personal driver and much, much more to Trevor during the last few years of the actor's life, allowed me to plunder his archives and provided invaluable help, hospitality and friendship. Sarah Bolt, formerly Sarah Miles, the star of *The Servant*, *Lady Caroline Lamb*, *Ryan's Daughter* and many other great films, lovingly described Trevor's humanity, humility and talent, all of which I vividly remember. For her continuing interest in this book, her friendship and true generosity of spirit I am most grateful.

Many, many thanks also to Tim Baker, Lord Attenborough, Leslie Bradbrook, Sheila Black, Peter Bloore, Robert Flemyng, Bryan Forbes, Jack Gold, Tom Gover, Dulcie Gray, Ernest Green, Sir John Gielgud, Dame Wendy Hiller, Sir Michael Hordern, Colin Ingleby-Mackenzie, Mike Johnson, Geoffrey Keen, Roger Knight, Euan Lloyd, John McCallum, Leo McKern, Michael Meyer, Robert Morley, Dilys Powell, Corin Redgrave, Sheila Reid, Paul Rogers, Philip Snow, Lieutenant-Colonel John Stephenson, Norman Travis, Reginald White and others too numerous mention. You know who you are. You have probably also guessed, correctly, that without your participation the finishing-line would still be a long way off.

Finally, I have a couple of apologies to make. To anyone who went to the trouble of giving me information, or personal memories, which I have not been able to include, I can only say that I wanted to use everything but, inevitably, space constraints had to be respected. It is a matter of record that Trevor encouraged me to write his biography in 1981 and gave his written permission to do so. In return, I promised him that I would. It has taken over twenty years to fulfil that promise. The delay has meant that several people who helped me in the beginning and who are thanked above have passed away since talking with me. I regret that most deeply and wish that they were here, as I wish that Trevor was here to see his words, along with theirs and mine, in print.

Terence Pettigrew
Digswell, Hertfordshire

CONTENTS

ILLUSTRATIONS

Between pages 156 and 157

1

IN THE LION'S DEN

Women went after him all the time. It got fairly bad. There was a time when he'd tell me that he was doing such-and-such a film and I would glance at the girls' names on the cast list and wonder which of them would be next.

– Helen Howard

My first meeting with Trevor Howard was one of those unplanned events that you kick yourself afterwards for not having planned. In 1979 I was notified by Associated Television's press office of a programme in production at Borehamwood which had among its stars Dennis Waterman and Trevor Howard. Waterman was a rising star of television, filling in time between finishing *The Sweeney* and the start of *Minder*, while for Howard it was an opportunity to work again after several months' inactivity.

Of the two stars, I chose Waterman, although it was unwise to try to conduct the interview in the studio canteen. Dennis kept vanishing into the hordes of studio workers at the bar, buying and bartering and slapping shoulders like a salesman down on his daily quota. Most of his conversation was tossed back over his shoulder as he ploughed through the thirsty hordes.

When an interview with another actor fell through at the last moment, I remembered that there was still a possibility of meeting Trevor Howard, who by that time had completed his assignment and retreated to his hideaway in the village of Arkley, near Barnet, north of London, to the considerable relief of the staff at ATV who had found him, to use their most diplomatic description, 'a bit of a handful'.

Would ATV like to arrange an interview, I inquired? No dice. If I wanted to talk to him, they would give me his ex-directory number, but that was all that they were prepared to do. Recent incidents on television made me wonder if it was wise to pursue him into his lair. As the mystery guest on *What's My Line?*, he had been so drunk that he called the quiz-master, Eamonn Andrews, a fool. It was the only time I ever saw the Andrews smile slide down his shirt front like a dollop of warm ice cream.

On Michael Parkinson's BBC show he shuffled into view pleasantly juiced, lost the thread of the conversation several times and was obviously at pains to coax his thoughts back into a straight line – not that they had been particularly straight when he arrived at the studio. Robert Mitchum, his house guest at the time, had made certain of that.

I phoned the great man one Saturday morning. The speed and spontaneity of his invitation to visit him at home took me by surprise. He made no attempt to check my credentials. I flattered myself that he already knew who I was, from my bylined articles in numerous papers and magazines. But that wasn't the case at all. He was simply being Trevor Howard. And in an age when stars tend to hide behind security fences, agents and neanderthal minders I found this openness and lack of pretension quite refreshing.

He simply said, 'Come on over, Monday morning around eleven. We'll talk then.' The informal invitation, the vigorous handshake that awaited me at his front door, the hand on my shoulder gently propelling me through the hallway and into the living-room and the speed with which a bottle of plonk was fetched from the kitchen – all these things added to my good feelings. I thought: This is no recluse surveying the world from a guarded mountain-top like Robert Redford or shooting at helicopters flying over his tropical island like Marlon Brando. This could be Ben Gunn rejoicing at the discovery of a fellow castaway after months of unwelcome isolation.

The large living-room was comfortably old-fashioned. Like its owners, you somehow knew that everything had been there a while. Everything around the house seemed larger than life. The wine glass that Howard jammed into my hand looked like a spherical street-lamp cut in half and welded on to a huge braided stem. When he started pouring, he did not stop until the bottle was equally divided between the two of us. 'It's French,' he explained, settling himself down. 'Rather good, if you like dry.'

Sometime in the middle of our rambling conversation – he wanted conversation, not an interview – I asked him if he had ever put pen to paper about himself. He reacted as if I had just sawn his leg off. 'For fuck's sake,' he snorted, 'I've never done that! Who gives a shit!'

'You could be wrong,' I told him. 'What about the personal experiences you've had. If you don't set the record straight people will come along years from now and make it up. Is that what you want – lies printed about you by people you've never heard of?'

He shook his head, and the crumbling superstructure of a face almost dropped into his lap. 'You'd only twist things like those other fuckers,' he grumbled.

He had every right to be suspicious of me. We had met only an hour before. But, then again, I wondered, maybe he was testing me. To see if I had any balls. I had the strangest feeling that the next couple of minutes would be decisive. If he took a liking to me, maybe – yes, maybe – he would listen to why I thought a biography would be a good idea. Not that I had any arguments prepared. It had only just occurred to me, but I suddenly felt that I wanted to do it, that here was a subject worth probing and picking at and that a biography of Trevor Howard could be good for both of us. But one thing was certain: he would never have anything to do with me after today if he believed that he could walk all over me.

I said to him, 'I've done a biography of Bogart. He had a life that was worth a book. How do I know that you have?'

He liked that reply. He liked people who spoke his language. A contented roar filled the room, and I found myself looking into the charcoal eyes of Lord Cardigan. He growled, 'I still think getting one of you pisspots to tell the truth is like asking a tart to give up the game.' But I sensed, from the near-joking way that he said it, that he was beginning to feel comfortable with me.

In the brief silence that followed I had an opportunity to study his face in detail for the first time. There was a deceptive stillness to it, I thought, like the surface calm of a lake, underneath which thousands of different life-forms busily devour, and are devoured, create and recreate, interlock and separate. It was the kind of stillness that exists before a bugle-call. Behind the dents and grooves lacerating that slightly pink, pebbledash face one could see the price ticket that went with living life to the full.

The image the public had of Trevor Howard, thanks to around fifty films, was that of a likeably gnarled, occasionally tarnished rebel whose handshake meant more than any legal document. The Howard character of popular perception was not the sleek motor-cruiser moored at St Tropez but an all-knowing, all-seeing old tugboat chugging along efficiently and without fuss, steered by an inner compass that was oblivious to everything but its own logic.

Howard's international popularity sprang from his ability to represent gritty opposition. During the 1940s and 1950s, at the height of the American movie incursion into Britain, at a time when, to boost their popularity within the burgeoning post-war European market, more and more American stars were persuaded to make films in Britain, Howard's name appeared on most producers' shopping-lists.

Back in his early screen career, around the time of *Brief Encounter* in the mid-1940s, he was never considered classically handsome, but he was clean-cut, sturdy, dependable. He wore tweed jackets in his films and often smoked a pipe. These were the props of middle-class reliability. A pipe indicated resonance of character, decency, tolerance, the kind of chap who would never kick a dog, jump a queue or avoid paying his fare. And many women at that time found a man smoking a pipe irresistible – they loved watching the rituals associated with it and the smell of the tobacco.

A pipe suited Howard. He would have been a superb Sherlock Holmes. Or Sexton Blake. Or, had the timing of the first James Bond movie been ten years earlier, a strong contender to play 007. There was nobody else in British films of the early 1950s who was better suited to be Bond. It would have been the casting coup of the decade. Howard had the class, and also the lived-in look, that made him absolutely right for the plush casinos, the sports cars and for those wonderful throwaway quips. When they compare Sean Connery to the later Bonds they always say that Connery was the best. But in the early days Connery's Bond lacked depth. Connery acquired it later, but when he started out as Bond he was a chancer, a fly-by-night, a kid from an Edinburgh slum putting on an act.

Howard was much closer to Ian Fleming's ideal Bond in both looks and manner. The face was by no means smooth. His skin had an appealing roughness that suggested he was a survivor, a man who been in rumbles and come out on top. He had been blooded. He knew the score. Sheila Black, who had known him as a child in Ceylon, told me that he had, as it were, a 'steel rod down his back'. That is what the Bond character needed on the screen and what Connery's portrayal lacked. That steel rod had been put there, according to Sheila, by Howard's upbringing, the colonial background, the rigid public school discipline. It was as if from early childhood he was being groomed not simply to play someone like Bond but to *be* him.

To give some idea of his versatility, Howard was formidable as a 'heavy', too. He had an unglamorous, square-jawed appeal and a physique that had been shaped on the sports fields at Clifton and at Stratford, certainly adequate for film acting and equally so for many of the great athletic roles in classical drama, had he been tempted in that direction. Sadly, he was not, with one glorious exception.

Like Spencer Tracy, the American film actor most often compared to him, Howard was infinitely more watchable and more subtle and more vulnerable and more real than many of his co-stars. Sometimes you can see him reining in so as not to steal their thunder. He dealt in truth. He was believable. When Howard was in a scene everything else fell naturally and reliably into place. To top it all, before the years and the booze caught up with him, he had enormous sex appeal.

Before the mid-1950s Howard had adored acting and applied himself to his craft with an enthusiasm that gave him no time for hobbies or domesticity. By the middle of the decade, however, around the time the studio system came to an end, something went out of the Howard performance. Laziness crept in; indiscipline, too. Mannerisms sometimes replaced the spontaneity. He became the Trevor Howard we remember, instead of the Trevor Howard who might have been.

After our first encounter Howard and I did not meet up again for several weeks – long enough for me to produce a rough outline of the biography I had in mind and for him to decide whether or not he wanted to become involved. I always hoped that he would, but it was not essential. One morning, out of the blue, he phoned me, sounding bright-eyed and bushy-tailed and eager to talk. He was a creature of impulse, I learned afterwards. Whenever he wanted something to happen, usually he wanted it right away. I stopped whatever I was doing and drove to Arkley.

He was in a buoyant mood. The script of *Staying On* lay on the settee and a trim moustache had appeared during the intervening weeks. Not only was he working again but the role was his juiciest for years, the overseas location was his beloved India, and the icing on the cake was the casting of Celia Johnson, his co-star in *Brief Encounter* thirty-five years before, as his wife. *Staying On* would be one of his last assignments of outstanding merit, although he was unaware of this in 1980, and, in retrospect, there could have been no better time to begin a biography.

Yes, he said, he had made up his mind, and he was happy for me to start on the biography. My outline had spurred him to 'look up a few things', and he pointed at some papers that he wanted to show me. Our collaboration began from that moment. To help loosen the tongues of people who knew him, he acknowledged in writing my role as his biographer and asked them to assist me in every way when I got around to making contact.

With his wife Helen Cherry away filming in the north of England, we had the day completely to ourselves, which was a tremendous bonus, because he was sober, alert, excited by his forthcoming trip to India and raring to go. The only interruption was a visit to his local pub, the Gate, for beer and sandwiches. By early evening we had covered an enormous amount of ground, and as I was about to climb into my car he put his hand on my shoulder in a gesture of spontaneous warmth and thanked me for reawakening some valued memories.

We met at his house many times over the next couple of months. Sometimes Helen was there, but usually she was working in television. She was always pleasant to me but never mentioned the biography, although she must have known it was the reason that I continued to come to the house.

Drink was, without a doubt, Howard's worst enemy, and despite Helen's determination to limit the damage it did to their relationship it frequently tested her iron will to the limit. More than once when I was at the house her attitude towards him seemed extremely cool. It seemed to me that by then they were living separate lives. No attempt was made by either of them to create a different impression. Helen had no shortage of friends, and she was frequently being phoned and invited out. By contrast, Howard appeared to have nobody really close to him. It seemed to me that she was away from Arkley as often as she was at home, dividing her time between stage work and meeting her friends. Unless he was filming, Howard rarely left the house except to visit the Gate. This role-reversal at the tail-end of their careers caused him a certain amount of pique, which, when he got drunk, he was incapable of concealing.

One afternoon he asked me to remind him when it was five o'clock because, he said, Helen was resting and wanted to be awoken in time to get ready for a night out. A car was due at six, he told me, to take her to *Nicholas Nickleby* at the Aldwych Theatre in London's West End. Shortly before five Helen appeared at the door, hands on hips, blood boiling.

'Trev,' she said furiously, 'You didn't wake me! The car'll be here any minute and I'm not ready. Honestly!' With that, she stormed into the kitchen. Nothing would have pleased her more, at that moment, than feeding parts of him into the blender. Howard called after her, in the voice of a husky angel, 'But, darling, I thought you said five.' But with Helen safely out of earshot the mask of innocence disappeared. 'Fuck Dickens,' he hissed under his breath. 'If she's late she'll miss fuck all!'

The couple never had any children, and observing their verbal skirmishes at close range one got the impression that when Helen married him she had, in one step, acquired a husband and a wayward child. The evidence suggests that when passion receded, or became either impossible or less of an occasion through Howard's non-stop drinking, Helen's maternal instincts, up till then denied a natural outlet, took over. And, in Helen, he had the perfect mother substitute. It would be guesswork to suggest that subconsciously he had married Helen to replace the mother he had scarcely known. Yet others who knew them well also noticed that as time went on Helen became the source of much-needed protection and reassurance and forgiveness, giving Howard a second stab at childhood, which proved much happier an experience than it had been the first time around.

It was no secret that around the house and garden Helen did the work and all the cooking, while Howard's half-hearted offers to help were never meant to be taken up. He was so useless that she felt safer with him in the local pub.

Eighteen years after I first met Helen I wrote telling her that I had reactivated the biography and wanted to see her. She remembered my earlier visits and agreed without hesitation. It was a strange feeling, parking my car in the driveway again after all that time and seeing again the porch on which Howard had put up a sign 'No children, pets or actors'. Helen, by then in her mid-eighties, was in a wheelchair following a stroke, but she was in excellent form and her memory was clearer than Howard's had been on the last few occasions that we had met.

She smiled when I reminded her how helpless he had been. 'He couldn't do anything,' she said. 'He didn't even know how many light switches we had. He said to me once, "Where's the light switch on the upstairs landing?" I said, "Where it's always been!" Quite early in our marriage, I went to Switzerland with Michael Denison and Dulcie Gray for a short skiing holiday. I came back to find the lights off and no water. Naturally I wondered where he was. The phone rang. It was a friend of ours with whom he'd been staying. Trevor came to the phone, and I asked him why he wasn't at home to meet me, which we had arranged. Trevor said, "The water froze in the bathroom. I couldn't have a bath." When something around the house didn't work he hadn't a clue what to do.'

I knew exactly what she meant. On one occasion at the house, Howard had been in good reminiscing form and, not wishing to interrupt his flow of thought, I allowed our conversation to overshoot lunchtime. At a suitable break I suggested that, instead of going to his local, the slowest pub in Britain, we might raid his larder, and I would make a sandwich from whatever was in there that was edible. 'Don't know if there's anything,' he said. 'I haven't opened that door for fucking weeks!' I took a chance and peeped into his fridge. When I returned to the lounge my car keys were already in my hand.

Another time Helen came back after visiting a friend, expecting Howard to be at home because he had promised that he would be, and for that reason she left her front-door key inside the house. However, when she arrived home there was no sign of him, the house was locked, and she could not get in. As she was about to call in help she noticed his door keys alongside a bush near the front door. She let herself in, sat down with a coffee and waited for the inevitable phone call. Howard, she was told in due course, was in hospital. Her alarm turned to amusement when she found out why. He had, apparently, nipped along to the Gate to have a few drinks, still planning to be at home when she arrived. He downed a few, then a few more, and by the time he reached the house – where, to his credit, he managed to arrive before she did – he was tottering like a duck on water-skis.

The hand-and-eye coordination needed to insert the key into the key-slot was, at that point, beyond him. After several attempts to enter his house he stood back from the door, hurled the keys at it, roared 'Fuck it!' as only he could and headed back to the pub to raise help. That, at least, had been the intention. But on the way back he tripped over something – his own feet probably – and crashed down on to the pavement. Someone called an ambulance, which whisked him off to the accident unit at Barnet General Hospital.

Howard's constant infidelity was something with which Helen had had to come to terms soon after their marriage. She told me, 'To begin with, yes, I was very jealous. What wife wouldn't be? But there comes a point where you either accept it or you get out. I'm not excusing it, but we are all at times attracted to other people. I was, too. The difference between myself and Trevor was that I could suppress it better than he could.

'You know how much he liked to be seen as a bad boy. He didn't mind at all being described as a hell-raiser. He wasn't one, but if others thought so he was quite pleased. Women went after him all the time. It got fairly bad. There was a time when he'd tell me that he was doing such-and-such a film, and I would glance at the girls' names on the cast list and wonder which of them would be next. I'm not making excuses for him. I'm not saying that he wasn't a womanizer, because he was, but he was also rather shy, and he would rarely make the first move. Once he got the come-on, it's true, he would respond.'

A journalist once asked Helen if she had ever seriously thought of leaving him. She replied, 'No, never. Whatever he got up to I always knew he would come home to me.' Helen told me, 'I got over being jealous. I knew that he loved me and nobody else. We also liked each other as well as loved each other. Trevor and I felt comfortable together, and that, really, was what mattered. That's the reason we stayed together for forty-three years.'

It seems to have made no difference to Helen whether he slept with other women, crashed his car while over the limit or got sued for non-payment of income tax; she was always there for him. She swallowed her pride, made excuses and came out fighting on his behalf whenever needed. To be the perfect wife for Howard, which she indisputably was, Helen seems to have put her own film career on the back burner.

Although she denies doing it, the arrangement made good economic sense. Helen was never likely to be as big a star as her husband. She was the opposite side of the coin to Vivien Leigh, whose earthy allure and blind ambition kept Laurence Olivier dangling on a string for years. Helen's classy looks belonged on a Gainsborough easel, not fuelling male fantasies. Her kind of sophistication and elegance had its place in the theatre, particularly during the 1930s, but the war had made elegance unfashionable, with even the likes of Noel Coward and Ivor Novello having to concede ground to a generation of socially conscious writers.

Howard's first film role after they married, as the true-blue romantic in *Brief Encounter*, made him a household name in 1945. His film stardom might have been a difficult pill to swallow had Helen not already decided that her career had its own path to follow, regardless of where his took him. She was also thrilled at becoming Mrs Trevor

Howard. She said that neither decision had ever cost her a moment's regret.

They were, undoubtedly, very different people. Perhaps that was why they attracted one another so strongly. Surrounded by the trappings of fame, Howard maintained a decidedly untidy attitude towards it. He saw himself primarily as a 'jobbing actor'. Film director Jack Gold confirmed this when he told me, 'Trevor was extraordinarily modest. Never thought of himself as special. He was always surprised when people treated him like a star.' Helen possessed both the desire and temperament for stardom but lacked the raw talent to rescue her from the groove in which her stunning good looks had trapped her.

Consequently, at the height of his fame, Helen behaved more like an international star than he did, in cultivating a certain distance from members of the public. Howard enjoyed a good rapport with people. He was a naturally courteous man and gave his time readily to people who approached him politely. For instance, when he found someone who enjoyed cricket, he would chat and joke with them, or grumble about the England XI, as if they had known each other all their lives.

Being on the receiving end of the public's attentions was something he was both flattered by and responded warmly to. Being good with people came naturally to him. He didn't have to work at it. Helen's interaction with the public was not nearly as smooth. She was never fully at ease with people she didn't know. Shyness had something to do with it, and because she disliked being an object of curiosity she was occasionally – and quite wrongly – accused of being aloof.

There was no shortage of stories about her so-called 'coolness' towards strangers. Geoffrey Keen told me that while filming *His Excellency* on location in Sicily in 1952 she always dined alone in the unit restaurant. Everybody respected this preference, except for one member of the company who had not heard about it. Seeing her at a table alone, looking, he thought, rather melancholy, he decided to cheer her up. 'Do you mind if I join you?' he asked. According to Geoffrey Keen, Helen looked him unwaveringly and replied, 'I'd rather you didn't!'

One got the impression talking to them that Helen would have been willing to work in films with Howard. Dozens of famous couples worked regularly together – the Lunts, the Hulberts, the Oliviers, Bogart and Bacall, Burton and Taylor. I asked Howard one day why he hardly ever worked with his wife. Why did he draw such a clear distinction between work and domesticity? Was the real reason that her presence on the set would curtail his fun? 'I didn't want us to be like Errol Flynn and Alan Hale,' he said, leaving open the question as to with which of them he was comparing Helen.

Howard came from the generation of actors who believed in speaking well of each other. It was the rule of the club. Even when he disapproved of someone's behaviour he would never criticize them. He had a rather individual way of expressing dislike for real or imagined enemies or injustices of the past. He simply forget who they were or what they were supposed to have done. And when he had made up his mind on this he would not be moved. I had read somewhere that there had been friction on the set of *Twinky* in 1969 between himself and Charles Bronson. When I mentioned Bronson's name Howard surprised me by asking, 'Who's he?' I explained that they had made a film together.

'Really?' he said, raising an eyebrow. 'Wasn't he that Mr Universe chap?'

I said, 'No, Trevor. That was Charles *Atlas*!'

I should have guessed that he was sucking me into his little game. But this was early days, and I hadn't yet learned to read the signals. So I babbled on about Bronson coming to London to make the film and how, for an oldie, he had become popular with young audiences of the 1960s for his uncompromising 'up yours' attitude, which, I pointed out, had made an even greater icon in the 1960s of Steve McQueen. Howard let me carry on, appearing to listen while he stroked his chin or sipped his booze. At the end, he asked, 'What was the film called?'

'*Twinky*, and Richard Donner directed it.'

A momentary gleam of recognition entered his face, and then it was gone. He said, 'Donner? Ah, yes. That rings a bell!'

It ought to have. Donner had also directed Howard in *Superman – The Movie* (1978). I realized then how cleverly I had been had.

By contrast, Howard hugely enjoyed telling stories against himself. In a famous incident, during the filming of *Richard III* in 1955, Laurence Olivier, doubling as the despot king and the film's director, was struck in the leg by a rogue arrow during the Bosworth battle scenes. The crew and extras were amazed to see Olivier, although clearly in pain, continue to play the scene impeccably until the take was safely in the can. Only then did he call for the unit doctor.

I asked Howard how he would have reacted in that situation. 'I'd be off that horse and on to my lawyer and fuck the film,' he snorted. He wouldn't, of course. That was just his way of debunking the idea that he was conscientious.

Howard was always a bit of an outsider. Robert Flemyng told me, 'I remember Trevor being slightly remote from the others in the cast of *French Without Tears* [1936–7]. Actors weren't his sort of people. He remained on the periphery, but I'm sure it was from choice.' In contrast to stars like David Niven, whose honorary membership of Bogart's Rat Pack meant as much to him as a good review, Howard never sought the company of the rich and famous. Fame, to him, was something that went with the job, and he was acutely suspicious of anyone who flaunted their success. Consequently, unless promoting a film or attending festivals, he avoided wherever possible the razzmatazz of show business, preferring pubs off the beaten track to West End restaurants and choosing his friends from outside his profession.

He certainly wasn't a prima donna. Seasoned actors like Howard and Flemyng understood that time means nothing to a conscientious director and accepted it. They devised their own schemes to counter the boredom between takes. Filming the beach scenes in *Ryan's Daughter* in 1971, director David Lean kept the actors and crew waiting around for weeks until the cloud formations created precisely the mood he wanted. Television moves at a different tempo. With inflexible budgets, usually pared to the bone, TV directors are under enormous pressure to complete their work as quickly as possible.

While Howard was making *Words on War* at ATV Studios in Borehamwood in 1980, he was waiting to be called for a scene when the director called 'Time' and the technicians immediately moved forward to dismantle the set. The reason was explained to him later. They had to be quit because the Muppets were due to use the same studio at six o'clock. *Words on War* was a modest one-off production, inconsequential compared with the money and the global prestige earned for the studio by Jim Henson's colourful hand-puppets. Howard was still smarting from the experience when we talked about it several weeks later. 'It's come to something', he groaned, 'when I'm upstaged by fucking *gloves*!'

2
THE LONG PASSAGE HOME

I had a dreadful time every summer,
absolutely hated it. I'd be sent off to some ghastly landlady.
That meant months of misery. – Trevor Howard

THROUGHOUT the earlier part of his life Trevor Howard felt unwanted. Being loved and cared for are things all children need to feel, but in Howard's case parental love was expressed through letters or not at all. He suffered from 'absent parents'. In Edwardian times it was acceptable, indeed fashionable, for parents living abroad to send their children thousands of miles to give them a good education at home or for the good of their health. They also expected the children to recognize that it was all done for their own good. Not many of the children shared this view.

For the young Trevor, the years between ten and twenty were profoundly difficult and unhappy. It was a period of almost unbroken separation from his parents, who lived in Ceylon while he attended school in England. The impact of this on the morale and self-esteem of a small, lonely child is much better understood today. Anyway, by the time he reached school-leaving age a considerable amount of damage had been done.

Adolescence for Trevor meant being looked after by a procession of strangers doing it strictly for the money. Love never entered the equation, and he hardly ever received displays of affection – hugs, kisses or an arm around the shoulder. Many children in similar circumstances had a worse time than Howard. Some suffered physically at the hands of so-called guardians. Neglect and beatings were commonplace. Anything could be tolerated, it seemed, in the name of discipline. No account was taken of the fact that these children were, for the most part, acutely distressed at being separated from their families and dumped in far-off places of which they had no knowledge, with people who often frightened them or treated them shabbily.

Most of them arrived in Britain with no idea who would be meeting them. It was an unnerving and humiliating experience, comparable to the distress felt by some of the child evacuees of the Second World War, who at least mostly had one or both parents in Britain. For Trevor, the trauma of those early years would have an enormous impact on many of his adult relationships.

The second decade of his life yielded him such little happiness that he found every excuse under the sun to avoid talking about it. I quickly learned that he had only a few memories of those times for which he had any affection. For the most part, they brought him no happiness at all, and he felt uncomfortable talking about them. I therefore did not press him too much for details of his childhood. What I have been able to glean about that period has mainly come from other sources.

He was born Trevor Wallace Howard-Smith in Cliftonville in Kent in 1913. Later he chopped three years off his age and pretended that he was born in 1916 – the year quoted by most reference sources – but school and other records disprove this. It was the first of many attempted deceptions, most of them trivial, but with one exception that almost landed him in prison.

His father, Arthur Howard-Smith, worked for Lloyds of London as an underwriter, and most of his working life was spent overseas. Not much is known about him, other than he was one of seven children and his hobby was collecting stamps. From photographs he appears to have roughly the same sort of physique as his only son. Trevor's mother, whose maiden name was Mabel Wallace, came from an even larger family in Canada – she was the youngest of ten children – whose ancestors were Scottish; among them, it is claimed, the thirteenth-century rebel clansman William Wallace. The English thought so little of Wallace that they cut off his head and shoved it on a pole for everyone to mock.

In the early years of the twentieth century opportunities for career advancement were relatively limited in Ontario, where the Wallace family lived, compared with the neighbouring United States, which welcomed young Canadians without restriction. Several of Mabel's elder brothers and sisters had vanished through this open door, so that when Mabel decided to become a nurse it was taken for granted that she would follow the others into the United States.

The fashion for rich Americans to travel overseas with a private nurse in attendance suited Mabel's ambitions perfectly. As soon as she qualified, she was eager to see the world and quickly got her wish. Mabel's travels eventually took her to Ceylon, where she met Arthur

Howard-Smith. The exact details of how they got to know each other are not known. Trevor had a vague recollection of his mother saying something about first meeting his father on board a ship, but Trevor's younger sister Merla believed it happened in Colombo, Ceylon. They got married in England and lived for a short period in Kent, where Trevor was born, but after so many years overseas Arthur found it impossible to adjust to the English way of life, especially the climate. He yearned for the job satisfaction and independence of running his own office, and when the opportunity arose to return to his old haunts in Colombo he seized it with both hands.

Not long after the family settled down in Colombo Merla was born. This not only completed the family circle but gave the children the longest uninterrupted period that they would have with their parents.

Colombo has been for more that twelve hundred years a bustling maritime capital. Today the city has about a million inhabitants, considerably more than during the 1920s. As early as the eighth century Arab traders established themselves there, trading in cinnamon, camphor, sapphires and livestock, including elephants. The city has an exceptionally long promenade, and Sheila Black told me that, in the 1920s what caught the eye, apart from the two rather grandiose hotels bookending the promenade, was a row of cannons facing out to sea, with their cannonballs stacked neatly alongside.

Those cannons provided a reminder of the centuries-long tug-of-war between powerful colonialist nations seeking to annexe Ceylon. In its turn the island had been overrun by the Portuguese, the Dutch and the British, who drove the Dutch away in 1796 and who retained sovereignty over Ceylon until granting its independence in 1948. For expatriate English business people, life in Colombo was not dissimilar to that of other middle-class colonials, which was a curious cocktail of refinement and boredom. In a typical household adults and children lived essentially separate lives. Children were taken to and from school by ayahs, or nannies, who also bathed and dressed them and who slept on cushions outside their bedrooms.

In many cases the devotion of these ayahs for the children in their care was extraordinary. And it was returned in full measure. Children often loved their ayahs more than their parents, because they were always with them, and they yearned for them deeply when the inevitable separations took place. Children knew that when they reached the age of ten or eleven they would be sent to English boarding-schools, but nothing prepared them for losing the love and closeness of their ayahs.

Socially, the affluent white residents of Ceylon kept mostly to themselves. Parties were frequent and lavish and everyone dressed formally. Children's parties were a regular feature, too, with up to thirty or forty children attending each one. For special occasions, such as a birthday, the nearby racecourse or the Hill Club, a popular golf venue, could be hired when otherwise not in use. Chips and cakes would be served with fizzy drinks, and then everyone would play games, such as musical chairs, tag and hide the cushion.

Although Trevor regarded all young girls as 'wet', he developed a soft spot for Sheila Black, the daughter of a company director living in the Colombo suburb of Mount Lavinia. They met at various parties, and Sheila recalled that he was 'a bit of a show-off'. He liked to issue challenges where the odds were in his favour and, when he won, he would jeer and point his finger in triumph. When he lost, he would sulk or call the winner rude names or insist on trying again.

One skill that Trevor developed into a fine art was 'high pissing'. He would challenge other boys to see which of them could urinate the highest up a wall or which of them could urinate the most leaves off a bush. No records exist of how many of these bizarre contests he won, but his fondness for them suggests an above-average success rate.

'Oh, yes, definitely, a show-off,' Sheila told me. 'I remember being at a party with him, and he challenged me to an eating contest. We were to stuff ourselves with food, and the winner would be the first one who was sick. I told him to go away and not be so silly.'

It was, she agreed, a 'curious' life in Ceylon. 'Some of the older white people who had been there a long time were prone to a bit of prejudice, but, on the whole, in Ceylon there was less colour prejudice than in any other mixed-race country. There were no barriers that I could see to integration between whites and the Ceylonese population, who were called Sinhalese because of their so-called descendency from the great God Sinhal. It was taken for granted, really, and we mixed with coloured children very easily and readily. The Tamils kept themselves apart, of course, and still do.'

At school sports were encouraged, and boys who were good at sport, irrespective of how high they could pee, were among the most popular in the class. Trevor cemented his popularity by being quite good at running. He was not a bully in any physical way, but had bullying tendencies and habitually ridiculed boys who could not run fast or would not fight when challenged.

'Trevor thought my brother Ian, a year younger than I am, was an awful sissy.' remembered Sheila. 'Ian cried easily, the girls would tease him and the boys would poke him with sticks. Trevor was very contemptuous of him, I remember, which was rather mean of him.'

While the boys were running races over the dusty tracks, the girls were groomed to become little ladies. Sheila recalled, 'We were taught to recite poetry and to sew and how to behave properly when we eventually married chaps from the Foreign Office.'

Howard's enduring recollection of his childhood in Ceylon was the annual Buddhist festival of the Esala Perahera, held each August in the hill country town of Kandy. One day I got him talking about it, and his eyes lit up as the vivid memories were stirred. The Perahera, or procession, remains to this day a very spectacular event, unrivalled throughout South East Asia. Kandy, which gets its name from 'kanda', the Sinhalese word for hill, is one of the island's best-known centres of traditional culture. For centuries it has stored, in a holy shrine built on the shores of a man-made lake, a golden casket said to contain the left eye tooth of Buddha. Each year a replica of the sacred tooth is taken on a procession through the city, and crowds pack the streets to pay homage.

The relic is carried on the back of a magnificently attired elephant with decorated tusks. Dozens of other elephants, some majestic bulls, others half-grown calves, make up the procession, all of them carrying emblems of the respective deities represented in the parade. Among the humans taking part are trustees and officers of the temple where the sacred tooth is stored, traditional dancers, acrobats and schoolchildren. Elephants were creatures Howard adored, and he kept many wood carvings and other mementoes of them at his home in Arkley. He also talked about the noise and the excitement and the music which continued, as he recalled, throughout the twelve or so days of the festival.

Sheila told me, 'I remember Ceylon then as a beautiful and happy island. There were four children in our family, and we had an ayah each. Trevor and his sister shared one between the two of them. Our ayahs really had the job of bringing us up. They were the nearest we got to mother love. When these ayahs could get us away for an hour or two, they would sneak us down to where their families lived, usually in a fairly run-down part of town. We loved being taken there. It was a treat for us. We'd sit on the mats and play games with the other children.'

A typical day in the life of a middle-class white family such as the Howards would be as follows. Awoken by their ayahs, the children would be fed, washed, dressed and taken to school by them. There would be little or no contact with parents in the morning. During the afternoon the mothers would meet up at each other's houses, sometimes to play bridge or to take part in a sewing circle, and they could be seen strolling in the sunshine in small groups, wearing long flowing skirts, colourful hats and carrying parasols. The women were discouraged from taking any part in the working lives of their husbands. Business was considered exclusively a man's realm.

Generally speaking, fathers would not work late unless the business was going through a crisis. After fetching the children home from school, the ayahs would bathe them and dress them for the evening. After they were clothed they would be taken to see their mother – literally, just to see them, with no hugs or kisses, because by then the ladies would be done up in their fine evening dresses and pearls, and the children would have strict instructions not to smudge their mothers' makeup or mess up their clothes. Accordingly, relationships with parents tended to be rather formal. Sheila recalled, 'I didn't miss the hugs and kisses at the time, but it was an extraordinary way to treat children. I seem to have come through it OK and never felt badly done by, but it affected my sisters and my brother in later life.

'I went to an English school which advertised a lot in the East, and quite a lot of the girls' parents were based in Ceylon and in southern India. Two girls I knew committed suicide, another fell in love with the gardener, and she committed suicide, too, when he rejected her, because after so much rejection as a child she couldn't bear it happening again. A great amount of unhappiness was created by the kind of lifestyle we had. It didn't make us resilient. God, no. Far from it.'

Sheila has no recollection of Trevor's parents, except that Arthur was not bald like her own father. She says, 'It was a joke to poke a stick up a frog's hindquarters, in the hope that it would spring up on to my father's bald head while he sat reading. There was no point in trying that trick with Howard's father. He didn't have a bald head so it wouldn't have been half as funny.'

At the age of six and a half, it was time for Trevor to leave Ceylon. He would never live there again. He was booked in as a junior boarder at Clifton College in Bristol, but instead of sailing directly to Southampton Mabel decided on a longer route that would take in Singapore, Honolulu and New York. She was particularly keen to introduce Trevor and Merla to her relatives in Brantford, Ontario. It meant her and Merla being away from Colombo for about two years, but lengthy family separations were commonplace among the white population of Ceylon, and none of their friends thought there was anything unusual about it.

As well as the benefits of an English education, parents sent their children to England for their health. Sheila told me, 'When Trevor and I were children in Ceylon, there was no calcium and very little lime in the water out there. Consequently the local children were prone to developing weaknesses in their teeth and bones. Later, of course, when calcium was given to expectant mothers and to children, the problem disappeared. But spending time in England when we were growing up made good sense from a health point of view.'

In 1927, together with her brothers and sisters – the youngest was just two and a half – Sheila was sent to England, where her treatment at the hands an arthritic aunt and a drunken uncle shocked and distressed her. On one of the few occasions when she and Howard met up as adults, at the fiftieth anniversary celebration of the opening of Pinewood Studios, she told him how awful it had been for her after leaving Mount Lavinia. He said to her, 'If I had five pounds for every child from Ceylon who had a miserable life after being sent back to England, I could retire tomorrow.' He did not disassociate himself from that group.

But they also had a good laugh remembering his childhood challenges. She told him, 'I don't think today is the time to eat so much that we'll be sick.' He replied, 'You'd win hands down. My lunch today will be liquid!'

By the time the Howard-Smiths boarded a liner for Southampton they had already taken eighteen months to get halfway around the world. Merla and her mother still had a further six months to reach Colombo again, but for Trevor the nightmare of being left behind in England was about to begin. He had been enrolled at Clifton College and was admitted in September 1921, when he was eight, into the preparatory school in Poole's House.

Knowing that her son would be devastated when he was told what was in store for him in England, Mabel put off telling him until she could delay it no longer. At first Trevor simply could not believe what he was hearing and wept uncontrollably. 'I hate England and I hate you!' he shouted at her. The more she tried to reason with him, to explain that it was all for the best and to allay his fears, the more hysterical he became. The trust between them, strengthened by the intimacy of their long journey together, had been destroyed, never again to return, and Trevor was heartbroken by his threatened loss of freedom and what he believed to be his mother's treachery. From entering the college in 1921 until he married in 1944, twenty-three years later, he was, in a very real sense, homeless.

At Clifton Trevor was a solitary figure at first, miserable, confused, unable to settle or communicate. He wanted nothing to do with anyone. Norman Travis, who was in the same year and knew him well, described his difficulties in adjusting from what had been evidently a free and easy life in Ceylon to the demands and disciplines of public-school life in England.

When I visited him at his country house near Hertford, Travis told me, 'Howard was very much a loner, totally lacking in self-confidence. Furthermore, he was indecisive and didn't make friends. I remember a chap called Tom Steiger-Hailey, who started at Clifton the same year as Howard, who was also from Ceylon, from Galle, which is quite near where Howard lived in Colombo. They were both English children from Ceylon, both the same age and both in the same house, but Howard wasn't the least welcoming when Tom tried to get to know him better. He didn't know how to respond. His social skills were almost nil.'

At the first day's assembly the new boys were informed that every minute would be creatively filled. By the end of the first week he was left in no doubt about the college's no-nonsense discipline. Everyone was expected to pull their weight at all times. Slowness off the mark meant a clipped ear and for more serious misdemeanours – such as telling lies or being impertinent to a member of staff, or stealing, or leaving the college grounds without permission – corporal punishment might be prescribed. On the other side of the coin, house points were awarded for good behaviour, proven self-discipline, victories on the sports field and so on; and with each of the college's four houses striving vigorously to be the Cock House – that is, the one with the highest number of points at the end of the year – it was expected that everyone would do their utmost to secure the highest possible score for their house.

From the moment they were awoken till lights out, established routines had to be observed. At first it seemed a breathless, intimidating, nightmare world of scurrying feet, gloomy corridors and bells, and some boys took longer than others to settle, but before long they adapted to it and to the disciplines from which there was no escape.

Lacking an 'English' education up to that point, Howard was at a huge disadvantage academically. His schooling in Ceylon proved to be an inadequate preparation for public-school life in Britain, and he suffered badly. Travis remembered, 'It was a struggle for Howard to keep up with the others. He had to work twice as hard as anyone else just to stay level. At times, it became too much for him. He was kept back a year because of low grades.'

While Howard hated the classroom, where the deficiencies in his earlier schooling were most obvious and for which he was often ridiculed, he found sports activities more to his liking. But, again, the absence of formal training made him look clumsy, and poor gamesmanship, mainly owing to frustration, alienated him there, too. That was the last thing he wanted, because having failed to impress in the classroom he needed to prove himself at sports. To be hopeless at everything was unthinkable, but the unthinkable happened to him, and for a long time his misery overflowed.

It was not easy, but Howard pushed himself as far and as fast as his body would respond. The results were unspectacular at first, but gradually a slow improvement was detectable. Travis recalled, 'At sports, he got by. No more than that. There was nothing outstanding about him that I remember.' So Howard's success in making any of the house or college teams – as he did towards the end of his period at Clifton – confirms how determined he was to overcome his lack of sports training in Ceylon.

Representing Dakyn's House at cricket during 1931, Howard was a better bowler than a batsman. For example, against School House, on 14, 15 and 16 June that year, Dakyn's made 156 in the first innings and eighty-three in the second. Dakyn's won by eighty runs in what appears to have been a low scoring game. Howard made twenty-two in the first innings, before going out leg before wicket to a bowler named Lapage. Another LBW in the second innings, to one of School House, and the college's star bowler, J.A. Coachafer, gave him a total of twenty-eight runs, a respectable enough figure in view of the game's total.

The archives report states that during School House's first innings Howard's bowling got the better of them: 'Howard-Smith [as he was known then] took six wickets for twenty-seven and performed the hat-trick.' Three important wickets in a single over at the expense of a single run was heady stuff. And sweeter still when one of his victims was the same Master Lapage who had clobbered him leg-side earlier in the match.

During School House's second innings he added a further three wickets to his total for the game, making him almost certainly the 1931 equivalent of 'Man of the Match'. The boy who had started at Clifton a long way behind the others had finally caught up with the pack.

On the strength of his appearances for Dakyn's, the following summer saw Howard elevated to the First XI. The competition was much tougher at this level, since the College XI faced mostly outside teams with players of considerable experience. By then he had acquired a taste for the game, although he continued to be more fluent at bowling than at batting which, to his way of thinking, was the wrong way around. He wanted to be a batsman, first and foremost, but the sides they played against were of minor counties standard, and when he found himself at the crease his determination to make a good impression often worked against him. He swung at deliveries a more intuitive player would have left alone. Walking off the field, he made no attempt to conceal his anger and disappointment over an early dismissal, of which, in the course of the season, there were quite a few.

Occasionally he had a good day, as against the visiting Clifton Club on 7 May 1932, when his batting stance with J.A. Coachafer saved the game. The archives state, 'Coachafer and Howard-Smith showed the best batting of the day. Picking the right ball they hit confidently and hard and not only won the match but put the hundred up before Howard-Smith was caught and bowled.' Howard's nineteen runs made him the second highest scorer for the college that day, the highest being his batting partner Coachafer. The archives stated, 'Theirs was a crucial innings in an otherwise rather disappointing batting display.'

On 14 May the college experienced its first defeat of the season, against the Somerset Stragglers, a talented club based in Taunton. Howard took two wickets for thirty-two in nine overs, bowling tightly and competently throughout. Against Liverpool, in a two-day game interrupted by bad weather, Howard performed quite impressively, getting five wickets for only thirteen runs.

The *Old Cliftonian* said of the tussle, 'Liverpool won the toss, and by dull batting against steady bowling made a first class start, forty going up without a loss of wicket. A change of bowling, however, proved a great success, Howard-Smith not only breaking the partnership but getting four other wickets before lunch when the total was sixty-one for five.' A steady drizzle then descended, but Howard had made his mark on the game and he strode off the field feeling satisfied with his performance.

The pattern of his playing changed little throughout the season.

On 31 May against the Worcestershire Gentlemen Howard took F.G. Wrighton's wicket for eleven runs off six overs, thanks to a superb catch by Norman Travis. The college won comfortably, by nine wickets. Against Cheltenham Rugby – which the college also won, by three wickets – Howard bowled eight overs, and although he failed to take a wicket on that occasion he bowled economically and pinned the Cheltenham side down to an average of three runs per over.

On 11 June Howard's side encountered tough opposition from a team calling themselves the Free Foresters. The *Old Cliftonian* report said, 'The Foresters played excellent cricket all through and were probably the best side that has played against the School for a considerable time.' Two weeks later, against the Old Cliftonians, Howard enjoyed a return to good form.

Opening the bowling in the first innings he got two wickets for fifty-six, and in the second he grabbed three more wickets for twenty-four off nine overs and helped his side to a decisive win, by four wickets. The match report stated, 'Howard-Smith and T.G. Kinnersley got some valuable early wickets cheaply.'

Other matches in which Howard played that season were against the Marylebone Cricket Club (MCC) on 20–21 June (game drawn); the Bristol District XI on 5 July (also drawn); and against Cheltenham on 8–9 July, which Clifton won. Howard bowled fairly economically in these games – typically bowling five maidens in twelve overs against Cheltenham and getting one for twenty-two – but his batting had no shine whatever and the runs simply would not come. His top score during this lean period was eight runs against the MCC.

At rugby no mention of Howard appears in the archives until 1932, when he was selected for the first time, as a forward. His first season as a rugby player occurred during his final year at the college.

The rugby season was, effectively, the autumn term, from September to December. Match reports of the 1932 games do less than cover the team in glory. They had occasional wins, for instance, against Blundells, but for the most part the team struggled, predominantly drawing or losing to squads such as Richmond 'A', Downside, Cheltenham – described as 'a most efficient machine' – Wellington, Marlborough, Harlequins 'A', Bristol United and the Old Cliftonians. The archives contain no reference to Howard other than listing him as a team member. It is therefore difficult to assess his rugby-playing abilities.

Boxing was a spring term activity at Clifton, and boys were encouraged to put on the gloves as it was considered 'character-building'. This doubtful recommendation earned many of them a good hiding and did nothing to improve their characters. Idly strolling through the gymnasium one afternoon during a training session, Howard was amused to see two skinny human windmills flailing and pawing each other with such raw passion that they both tumbled out of the ring. A gym instructor spotted Howard laughing and yelled at him, 'If you think they're funny, perhaps they should have a chance to laugh at you!' Howard gave them that chance and, yes, they laughed at him.

There were two boxing competitions – the Inter-House Tournament, in which teams from each house challenged each other, and the Inter-School Tournament, where the best boxers from the various houses would take on another college. In the inter-house battle of 1931 Howard won through without having to land or take a single blow. He could scarcely believe his luck. He was the sole entrant at middleweight. On 3 March he was crowned as the middleweight champion of Dakyn's, without having to lace up a glove. The *Old Cliftonian* called him 'the winner of the weight where he beat nobody'.

The following year the organizers were determined that Howard would not get off so lightly. They persuaded a lad named Van Reynon-Marr to drop down to middleweight in order to challenge him. It was a close contest, but Howard scraped home the winner.

His victory got him a place in the Inter-School Boxing Competition of the same year. However, this time there were plenty of fists eager to thump him. His moment of truth arrived on 1 March when he squared up to the brawny W.G. Worrall of Downside. What happened during the next few minutes convinced Howard that boxing was for madmen. The report of the bout stated with delightful ambiguity, 'Howard-Smith was no match for his opponent', but those who witnessed the massacre knew exactly what it meant.

Having his parents thousands of miles away created problems for Howard during the summer holidays. He could not remain at school, but he could not go home. His mother made the journey to see him only once during the nine years he was at Clifton. Every year he had to cool his heels in England, for what seemed interminable weeks holed up in seaside boarding-houses in the West Country. The college had a list of 'suitable' boarding-houses where long-distance pupils were farmed out for the holidays, but little or no prior vetting of these establishments appears to have been done. Consequently, it was a lottery, with more losers than winners if complaints can be believed.

Children arrived by train clutching their belongings and were allocated a room – usually the smallest in the house, too small to be rented to an adult – and then given a list of rules and regulations that had to be strictly obeyed. The mental scars inflicted on Howard remained with him all his life.

'I had a dreadful time every summer. Absolutely hated it,' he told me. 'I'd be sent off to some ghastly landlady. That meant months of misery. Being locked out all day with nowhere to go, even in the pouring rain. I had no friends my own age, because they were off, you see, gone the minute the school closed. I had no friends at all, really. And the landladies didn't care. I remember one year, roaming the streets of Weston-Super-Mare; sitting on the beach watching the tide come in and out. In and out. All fucking day. I didn't even have sixpence for a donkey ride!'

He recalled having countless bad dreams, stifling his sobs in the middle of the night by shoving a corner of the bedsheet in his mouth, exactly as he had done during his first few weeks at Clifton. There seemed to be no end to his misery. His mother appeared frequently in his dreams during that first lonely summer of 1922, and her face would change, he said, progressively becoming, as the dream recurred, more gaunt and hardened like the face of someone dehydrating during a terminal coma. These frightening images, which he said he had never mentioned to anyone before describing them to me, he thought afterwards might have been a subconscious reaction to the pain he was feeling – Mabel's face becoming less recognizably the mother that he knew and more and more an alien creature on whom he could pour all his rage and frustrations and resentment. He did not appear to apportion any of the blame for this misery on his father.

But rescue was at hand – at least for one or two weeks of the summer. Martin Hardcastle would have been just over twenty when Howard came to Clifton. He had been educated at Winchester and at Oxford and was new to teaching – Clifton was his first job – when he met Howard during the boy's years in the pre-school Poole's House. The *Old Cliftonian* described Hardcastle as having 'throughout his life a sympathetic understanding of the needs and aspirations of the young'. When he learned of Howard's miserable school holidays he promptly invited the boy to stay at his house in Canterbury for a couple of weeks each summer. Those short breaks provided a lifeline for Howard, who never forgot Hardcastle's generosity.

Tom Gover, secretary of the Old Cliftonian Society, told me, 'I remember Martin telling me about Howard being farmed out and having the dreariest of times. Martin, without doubt, took pity on the poor chap and invited him home.'

Hardcastle's home was in the precincts of Canterbury Cathedral, where his father was the Archdeacon. During the holidays he organized the Canterbury Chestnuts, an amateur concert party staged each year to entertain the Friends of the Cathedral. He was a light entertainer in his own right, with an excellent singing voice, and took part in these shows himself, leading the audience into song – one of his favourites, apparently, was 'Come into the Garden, Maud' – as well as being the producer. This was, traditionally, a robust, knockabout musical show, combining end-of-pier variety with community singing. The Ralph Reader Gang Shows of the wartime years had much in common with them. While staying with the Hardcastles Howard would almost certainly have attended the shows, possibly also the rehearsals. He could have been roped in to help and, if so, this would have been his introduction to the performing arts, because although Clifton College had a thriving dramatic society – Sir Michael Redgrave and John Cleese are among its alumni – Howard took no part in college plays.

Gover recalled, 'Knowing Martin as I did, I think he would have encouraged Howard to have a go and, given the circumstances, he would have jumped at it. A bit of a card was Martin, very colourful, lots of vitality, somewhat aristocratic and very well connected. He did an enormous amount for Howard. Martin was also a great outward-bound man, and he would have been attracted to the sort of character that Howard was. Howard owed him a huge debt of gratitude, which I'm pleased to say he acknowledged over and over again.'

Hardcastle was, inadvertently, responsible for Howard's first brush with celebrity. The boy's cricketing hero was C.C. Macartney, the great Australian batsman of the 1920s whose reputation was created when, on a hot sticky day at Trent Bridge in June 1921, he cut, hooked and drove his way to a total of 345 runs, at the time the highest individual score in a single day's play in Britain by an overseas cricketer. Reporting on his remarkable achievement, *The Times* applauded 'the pace at which the runs were obtained'.

At breakfast one morning Howard overheard the Archdeacon say that he would be officially welcoming the Australian tourist team to Canterbury that afternoon and escorting them around the cathedral. Howard listened with his heart pounding. Seeing Macartney in the flesh would be the thrill of a lifetime. Minutes seemed like hours as he waited around to catch a glimpse of the visitors. Finally the team arrived and, sure enough, Macartney was among them.

Howard took up the story. 'I would have been about ten. Macartney was Number Three for Australia at the time and one of the very few who could score a hundred before lunch. I was desperate to get his attention. Nowadays, of course, I would have an autograph book, but we didn't have autograph books then. So I just bumped into him on the steps of the cathedral and trod on his foot. I badly wanted him to speak to me, to notice me and maybe pat me on the head. It was a bloody idiotic thing to do. Anyway, he seemed to think it was his fault, for he apologized to me. "Sorry, old chap," he said. I was ecstatic.'

Another primary influence in Howard's life during his stay at Clifton and for many years afterwards was his housemaster at Dakyn's, Richard Prescott Keigwin, who had been a scholar at the college and who had represented Cambridge at cricket, racquets, football and hockey. Keigwin, a teacher of modern languages, was an outstanding sportsman. He played county cricket for Essex, football and hockey also for Essex, cricket and lawn tennis for Gloucestershire and, to top it all, hockey for England.

During the Second World War Keigwin became a lieutenant in the RNVR and had a distinguished war record, earning the Chevalier Belgique, Order of Leopold and being created Knight of the Order of Dannebrog by HM King Christian of Denmark for service to Denmark. Howard hero-worshipped him, describing him to me as 'perhaps, second only to C.B. Fry, who was the best all-round sportsman ever to go through university', and kept in touch with his former house master until he died in 1980 at the age of ninety-one. Sir Michael Redgrave, who attended Clifton College around the same time as Howard and who also belonged to Dakyn's House, recalled Keigwin as 'the best mixture of scholar and athlete, one of the few masters [at Clifton] who had any semblance of being up with the times.'

During Howard's later years at the school, when he was a house prefect or head of dormitory, Howard frequently risked getting into trouble by shinning down the fire escape located temptingly outside the window and disappearing to Bristol disguised as an adult.

Sometimes he went to a concert at Colston Hall. The false moustache and beret pulled down to his eyes would have fooled nobody, he admitted to me, but at the time he thought he looked about twenty-five. There could be only one explanation why Howard was never hauled before the Dean or given his marching orders – Keigwin did not report him.

When I asked him why, Howard had no answer. 'He knew I was doing it, but he said nothing. He took a hell of a risk. If I'd been hit by a bus outside the gates he'd have been in serious trouble. Perhaps he had done the same kind of thing when he was at school. Who knows?'

Tom Gover confirmed that Keigwin was capable of turning a blind eye when pupils broke college rules. 'Yes, indeed,' he said. 'Richard Keigwin was a brilliant scholar and games player, and he was greatly admired. But he did have a rather laissez-faire attitude towards discipline, which was unfortunate. If you misbehaved in his house you had a much greater chance of getting away with it than in any of the others.'

The subject of sex gave many of the boys at Clifton their first moments of real panic. Stuck thousands of miles from home, in an institution where the subject of sex was taboo, as if men and women got babies by filling in a form, Howard was totally unready when puberty jumped on him wearing hobnailed boots. Consequently, he blundered into adolescence completely confused.

All manner of lurid rumours about how babies were made floated back and forth around the dormitory after lights-out, including, more by luck than judgement, the correct one. Howard recalled taking this news rather badly at first, convinced – and not for the first time since leaving Ceylon – that his parents must be monsters. One boy in his house became so alarmed that he buttonholed the assistant housemaster, Mr Gee (known throughout the college as Gee-Gee), and asked him, point-blank, 'Did my mother and father do that to have me, sir?' 'In your case, probably not,' replied Gee-Gee, walking on swiftly. There was a strict no-contact-with-girls rule at the college. I asked Howard if he had managed to circumvent that piece of legislation, too. The question provoked a growl of impatience.

'No chance of losing my virginity at Clifton,' he said. 'No one to give it to. No girls, anyway. Nowadays, it's different. They can invite girls into the houses and presumably into their beds. The attitude in my day was totally the opposite. We couldn't even talk to girls. For our own good, apparently. Can you believe that? For our own good!' The snort that followed was loud enough to be heard in nearby Barnet.

3

STRATFORD-ON-ALE

Give up the drink, lad. You don't want to end up like me.
–Wilfrid Lawson's advice to Trevor Howard in 1953

ALTHOUGH Howard cultivated no enduring friendships during his stay at Clifton, his international stardom many years later did not pass unnoticed by a number of former classmates. One day he had a phone call from someone who had been at Dakyn's who had later joined the Calcutta Light Horse Infantry, the regiment featured in Howard's film *The Sea Wolves* (1980). Howard told me, 'He reminded me of things I had forgotten, like how I used to read ghost stories to the other boys before lights out. And sing, too. Unbelievable.'

One of the college's most prestigious leisure activities was the annual school play. Pupils chosen to take part were expected to attend rehearsals in their own time. This was one of several reasons why Howard gave the stage a miss at school. It is reasonably likely, however, that in discussions about his future during his final year at Clifton Howard asked Martin Hardcastle to help him get a job and equally likely that Hardcastle recommended acting as a possible career. Of all the masters at Clifton Hardcastle was the one of whom he took the greatest notice. Howard must have got the idea from somewhere, and Hardcastle would have been the most likely member of staff to have pointed him in that direction.

Despite being reluctant to take part in stage productions within the college, Howard's visits to Colston Hall had given him a taste for performance. More than anyone, Gerald Du Maurier, whom he saw once at Colston Hall, convinced him that acting was simple. Du Maurier performed as if he was just being himself, with a complete absence of theatrics. Laurence Olivier thought so, too. He said, 'Brilliant actor though Gerald was, he had a most disastrous influence on my generation, because we really thought, looking at him, that it was easy. And for the first ten years of our lives in the theatre nobody could hear a word we said. We thought he was really being natural. Of course, he was a genius of a technician giving that appearance, that's all.'

Howard reached adulthood during the heyday of the matinée idol, that droll almost absurdly handsome lynch-pin of dozens of frothy comedies and musicals, the epitome of male glamour and sophistication. This was a path along which Howard could not see himself going. If he were to be persuaded to try his luck at acting it would be in the style of craggy-looking, debonair rogues such as Du Maurier, who was no saint either on or off the stage.

Immediately after leaving Clifton Howard had a series of stop-start jobs, none of which amounted to anything or lasted for long. It is not clear whether he contemplated returning to Ceylon or, indeed, if the invitation to do so was ever received. He was nineteen when he left Clifton in December 1932, and at nineteen a young man was deemed to be an adult and expected to be self-sufficient, although for working-class people caught in the early post-slump years it was not always easy to find work.

Howard enrolled at the Royal Academy of Dramatic Art (RADA), because, he told me, he thought 'the word academy would go down well with my father, who would be footing the bill'. At his audition he inquired if he would have to learn long speeches. Not necessarily, he was told. The texts also contained short ones. Excellent. And girls? Would girls be there? Yes, he was told. Girls applied in far greater numbers than there were vacancies. The lucky few were selected on the basis of an audition. Even better, thought Howard. And the men? Too few men applied, he was told. The standard for entry was much lower. Perfect.

Eyeing his fellow students on the first day, Howard could understand why. 'There was Bob Digby, who later ran the Colchester Repertory, who was an overweight six-footer, bless him, lovely man but no actor. There was a fellow who tap-danced and another who turned up wearing a monocle like some fucking Lord who'd lost his way.' RADA's official records contradict Howard's recollection of events. It lists a total of twelve young actor-hopefuls, although, apart from Howard and Francis De Wolff, none of the others appears to have made the grade. It was true, however, that the bulk of the applicants in 1932 were young ladies, mostly from well-to-do families. Among them was Margaret Lockwood.

Howard entered the academy in January 1933, a month after

leaving Clifton College, financed by a money order from his parents. He remained there for five consecutive terms of approximately three months each, all but the first and last of them secured by a RADA scholarship. His final term was funded by a Northcliffe Scholarship, and there was an additional £5 prize from the BBC for being, in the Corporation's view, the most promising male newcomer of the year.

One of the first problems he had to resolve was his name. Trevor Wallace Howard-Smith was too long, sounded stuffy and was better suited to a nameplate in Harley Street than on a theatre poster. It went through three variations before finally 'Trevor Howard' was settled on. A year after entering RADA he was billed as Trevor Wallace and played a scene from Act One of *King Lear* at the Theatre Royal as that. The director on that evening was Dorothy Green, a tutor at RADA who was also a leading actress at the Old Vic in Waterloo Road. She later was one of the stars of the 1936 season at Stratford-upon-Avon in which Howard was, in his own words, a 'spear-carrier'. He also toyed briefly with the idea of calling himself Trevor Howard-Smith and appeared under that name in Ronald MacKenzie's play *Musical Chairs* directed by Gertrude Bennett.

The focus at RADA was strongly on the classics – Shakespeare, Chekhov, Ibsen, Turgenev – with an occasional modern playwright thrown in for light relief. All but one of the plays were performed within the academy and without an audience, the exception being the end-of-term performance attended by theatre representatives, agents and other invited guests. This show usually transferred to the Theatre Royal in London's Haymarket for a single performance attended by the cream of the West End's theatre-goers.

According to Howard, his conversion from 'idle bugger' to someone who enjoyed performing was a gradual process. For the first three months he showed little interest in learning to act. Rebuked once in front of the entire class for not learning his lines, he sulked and went missing for three days. This kind of behaviour was not tolerated; he received a severe reprimand and was warned that he would be thrown out instantly if it happened again. He conceded that he probably was 'a handful', but the real cause was lack of self-confidence, the same problem that had blighted his early years at Clifton. He always had difficulty adjusting and took a while to acclimatize to new things. He made few friends at the academy, with the exception of Bob Digby, who, more than himself, was ill at ease performing in front of an audience.

Despite his rebellious behaviour, Howard was not booted out. He survived the warnings and successfully graduated, earning the award from the BBC as the year's most promising newcomer, which took everyone by surprise including Howard himself. By then he felt competent enough to tackle minor roles in the commercial theatre around London, partly because he had warmed to the profession and partly because he needed to earn money. His wages, on average, were around three pounds a week, but, as old men are keen to point out, three quid was three quid in those days.

'During the holidays and weekends I was game for anything that was going. You simply wrote off and if they wanted to see you they said, "Come on." There used to be Sunday shows put on by the Repertory Players, which was run by a committee of actors, nothing to do with repertory. These shows would be seen by producers and agents searching for new talent.'

These try-ons could be hugely successful. One play given a trial run at the Repertory Players, *George and Margaret*, written by Gerald Savory, was picked up by a commercial management and ran for 799 performances at the Wyndham's Theatre in London. By the time it was taken off, its leading player, Nigel Patrick, had established himself as a star.

Taking into account the number of productions Howard failed to get into, his curriculum vitae for 1934–5 is impressive. His first appearance outside RADA was in a small part in *Revolt in a Reformatory* at the Gate Theatre, directed by Peter Godfrey who later went to Hollywood where he directed, among others, Humphrey Bogart and Errol Flynn. At the Embassy Theatre in Swiss Cottage – a favourite venue for Sunday shows presented by John Fernald – Howard played Schwenk in *The Drums Begin*, and in September 1934 he had a walk-on part in *Androcles and the Lion* by George Bernard Shaw at the Winter Garden Theatre.

After two roles at the Westminster Theatre towards the end of 1934 (Sagisaka in *The Faithful* and Harry Conway in *Alien Corn*), Howard moved up the rankings a bit, being cast as Jack Absolute in Sheridan's comedy *The Rivals*. The production, at the Q Theatre in February 1935, gave Howard his first on-stage blooper. Midway through the first act the seams of his satin breeches suddenly parted at the back as he sat down. No one else in the cast suspected that anything was wrong, but

Howard knew that if he stood up again before the curtain the rest of the evening, and his face, would take on a different complexion. Ignoring the puzzled glances from the other actors Howard took root on the sofa and delivered his lines without losing his dignity.

Francis De Wolff, who graduated from RADA at the same time as Howard and knew the play backwards, was in the audience and thought Howard must have pulled a muscle. Afterwards, when Howard told him what had happened, De Wolff grinned. 'You should be glad of any extra exposure.'

Later that month Howard was back at the Embassy Theatre in Swiss Cottage for another John Fernald production, *Crime and Punishment* by Gaston Baty, in which he played Dmitri, and the following month he was cast as the Honourable Willie Tatham alongside Frederick Lonsdale and Marie Lohr in *Aren't We All* at the Court Theatre. Shortly after its brief run Howard was invited to take a film test in London for Paramount Studios. Hollywood producers were constantly on the look-out for English stage actors to follow in the footsteps of Leslie Howard and Ronald Colman. Howard passed the test but refused to sign a seven-year contract.

Howard told me, 'I wasn't a Colman or a Niven type, which was what they were looking for, so I said no, and that was that.' Instead of sailing to the United States with his expenses paid and a long-term contract in his pocket, Howard caught a bus that evening to the Playhouse Theatre to appear in *The Skin Game* by John Galsworthy, wearing a dinner jacket he had borrowed because nothing backstage fitted him. Olga Lindo, who played his mother, was actually two years younger than he was. Howard gritted his teeth and tried to forget Hollywood.

When *The Skin Game* ended he was retained at the Playhouse for two other Galsworthy plays. In *Justice* he played Walter How, and in *A Family Man* he had a small role as a journalist, but, more importantly, he understudied Wilfrid Lawson. This was Howard's first encounter with the brilliant, erratic Lawson and the start of a lifelong admiration which proved disappointingly one-way. Howard recalled an occasion during *A Family Man* when the curtain went up and Lawson should have been on stage but he wasn't. The other players were on their marks, looking about in embarrassed silence. Howard was dispatched into the traps to find him. Lawson was on his feet – only just – when Howard arrived at his dressing-room. Lawson patted him on the shoulder as he strolled nonchalantly towards the stage and said in a conspiratorial whisper, 'Never hurry, dear boy. Never hurry!'

Lawson ended up, like Robert Newton, virtually forgotten and unemployable in later life because he drank too much. In his younger days he had been a highly respected performer, with a brilliant self-taught technique, but a punishing diet of booze and eel pies had worn him down. The end, literally, came after he had weaved unsteadily through Bryan Forbes's movie *The Wrong Box* in 1966. Forbes recalled that Lawson's contribution to the film was not really a performance but a 'reading of individual lines in a language that only he spoke'. With stage and film productions getting more expensive and insurance costs spiralling, the careers of actors who were not reliable had only one direction to go. As early as 1935, the year Howard understudied him, Lawson's drinking was widely known and managements were wary of employing him.

Howard recalled, 'Wilfrid used to cycle from Notting Hill, where he lived, to the theatre, and he'd march in with about a minute to go, wearing plus-fours, his favourite cycling attire, and he'd say "Good evening" in that strangled voice of his to everyone he bumped into between the door and the stage. He would walk on in his street clothes, with no make-up. As his understudy I had to watch every move he made or, more to the point, didn't make! I went through the agonies of the damned because I didn't know until the last minute if he would show up or not. He was unpredictable, contrary and drove everyone crazy. But he was a genius. I loved him dearly.'

Their paths crossed again, in 1953, by which time Howard had become a major star and Lawson was virtually on the scrap-heap. Howard accepted the lead role in *The Devil's General* by Carl Zuckmeyer, a production described by the *Sunday Telegraph* as 'one of the greatest post-war theatrical memories'. The role of General Harras's grizzled old attendant Korrianke could have been written for Lawson. Howard pointed this out to the management when he asked for Lawson to be hired. They refused at first, but Howard's offer to repay any losses that Lawson's erratic behaviour might incur persuaded them to relent. The offer was made on the strictest understanding that Lawson must not be told that his job had been underwritten.

'They wouldn't put Willie's name up at the theatre because he was always suspect,' recalled Howard. 'I can only say that he was OK with me. He never stepped out of line. A bit slow once or twice, but he never objected if you jumped in on his lines when he needed saving. He'd come over and clown a bit afterwards and say, "You cut me out", and I'd say, "Yes, Willie, old love, you were a bit slow", and that would be that. He didn't mind the truth, but he hated compliments.

'I remember once, during rehearsals, saying to him that I thought he had been bloody marvellous in Strindberg's *The Father*, which I had seen about five times because I so admired his technique. He was just sitting there, enjoying his beer and his chaser. He got to his feet, said to me, "Is that right?" and that was the last I saw of him until the minute before the curtain went up the next day. Criticism was fine, but he never liked or sought or, indeed, believed praise of any kind.'

The Devil's General toured Britain before arriving in the West End. In Newcastle Howard had a beer too many before the start of the performance, and during the opening scene cut himself rather badly on a wine glass which shattered in his hand. He spent the remainder of the scene trying to disguise his wound and played the last fifteen minutes with his damaged hand submerged in a bowl of lettuce where the blood could seep unseen into the green leaves. The interval allowed the hand to be bandaged and order restored. It appears that Lawson, an unlikely advocate of sobriety, took Howard to one side and said, 'Give up the drink, lad. You don't want to end up like me.'

During October 1935 Howard appeared in *Lady Patricia* at the Westminster Theatre. Shortly afterwards he played the Aldwych, home of the famous Tom Walls–Ralph Lynn farces, in *Legend of Yesterday*. In November he returned to the Westminster as Lucillus in Shakespeare's *Timon of Athens*, a role that proved prophetic. For much of the following year Shakespeare occupied a large slice of his professional life. It was during the run of *Timon of Athens* that he was accepted as a junior member of the Royal Shakespeare Company's 1936 season at Stratford-upon-Avon.

At the time of Shakespeare's death in 1616 play-acting was forbidden in the ancient Midlands town of Stratford-upon-Avon. The first attempt to honour Shakespeare by turning it into a theatre town occurred in 1769, when the leading actor, David Garrick, organized a three-day jubilee celebration. The Memorial Theatre was established in 1879 by Charles Edward Flower, a prominent local brewer whose company took over the theatre's running costs. Seven years later Frank Benson became festival director, and it was under Benson's guidance that the Shakespeare 'industry' began to take shape. Ronald Harwood, in his biography of Donald Wolfit, noted that 'Benson created an atmosphere of athletic conviviality that still pervades the Warwickshire air'.

After thirty-five years Benson handed the job over to W. Bridge Adams, who oversaw the rebuilding of a new Memorial Theatre in 1932 after the original building was destroyed by fire. The new building accommodated a thousand people, 250 more than the old one, and had the additional advantage of a moving stage.

When Howard arrived in Stratford in the spring of 1936 he found that the Festival Company had become a refuge for several over-the-hill actors who lived in pretty thatched cottages in and around the town and who had long since become part of the Warwickshire countryside. When the season ended they returned to their allotments and grew potatoes and cabbages. It was a comfortable, undemanding way of life, as far removed as one could imagine from the noise and bustle of the mainstream commercial theatre.

As a result, the Memorial Theatre lacked artistic bite and seemed in danger of becoming a side-show of the Shakespeare circus. People travelled to Stratford to see the sights, look at the birthplace, trail through Anne Hathaway's cottage, drive to the Forest of Arden, stroll beside the Avon and then, when they had seen and done everything else, if there was time left over, they might visit the theatre. Equally, they might not. The plays were not the high spot of the trip. Inevitably, standards had been allowed to decline, but because their revenues were unaffected Flower's Breweries lost no sleep over it.

However, following the 1932 reopening, Bridge Adams decided that it was time to revitalize the artistic side. Invitations went out to ambitious new directors in classical and modern drama and to new actors to replace, or at least augment, the old retainers. It was an experiment in which the owners saw little value, since their parochial interests were already adequately served. But Bridge Adams would not be denied, and of the talented outsiders whom he attracted to Stratford one of the most audacious was Theodore Komisarjevsky, whose innovative set designs sent shock waves all the way down to Shaftesbury Avenue in London.

In 1933, for example, he staged *Macbeth* in a modern setting for the first time and two years later put lighted candles in the tiaras of the fairies in *The Merry Wives of Windsor*. Ben Iden Payne, who took over as creative director in 1935, was an admirer of Bridge Adams and vowed to keep faith with his predecessor's ideas. True to his word,

Komisarjevsky was brought back to Stratford from his native Russia in 1936 to revolutionize the season's attractions.

Among new faces to arrive in 1936 were several destined to achieve success in the cinema in later years. Donald Wolfit was one; Norman Wooland another; Trevor Howard a third; and a fourth was Rosamund John, who later co-starred with Howard in *Green for Danger* (1946). He had a small part in Komisarjevsky's production of *King Lear* in which the mad old king was played by Randle Ayrton, one of the Stratford old-timers. Donald Wolfit was also in the play, as Kent, and received deserved acclaim, the *Daily Telegraph* complimenting him for his 'vigour, poetry and intelligence'. This was, of course, many years before Wolfit slipped into giving what Leslie Halliwell called his 'enjoyably hammy performances'.

Wolfit's were the leading roles of the season – Lear, Julius Caesar and Hamlet – which, apart from the merits of his acting, represented a huge feat of memory. Not surprisingly, he seemed preoccupied for most of the time. He was an actor who lived every moment of a performance as intensely as he lived his life. One evening, during the hectic sword fight between Hamlet and Laertes, Raymond Raikes, who was playing Laertes, thrust when he should have parried and accidentally drew blood from Wolfit's leg. The duel continued as if nothing had happened. In Wolfit's mind, nothing had. Anything that was not in the play escaped his notice. It was once said that if he ever played Lord Nelson he would have insisted on having an eye removed for realism.

Howard appeared in all but one of the season's productions, so he had few evenings off, although the size of many of the roles confined him to prowling the untidy dim-lit backstage for much of the time. He was one of the crowd in *The Taming of the Shrew*, Fortinbras in *Hamlet*, Paris, the son of the King of Troy, in *Troilus and Cressida*, a servant lad in *King Lear*, Salanio in *The Merchant of Venice*, doubled up as Octavius and Cinna in *Julius Caesar* and Fabian in *Twelfth Night*. The play that he 'rested' through was *Much Ado About Nothing*. It was, by any standards, a remarkable year for the company, with improved attendance levels and cash receipts which the local newspaper, the *Stratford Herald* doubted could 'ever be beaten except by perhaps by a few shillings'. Those, of course, were the days when the word 'inflation' had more to do with tyre pressures than the national economy.

The undoubted star of the season was Komisarjevsky, who seemed genuinely puzzled when his designs aroused controversy. Lecturing at the Repertory Players Society, he described the company as 'nothing extraordinary, just workers who work hard', and the only comment he would make about his productions was 'I don't know if they're good or bad, but I hope they're different.'

Newly back in London after his first Stratford season, Trevor Howard started looking for work. He auditioned for, and won, a small part in the West End production of *French Without Tears*, which ran for almost two years. For a play destined to make the record books, it had an unpromising start. In the spring of 1935 an unknown and penniless Terence Rattigan had persuaded John Gielgud to allow him to adapt for the stage Dickens's *A Tale of Two Cities*. At the last minute, the production was withdrawn and Gielgud became involved in *Romeo and Juliet*, in which he and Laurence Olivier would alternate the roles of Romeo and Mercutio. Bronson Albery, the impresario who had cancelled *A Tale of Two Cities* (having been told by Gielgud the delicate state of Rattigan's finances), sent the disappointed playwright a cheque for £50 and asked what other plays he had up his sleeve. Rattigan sent him a newly written three-act comedy called *Gone Away*.

Albery hesitated until the director Harold French, who had also been sent a copy, suggested it as a replacement for Albery's production of *The Lady of La Paz*, starring Lilian Braithwaite, which nose-dived at the Criterion, a small theatre opposite the Eros statue in Piccadilly Circus. Albery agreed, but with certain conditions. The production must be mounted for less than £1,500, the financial risk must be shared and Harold French must choose 'a young, unknown cast'.

On 16 October 1936 Rattigan signed the contract for the play to be produced at the Criterion. Albery had specified 'no stars', but the cast assembled had acres of potential. Rex Harrison, Kay Hammond, Jessica Tandy, Roland Culver, Robert Flemyng, Guy Middleton and Trevor Howard were all on their respective routes to a bright future.

At the first dress rehearsal, however, on Guy Fawkes' Night 1936, omens were not good. Harold French recalled, 'Rex played as though he were constipated and didn't care who knew it. Culver stammered more than at any previous rehearsal, and Jessica Tandy was so slow she might have been on strike.' Howard forgot his lines, despite not having very many to cope with. Albery was furious, retreated to his office muttering, 'It won't last a week!' and immediately committed himself to replacing this replacement. But all was not lost. The second dress rehearsal went much better, and the other backers of the play kept their nerve. By the time the curtain rose on the first night the difficulties had been eliminated and the play had been renamed *French Without Tears*.

Robert Flemyng told me, 'Many of our individual careers were shaped by that one success. Poor old Trevor had rather a small part, and night after night, month after month, that can be frustrating. I remember him pacing up and down backstage waiting to make his entrances.'

However, there were opportunities during the marathon run of the play to display his talents in, for example, Sunday shows, and he appeared at the Arts Theatre in *The Waters of Jordan* in October 1937, and in May the following year he appeared in *The Star Comes Home*.

For some reason that Flemyng could not recall neither he nor Howard were invited to the triumphant first-night party at Kay Hammond's house. As Flemyng left the theatre with his girlfriend Carmen Sugars, whom he later married, he spotted Howard stepping out across Piccadilly Circus. They promptly invited him to join them for supper at the nearby Café de Paris, where Flemyng remembered, 'We sat in the balcony and were entertained by Lucienne Boyer, a French singer who had what you might call a big hit at the time called "Parlez-Moi d'Amour". After the pressures before the opening night, and feeling that our jobs were secure, I'm delighted to say the three of us got plastered.'

After our enjoyable lunch together at the Wig and Pen Club in the Strand while Howard was still alive, Flemyng wrote to me saying, 'I fear I talked far too much. I am somewhat nervous that I was highly indiscreet, but I do trust that I said nothing that could detract from my great affection and deep admiration for Trevor. He has unique qualities as an actor, and there is a certain uniquely masculine honesty about his work which has always been outstanding.'

French Without Tears was the first play attended by the recently widowed Queen Mary following the country's official period of mourning. Early in the play Rex Harrison declares about another character, 'She's a bitch', a line considered *risqué* for 1930s' audiences and possibly unsuitable for a rather starchy queen who had so recently been bereaved. Heads turned to the Royal Box when the line was delivered, nobody daring to laugh in case Queen Mary did not. When it became obvious that she had not been offended the audience rose to its feet and applauded.

A long-running play creates within members of the cast the intimacy of a close-knit family, and *French Without Tears* proved no exception. But, according to Flemyng, the only one who remained outside the cosy little circle was Howard. His role in the play was, of course, relatively minor, and at twenty-three he was younger and less experienced than the other actors. These were factors which would tend to keep them at arm's length socially, and Howard was not someone who would ever break down a door to get to know anybody.

Flemyng told me, 'Trevor didn't swap confidences. He had very little to say really. I remember he and I were guests, once, at a golfing weekend with Rattigan and a few of Rattigan's friends. Being homosexual, Rattigan's friends were a bit arty, not Trevor's bag of tricks at all, yet he coped magnificently. He was totally unpretentious.'

Flemyng succeeded in negotiating his release from *French Without Tears* after sixteen months and moved several hundred yards to the Strand Theatre to appear in the Ben Travers farce *Banana Ridge*. He was appearing on Broadway with Laurence Olivier and the American actress Katherine Cornell when war was declared in September 1939, and that brought him hurrying back to London to volunteer for military service.

French Without Tears was the only occasion that Howard and Flemyng worked together, although their paths crossed several times. One encounter Flemyng never forgot took place in 1949 in the smoky basement of a New York bar called Clark's, which was popular with actors. Flemyng had taken a couple of friends there while he was appearing on Broadway. They had just sat down and ordered drinks when out of the gloom of a crowded corner booth came the sound of a familiar gruff voice.

A closer look confirmed it was Howard, red-eyed and stubble-jawed, holding forth among a group of young American actors. Recognizing Flemyng through the smoky atmosphere, Howard banged his glass heartily on the table and shouted an obscene greeting. After he had recovered from his surprise, Flemyng walked over to him and asked, 'Trevor, what on earth are you doing? Look at the state of you. How long have you been here?'

An evil grin spread across Howard's face. 'Three days!' he roared.

4

LOVE CARAVAN

Even in a bad film you couldn't take your eyes off him.
– Dulcie Gray, 1981

THE 1939 season at Stratford-upon-Avon provided Howard with as welcome a contrast to *French Without Tears* as the Rattigan blockbuster had been to his earlier Stratford season. Instead of being locked into a single play that went on interminably until he almost died of boredom, Howard went back to acting in a different play every night of the week. As it was his second Stratford season, he had moved up the ladder and had many more lines to remember, but, as he explained to me, 'Shakespeare is a bit like music. It has a recognizable tempo. Once in your mind, it sticks there. The speeches keep coming back to you.' Within days of arriving, he had knuckled down to the task of learning his lines, occasionally, he said, 'with the help of a towel soaked in cold water wrapped around my head' – presumably to stop his brain overheating.

Many of the older actors who had been there in 1936, such as Stanley Howlett, Kenneth Wicksteed and Gerald Kay Souper, were still around, and they greeted Howard like a long-lost son. The new leading man at Stratford was John Laurie, who would share the leading roles with Alec Clunes. Laurie, a quirky Scot, who appeared in many films of the 1940s and 1950s and later became widely known as Private Fraser in television's *Dad's Army*, brought some elegant touches to his work, and twelve years earlier his Hamlet at the Old Vic had been judged one of the finest interpretations ever staged. Clunes was a completely different sort of character. He adored the classical theatre, to which his strong resonant voice was ideally suited. He was eccentric and impatient, and no role, however taxing, was beyond his talents. With his faultless diction and a fondness for the overdone gesture, he was ideally suited to the Memorial Theatre.

Two young actors new to Stratford were Michael Goodliffe and

Geoffrey Keen. Both became popular in television series during the 1960s. Goodliffe was the original spy-master Hunter in *Callan* with Edward Woodward, and Keen played the acerbic boss of an oil company in *The Troubleshooters*, a successful series that ran for seven years on BBC television. Lower down the ladder – playing footmen, courtiers and the like – were Richard Wordsworth, Michael Gwynn, Paul Rogers and John McCallum; the latter was to become a star of British films during the 1940s. Howard found the class of '39 more to his liking than the 1936 company.

As a young freelance photographer Ernest Green arrived in Stratford in 1936. He liked the town and decided to remain. A room in Scovers Lane, behind the Falcon Hotel, was available for hire at 10 shillings (50p) a week. Green took it over and promptly set up a small studio. The official photographer of the Memorial Theatre was Gordon Anthony, but, with the Shakespeare company one of the local attractions, Green was determined to carve himself a slice of the action. He approached the actors, one by one, and got them to pose for pictures which he then arranged for another man to sell to visitors from a stall outside the theatre; the profits from this were shared equally between them. This enterprise, plus occasional freelance work for the *Stratford Herald*, helped him earn a 'fair living'. When Green was not working he could be found in the Swan's Nest pub at Clopton Bridge. Howard was also a regular there, and it was inevitable that the two would meet.

Green, who when I met him was a sprightly 82-year-old living in comfortable retirement in Harlow, Essex, told me, 'I met Trevor in 1936, but I didn't arrive in Stratford until nearly the end of the season, so I didn't have much to do with him then. But when he came back in 1939 I was established. We both liked cricket, and when we got chatting one night at the Swannie everything clicked.'

Howard rented a room with John McCallum and Michael Gwynn at the Dower, an actors' boarding-house on the outskirts of town. The landlady had old-fashioned views about visits from lady-friends, and a strict curfew was enforced. One morning, while dusting under Howard's bed, she found a lady's bicycle. His excuse, that it was there for 'safe keeping', cut no ice with her and he was asked to leave. But it proved a timely eviction, coinciding with Green's move to a rented house in Quinneys Road in Shottery named Glebe House. After his fifth beer of the evening in the pub, Howard said to Green, 'I'd best be off, old sport. Got to find somewhere to sleep tonight. Some tosspot of a landlady has chucked me out.'

Green had a suggestion. 'You can stay with me. I've got an empty flat downstairs. In fact, you could move in. We could split the rent.'

Howard shook his head. 'Dunno about that, Greenie.'

'It's opposite the Flower's cricket ground.'

Howard thought for a moment, called over the Swan's Nest proprietor, George Sampson, and said, 'Two beers, George. I think you know my landlord!'

Green recalled, 'Then he asked me, "Do you play cricket?" I said, "Yes, but I'm not even a club-level player, although I follow the game a lot as a member of Lancashire." Trevor said, "I'm forming a team and we need more players. If you want in you'd be very welcome." I thanked him and replied, "I'd like a game or two, but I'm not very good." He looked me up and down like an officer on parade and said, "You're not too fucking old to learn, are you?"'

At the theatre it was business as usual. Apart from the welcome new faces, nothing had fundamentally changed. Even Theodore Komisarjevsky was there, with a daring production of *The Taming of the Shrew* about which the normally unexcitable *Times* went wild, declaring 'the important thing is not that Shakespeare wrote it but that Komisarjevsky produced it' and stating that the production 'never fails to delight the eye'. Clunes played Petruchio opposite Vivienne Bennett's Katharina, with Howard as Tranio.

John McCallum, who understudied Clunes, stepped in when Clunes developed laryngitis and quickly made his mark. Paul Rogers, who understudied Howard, got his chance when a motoring accident left Howard with cuts and bruises to his face. For Rogers it was the opportunity he had been waiting for. Later he became convinced that Howard had deliberately exaggerated his injury to give him a shot at the role. According to Rogers, the injury was insufficient to put him out of action, but Howard insisted that he could not perform. At the time, Rogers was unaware that a figure from his student past, Dennis Lenning, had known Howard when he was at RADA. When Lenning learned that the two of them would be at Stratford together he suggested that Howard keep a 'friendly eye' on Rogers, whom he described as 'raw and new'. Rogers was unaware of the connection until after the war. He then became convinced that Howard had intentionally used his accident to launch Rogers on the Stratford stage.

Howard, as Tranio, played Geoffrey Keen's servant. In one of their scenes together Komisarjevsky told them to yell their lines at each other at the tops of their voices, which he thought hugely funny at rehearsal. Neither actor saw the joke but did as they were told, hoping that the eminent director would be proved right, as he so frequently was. Geoffrey Keen told me, 'The audience didn't think it was funny, at all. They just sat there looking bewildered. Everyone had been telling us how brilliant a director Komisarjevsky was, but what he made us do made no sense at all.'

In *As You Like It* Keen as Orlando wrestled on-stage with Howard in the role of Charles. The *Observer* critic described the bout as 'one of the best features' of the evening. Another reviewer said that Howard 'looked a very tough champion'. Keen recalled, 'Trevor had an ideal physique for the part. I'm quite small and he hoisted me on to his shoulders with ease. One night his understudy, Michael Gwynn, took over. Michael was a tall, spindly guy with nothing like Trevor's strength. At rehearsal he got me off the ground OK but then collapsed with me on top of him. We were helpless with laughter. Komisarjevsky wasn't amused.'

Howard played Lord Hastings to John Laurie's *Richard III*. Hastings is a sad, unlucky character who gets beheaded on Richard's orders after being accused unjustly of treason. It was a sympathetic role, and Howard's performance drew snippets of praise from a couple of reviewers. The *Birmingham Mail* said that he was 'exceptionally good', while the *Birmingham Post* complimented him on an 'excellent piece of playing, better than anything Mr Howard has done previously at Stratford'.

In his next production, *A Comedy of Errors*, Komisarjevsky came up with more of a pantomime than the farce Shakespeare intended it to be. The stage was decorated in toy-town colours, and the costumes were equally audacious – doublets and hose held up by modern braces and characters dressed in Roman togas and green top hats. Shades of *Charley's Aunt* and *Gulliver's Travels*, with more than a hint of Edward Lear, were lumped together to form an eye-catching, chaotic, memorable night in the theatre. Its extraordinary vivid and striking colours in many ways anticipated set designs now commonplace on television, but at the time they were revolutionary, and the audience was mesmerized by them. The *Birmingham Gazette* called it 'more alive than most things one now sees in the theatre'. Praise was divided fairly evenly between the cast. The *Birmingham Mail* noted that Howard, who played Aegeon, a Syracuse merchant, overcame the character's tendency to talk too much 'with effective changes of tone and tempo'.

Off-stage, Howard continued to pursue his three main interests – drinking, womanizing and playing cricket – with enviable vigour. The drinking got him into trouble on numerous occasions. One day he and Ernest Green decided to attempt a drinking feat, which, had they achieved it, would have made them Stratford legends. Some would say that they were not far off that already. On market days, which were Tuesdays and Fridays, all forty-eight pubs in the town remained open from ten o'clock in the morning until ten at night. The plan was for the two of them to drink a pint alternately in each of the pubs between opening and closing time. Forty-eight pubs, twenty-four pints each. There had never been a pub-crawl like it in the history of the town. Even the brewing trade could not believe it.

'Can't be done,' said the Swan's Nest's landlord, George, emphatically.

'Nonsense,' replied Howard. 'It's only one pint every thirty minutes. Nothing to it.'

'Maybe,' said George. 'But you're forgetting something.'

'What's that?'

'You won't be on your feet for the last half of the trip.' Howard had taken that into account, too. 'Volunteers will pour it into us. We didn't say we'd be fucking *conscious*!'

In the pubs owned by Flower's Breweries, which accounted for most of them in Stratford, beer cost fivepence a pint. When the news of their challenge got around there was no shortage of people eager to put sixpence in a jug to help with the expenses. They would meet at the Swan's Nest at ten in the morning and round things off at the Railway Tavern at just before ten that night. A day was agreed upon, and the two were given a rousing send-off.

Not surprisingly, they failed to complete the circuit. But it was an honourable defeat, Green recalled, for they managed to sink about fifteen pints each before sliding into a gentle coma. Warming to his theme, Green went on, 'There was a pub, I remember, called the Merry Wives, which was on the banks of the Avon, and the people who owned it had a caravan parked at the end of the garden, almost on the bank of the river. Trevor and I used to drink there. One night it started to piss with rain, really slamming it down, and we couldn't get back to

Quinneys Road, so the woman who owned the Merry Wives said to us, "If you want to stay over tonight you can have the caravan."

'We did that, and when we woke in the morning, still half-pissed, we noticed water about a foot deep sloshing around inside the caravan. We were soaked. We scrambled out and banged on the doors of the Merry Wives. It was about six o'clock in the morning. They opened the window and the woman shouted down, "What do you want?" We told her, "We can't stay there. We're bloody drowning!"

'She unlocked the pub and gave us some breakfast to warm us up, and we could see the water level still rising around the caravan. Trevor hated rain. He was in a foul mood. The people who owned the Merry Wives were very fond of rifle-shooting, which we knew fuck-all about. When the caravan was almost totally submerged, a cockerel flew on top of it and stood there, chest out, looking very pleased with itself. That sodding bird preening itself was the last straw as far as Trevor was concerned. He barked at the woman, "Let's have the bloody gun." When she handed it to him, he took aim, fired and said to her, "That'll teach the bastard." He didn't even wait to check if the bird was hers, which, luckily, it wasn't.'

Accounts of his womanizing vary from Ernest Green's assertion that he never brought girls back to the flat in Glebe House to Geoffrey Keen's recollection that he and a female member of the company were frequently late for rehearsals because they were making love in another room. Keen recalled that on one occasion the room they occupied was directly above the rehearsal room. He told me, 'We couldn't concentrate on our lines for the noise made by Trevor and this girl he was screwing on the floor directly above us.' Randle Ayrton, who had quit the company after the 1936 season, had established a drama school in the town at which a number of attractive young women had enrolled. One evening Howard strode into the dressing-room with a huge grin on his face. A visit to Ayrton had added several names to his little black book.

'Trevor liked to create the impression that he was servicing the whole damn school,' recalled Geoffrey Keen. 'But he didn't get his hands on one particular girl. I know, because she was going out with me.' Green told me that Howard had at least one serious affair, with an actress in the company who quit to become a nurse during the war and who subsequently made her career in medicine. Green's main reason for suspecting that their relation ship went deeper than either of them would admit was the way they covered their tracks. Howard was never usually shy when it came to identifying, or discussing, his romantic targets. But of this young woman nothing was ever said, and none of Howard's close friends, including Green, had any idea that they were a 'couple'. It was several years later, with the affair long forgotten by both of them, when Green saw the woman in question at a hospital in which she was working and in the course of their conversation she let it be known that she had been Howard's secret passion during the summer of 1939.

Flower's Breweries had a long association with cricket, with its own cricket ground at Shottery. According to the *Banbury Guardian*, the ground was a in 'delightful setting'. At the start of the 1939 season, however, the team badly needed someone to grab it by the scruff of the neck and knock it into shape. Howard was an obvious candidate, and when approached he jumped at the chance.

Cricket brought out the best and the worst of Howard. Nothing plunged him into gloom faster than the England First XI getting slaughtered in a test match, especially by the Australians. Howard loved the Australians, but he loved it even better when England knocked them for six. Until age took its toll he thought nothing of flying halfway round the world to see the national side in action, and work was never permitted to interfere with cricket. His contract contained gaps which allowed him to attend important international matches.

Howard's objectives at Stratford were, he told me, to build and motivate the team and to make sure that everyone was fit enough to play at his best. He was a captain who led from the front, trained as hard as anyone and regularly opened the batting with John McCallum. During his captaincy the team rapidly improved in all directions, and by June 1939, mere weeks after its formation, the *Stratford Herald* wrote, 'Onlookers who have watched the Festival cricket teams since Benson's day say they have never seen an actors side so strong in all departments – batting, bowling and fielding.'

Three of the survivors of the 1939 team told me that that it was Howard's persistence, his ingenuity at getting the players to train regularly and his patience with those who needed coaching that gave the team its cutting edge.

An opposing team, in mid-July, was the Derek Salberg Repertory Company team from Wolverhampton. Salberg had been at Clifton

College while Howard was there, although, according to Tom Gover, they barely knew one another. Among Salberg's players was a young unknown cricket-mad actor named Kenneth More. One or two of the matches were played for amusement only, such as the one held in August against the Malvern Festival team, which included Alexander Knox and Alastair Sim. They played with bats half the regulation size and instead of cricket balls the batsmen had to contend with 'soft balls of varying dimensions' as well as an orchestra playing strict-tempo dance music at the edge of the field.

Another pleasure, fondly recalled by Howard, was his exploration of the Cotswold countryside by bicycle and riverboat and sometimes by car. Alec Clunes could afford to run a car, and the two of them would drive to places such as Evesham and Stow-on-the-Wold. Sometimes they would hire punts and see how far along the river they could get. Howard was particularly proud of the occasion when they got as far as Tewkesbury, a journey encompassing ten different weirs. Richard Wordsworth, a descendent of the poet who was also a junior member of the company, set off with them but was forced to abandon the trip and thumb a lift back to Stratford when his punt collided with a bridge.

With the outbreak of war on 3 September 1939 all theatres and cinemas were closed by order of the government. At Stratford *A Comedy of Errors* ended the season, the enormous colour and vitality of Komisarjevsky's production contrasting starkly with the pessimistic mood of the nation. Moreover, closure meant a loss of revenue running into many thousands of pounds for the theatre companies affected.

Immediately after Stratford Howard joined Colchester Repertory, where two friends from his RADA days, Bob Digby and Beatrice Radley, were setting up the company. Howard stayed on to help the new venture get started, and then he moved on to a longer-established repertory company in Harrogate. Part of the reason for his move north was the uncertain state of the London theatre after the order enforcing the initial closures had been rescinded. Theatre-going went out of fashion, a trend that benefited cinemas. In the regions, however, where people felt safer, theatre revenues were down but by a smaller percentage. Out-of-London repertory companies and touring productions moved away from the cosy, pre-war confections that appeared to have had their day and which were out of step with the prevailing national mood. As well as reviving the classics, which were always popular, a much grittier, more robust, more truthful style of drama developed in the provinces, which some believe gestated the realistic 'kitchen-sink' theatre that was to materialize fifteen years later.

With two Stratford seasons and a major West End hit to his credit, Howard was the White Rose Players' most experienced performer. His leading lady for the first couple of productions was Sonia Dresdel, who later appeared with him in *The Clouded Yellow* (1950). Before leaving Harrogate to make a film, Sonia wrote to a young actress who had recently married, who had been with her at her previous rep company and who she knew wanted desperately to work in Yorkshire because her husband, a royal signalman, was stationed there. The newly-weds were Dulcie Gray and Michael Denison.

I met Dulcie Gray backstage at the Haymarket Theatre in London. She told me, 'I had been at H.M. Tennent with Sonia, and before she left Harrogate she said she might be able to get me in there. Michael was stationed at Ossett, and I wanted to be as near to him as I could, so I said to Sonia, "Please, please try." The next thing I knew, I was there.'

It was only her second job and, feeling apprehensive, Dulcie made a mess of her first reading, which added to her embarrassment. Howard was the first to try to ease her discomfort. He led her to one side, and said, 'If you like a bit of fun, I have bad news. You won't find it with this dreary lot.' The joke did its job. It cut the ice. He had already noticed her shiny new wedding ring and had not intended the remark as a chat-up line, but she thought instinctively that she would need to watch her step with this man.

She need not have worried. According to Dulcie, 'Trevor was very much in love with a pretty blonde named Mavis Labatouche.' When he wasn't seeing Mavis, he would take Dulcie to dances and cabaret nights at the Grand Hotel, where Howard's friendship with the resident band leader got them complimentary tickets in return for free admission to the theatre. Their relationship was close but proper. Not once did Howard overstep the mark.

She told me, 'It's no secret that I liked Trevor enormously. He was like Michael in many ways. After a performance, if we were both free, we would spent time together, just the two of us. I enjoyed his company. We were good friends. It was all that either of us wanted.'

The White Rose Players went in for revivals in a big way. Among the 1941 season of plays were *The Lady with the Lamp*, with Dulcie as Florence Nightingale and Howard as Sidney Herbert, and *The*

Importance of Being Earnest, with Howard playing Algernon opposite Dulcie's Gwendolen. Despite it being a big step-up for her, Dulcie was miserable at Harrogate. She could not meet Michael very often and, to make matters worse, a director of the company kept touching her bottom. She told me, 'I asked him to stop, but that didn't work, so I tried another tack. I told him I didn't mind the bruises but I objected strongly to the monotony.' She declined to name him but said that he had become quite a well-known name in the theatre. One hopes that it was for producing plays.

As a comparative newcomer eager to learn, she frequently sought Howard's opinion of her acting. In one production Dulcie played a young woman with a terrible secret, which the audience did not know until the end, when in a tearful confession to her pastor, played by Howard, she admits to having murdered her baby by throwing it on a fire. It was the kind of over-the-top moment that generally gets a laugh, and Dulcie wanted to prevent this reaction.

Howard suggested that she said the lines with her back to the audience and that she should muffle the words in huge sobs except 'baby' and 'fire'. The audience, he said, would be straining to hear what she said, They would be too busy figuring it out, and when the penny dropped it would be too late. She followed his advice and, to her relief, the confession was received in total silence. Dulcie told me, 'That was an important lesson for me, one I never forgot. He was saying that I should give an audience only what it needs. Just enough to let them form their own opinions, to use their imaginations. He was ahead of his time in that respect. It became his hallmark. That's why even in a bad film you couldn't take your eyes off him.'

While at Harrogate Howard received a cry for help from Paul Rogers. His young protégé from Stratford was desperate for work. Rogers's wife was pregnant, and the couple were surviving on money gifts from his parents. Rogers told me, 'The war had begun. I had volunteered for the Royal Navy, but nothing had happened. I applied to join the Marines, but I hadn't heard from them either. I had been brought up not to ask friends for favours, but my situation was intolerable. When we parted company after the outbreak of war Trevor had told me he was going to Colchester, and I rather hoped he was still there. Obviously my letter was forwarded on to him.' Within days, Rogers was offered a job as comic relief in a concert party that Bob Digby had put together to entertain servicemen stationed in

Colchester, a long-established garrison town. Howard had wasted no time coming to the rescue.

By any standards Helen Cherry was a beauty. A tall, elegant redhead from a wealthy family in Cheshire, she had fallen into acting by default. She had wanted to be a theatre set designer, but when she turned up at Manchester Theatre offering her services, after graduating in stage design at Manchester University, she was told, 'Sorry, we have someone who does that.' The manager had something else in mind for her. Two things, possibly, but he settled for offering her a job on the stage, as one of the girls in his forthcoming Christmas show. Helen told me, 'I had no experience, which didn't really matter. I had no lines to say. I just had to sit on somebody's lap and sip a glass of champagne. It was a typical thirties musical comedy. After the show ended they invited me to stay on. I was about nineteen. I'd thoroughly enjoyed myself, so I agreed.'

Several months of working in rep and touring followed, valuable time for Helen as she learned the business from the ground floor upwards and gradually became self-assured. But, despite the exciting work going on in the provinces, London was still thought to be the centre of the British theatrical universe, and Helen could not wait for an opportunity to work in the West End. However, for a time, fate got in the way. After the theatres closed in September 1939 they remained so for several months. Helen stayed in Cheshire until they reopened. The war had just entered its second year when, in September 1940, she made her London début in a frilly musical revue, *In Town Tonight*, wearing a costume no larger than 'three oak leaves and a bit of blue chiffon'.

These were exciting, glamorous and dangerous months for her. The Battle of Britain coincided with her London appearance, and Helen told me that both the Criterion and Lyon's Corner House, on the other side of the Eros statue, were bombed during the run of the show. But Londoners and the acting profession had no desire to hide in corners. Theatres and cinemas provided a valuable morale-booster to the nation. After a short trip up north to see her family and to appear at Altrincham Rep, she returned to London and did two consecutive summer seasons at Robert Atkins's famous Shakespearian venue, the Open Air Theatre in Regent's Park. By then she had progressed to leading parts, as Olivia in *Twelfth Night*, Titania in *A Midsummer Night's Dream* and the Widow in *The Taming of the Shrew* in

1942 and as Rosalind in *As You Like It*, Miranda in *The Tempest* and Rosaline in *Love's Labour's Lost* between June and September 1943. During the second season she became friendly with a young married woman in the cast who had come to London more recently than she had and who was eager to learn the ropes. Helen gladly took the new girl under her wing. As their friendship grew the two became inseparable and regularly swapped confidences.

A regular visitor every year to the Open Air Theatre was the classical actor and Shakespeare enthusiast Alec Clunes. He had registered as a conscientious objector in 1939, and his principled stand had unfortunate repercussions, never becoming the star for which his talents had been more than sufficient. (This injustice was to some extent rectified when his son Martin achieved success on British television during the 1990s in a number of dramas and especially the situation comedy *Men Behaving Badly*.) Finding acting work difficult to come by during the war years, the now almost forgotten Alec Clunes kept himself busy producing plays at the Arts Theatre in London.

He invited Helen, when her Regent's Park season ended in September 1943, to play Sylvia in Farquhar's Restoration comedy *The Recruiting Officer* at the Arts Theatre. Feeling pleased to have secured ongoing work in London, she told her friend at the Open Air Theatre about Clunes's offer. The actress wanted to know who her co-star would be.

Helen said, 'Oh, it's someone Alec knew before the war. He's called Trevor Howard.'

The other woman pursed her lips and said, 'Helen, you are going to meet the most enchanting of men, I promise you.'

'How do you know?' asked Helen.

Her friend, Dulcie Gray, replied, 'Because I acted with him in Harrogate.'

The love affair between Helen and Howard had an unpromising start. In the cold rehearsal room Helen did a double-take when Clunes pointed him out. She took one look at Howard, in his drab raincoat that reached almost to his shoes, with the collar turned up and a hint of stubble on his chin, and thought to herself: Goodness, that can't be him! However, those early, negative impressions quickly evaporated as she got to know him. For Howard, the elegant redhead started out as another conquest, not yet married but involved with a Navy officer. He drew the line at seducing married women, but someone unattached, however much they claimed to be in love with another man, seemed fair game. His dislike of Navy officers provided a further incentive to court Helen.

The Recruiting Officer opened in November 1943 and finished its run in January 1944. They stayed on at the Arts Theatre in *On Life's Sunny Side*, with Howard as Joachim Bris opposite Helen's Wendie. The title of the play neatly summed up how they were feeling, and towards the end of the twelve-week run Helen decided to finish with her Navy man because she had fallen in love with Howard. A period of separation followed, with Helen in Stratford for the 1944 season, appearing as Portia in *The Merchant of Venice* and repeating her Regent's Park performance as Rosalind in *As You Like It*.

As it was wartime and the authorities were fearful of infiltration by fifth columnists, people were barred from staying in hotels for longer than five days. Helen told me that she could not afford to rent anything in Stratford except a tiny, one-berth caravan with no mod cons, parked in a field near the theatre, but her blushes were spared thanks to the backstage facilities at the Memorial Theatre. However, a decent sense of timing was essential because the theatre's doors were locked every night at 11 p.m.

Before they married Howard would visit her at most weekends, and they shared the caravan, which was cramped but serviceable. Their wedding, which took place on 9 September 1944 at Birmingham Registry Office, immediately after the Stratford season ended, seems to have been prompted by the discomforts of their love-nest on wheels. Helen told me, 'We didn't want a lot of people to know about the wedding. We had lived together for a time before getting married, and we didn't want a lot of people to know that, either. My parents, as you can imagine, were absolutely staggered. They wanted to give me a big wedding with a white dress and everything. They felt cheated. We started our married life in a small flat in Pall Mall when the Stratford season ended. A lady let it to us. Then she came back and we had to move somewhere else. While Trevor was away, doing a play, I think, we moved to another place near Regent's Park.'

After they married, the couple came to London to further their careers. Helen saw her future in the theatre; Howard thought that he would try his luck in the modestly reviving film industry. Winter 1944 was approaching, and resources were limited, but the Germans were no longer the invincible force they had seemed to be a couple of years before. A sense of optimism prevailed, not just in the film industry but everywhere. People had started to believe that the war would soon be over and were gearing up to make the most of the peace that would follow.

After knocking on many doors and having them slammed in his face, Howard succeeded in landing a small film role. On paper, it seemed fairly trivial, barely worth doing in fact, and for a while he could not make up his mind. Then he decided that he wouldn't do it and headed to Yorkshire to appear in a play. By a quirky coincidence Catterick military training camp in Yorkshire had been chosen for exteriors in the film he had turned down. When the unit arrived at the location in September 1944, associate producer Gordon Parry made a second approach to Howard. Since he was already on the doorstep, and the work would provide extra cash, Howard changed his mind. The film was *The Way to the Stars*, and it set him up for the greatest triumph of his career. Yet he came within a whisker of not being in it.

The Way to the Stars began as a film story by Terence Rattigan to salute the success of Anglo-American military collaboration during the war. Although the collaboration applied to all the armed services, the Air Force was a logical choice for Rattigan, then a flight-lieutenant in the Royal Air Force. He was given extended leave by the Ministry of Information to work with an American screenwriter in the United States Air Force, Captain Richard Sherman, on a film showing the Alliance in action.

Merle Oberon had been pencilled in to star, and William Wyler, who had directed *Mrs Miniver* (1942), was released by Metro-Goldwyn-Mayer to make the film. Wyler shot miles of footage covering the preparations for a bombing raid over Germany and the flight itself, but he later changed his mind about the film, preferring to use the material as the basis for a documentary, which became *The Memphis Belle*, one of the war's most compelling film documentaries. It was remade as a feature film in 1990 by David Puttnam. Wyler and MGM's withdrawal left the Rattigan–Sherman script without a budget or a director. With the help of producer Anatole De Grunwald, the Ministry of Information approached Two Cities Films with an offer they could not refuse, and the project was revived, with Anthony Asquith replacing Wyler.

By the time the project was up and running again, the war had entered its final stages and, although the end wasn't yet in sight,

De Grunwald had to face the fact that by the time the film was released the war in Europe might be over. Were that to happen, Anglo-American military collaboration would be yesterday's news. Rattigan suggested that they could cover both options by turning the core of the film into a flashback, with the beginning and ending taking place after peace had been declared. If the war ended before the film's release, the story would appear to be hot off the presses. If not, the futuristic setting, and its confident prediction of an Allied victory, could hardly fail at the box office.

Rattigan produced an outline in which the airfield where the action takes place is first shown deserted and abandoned, with the camera lens lingering on graffiti and on personal possessions discarded by the pilots. A voice-over links the present with the past, and the deserted airfield becomes, in flashback, the bustling fighter station of a few years before. The film was made precisely as Rattigan planned it.

Another clever device was the inclusion, again at Rattigan's suggestion, of the John Pudney poem 'For Johnny', which had first appeared in the collection of poems *Dispersal Point* in 1942. The storyline has the poem written by a squadron leader, played by Michael Redgrave, later killed in action, recited with considerable dramatic and emotional effect at the end of the film by another flying officer, played by John Mills:

Do not despair for Johnny-head-in-air.
He sleeps as sound as Johnny underground.
Fetch out no shroud for Johnny-in-the-cloud;
And keep your tears for him in after years.
Better by far, for Johnny the bright star,
To keep your head and see his children fed.

The film traces the fates of three flying officers – two British, one American – between air raids, against a background of culture differences and misunderstandings between the British and American airmen and between the American airmen and the townsfolk on whom they have, literally, dropped in. Howard appears briefly as the pipe-smoking commanding officer, complaining bitterly about the inexperience of the pilot replacements and later proving that experience is no substitute for luck when he fails to return from a bombing mission.

Although technically a war film, *The Way to the Stars* does not show men in combat. Flyers are glimpsed at the start of a raid and wearily returning. A name board in the ops room shows who is killed or missing. By concentrating on the love stories, and having the deaths of Howard and, later, Michael Redgrave occur off-camera, their sacrifice is tidied up and some would argue suffers a reduced impact because of that. The love stories are interwoven skilfully and the heroism and sacrifice ring true, thanks to Rattigan's sensitive writing and several sturdy performances.

In its depiction of the Anglo-American alliance the film taps a rich vein. The contrast between the British and the Yanks, which initially provokes mutual dislike and ridicule, is humorously dealt with, as when cricket-mad Basil Radford is defeated by the complexities of baseball. By the end the Americans have acquired a grudging respect for the British, who reciprocate by 'civilizing' them. Although burdened by dated attitudes, the film is realistic and the moods and emotions of the central characters strike few false notes. The film's impact was huge at the time of its release. The *Daily Mail*, which called it a 'gripping, tense and vivid production', polled its readers in 1945 to find out the most popular film of the war years, and *The Way to the Stars* won by a margin of half a million votes. The *Daily Mirror* called it 'very convincing and a nice mixture of laughter and tears; these are real people doing real things'. C.A. Lejeune in the *Observer* praised its 'great merit of emotional restraint. The intimate scenes are beautifully charged with a feeling that never spills over. These people are real people and like real people they do not make much of their private emotions. Again and again the audience is left to resolve its own tensions.' Dilys Powell in the *Sunday Times* nominated director Anthony Asquith for individual praise. She wrote, 'Asquith has achieved a delicate balance of timing throughout the stumbling, clipped speeches of the characters in emotional sequences, the easy rapid flow of talk and laughter in the intervals of hilarity combine to evoke with scarcely a false touch the atmosphere of wartime. It is inexpressibly moving.' The general view was that Terence Rattigan had provided a talkative although consistently thoughtful drama which kept its wheels firmly on the runway despite the evocative up-up-and-away title. Howard's was only a small role, quickly seen and gone, but it was an important milestone for him. The craggy face and strong voice had been discovered.

5

ENCOUNTER AND AFTER

He later became a wonderful actor, but, oh dear,
there were a lot of things that went straight over his head.
– David Lean, during the filming of *Brief Encounter*, 1945

ALEXANDER Walker has written, 'To several generations of filmgoers, Howard had always been the romantic Englishman – his reputation as such sealed by one film, *Brief Encounter*.' Howard a romantic? Well, not for very long. He was thirty-two when *Brief Encounter* was made and Celia Johnson eight years older. Yet *Brief Encounter* has a passion and power that lifts it head and shoulders above the conventional love story. It is simply one of the best films ever made.

Written originally by Noel Coward as a forty-five-minute dramatic sketch called *Still Life*, it took place in a single setting, the refreshment room of the fictitious Milford Junction train station. In the original 1935 stage production Coward played Alec, the married doctor, opposite Gertrude Lawrence, for whom he had written the piece, who played the respectable suburban housewife Laura. It was Coward's private joke to make the housewife's first name the first half of his glamorous co-star's surname.

Alec and Laura meet originally by accident in the refreshment room while waiting for their respective trains. Laura gets some grit in her eye and Alec, displaying his doctorly skills, comes to her rescue. During further encounters a strong mutual attraction develops, and they start meeting by arrangement. Their friendship blossoms into love, but, realizing that they will hurt people close to them if they continue their affair, they decide to part. She returns to her family, who suspect nothing, and he departs to a new life in Johannesburg.

Coward had discovered during the filming of *In Which We Serve* (1942), his first collaboration with the triumvirate behind Cineguild – director David Lean, producer Anthony Havelock-Allen and screenwriter Ronald Neame – that although he enjoyed having his work turned into movies he disliked film-making. He had faith in Cineguild and gave it a free hand to interpret his work as the company saw fit, but he insisted on being consulted before the cast was finalized. *Brief Encounter* was their fourth collaboration, following on the heels of *This Happy Breed* (1944) and *Blithe Spirit* (1945).

Lean had originally wanted to sever his links with Coward after *Blithe Spirit*. The Maestro's ascerbic comedies had helped him to make a name for himself and had been fun to do, but it was time for a change. He wanted to move on. But when he told Coward of his plan to adapt and film a historical drama, *Mary Queen of Scots*, Coward looked aghast. 'What do you know about costumes?' he demanded to know, and when Lean hesitated for a moment Coward answered his own question. 'There, you see? Nothing. And I know nothing either! For heaven's sake, David, don't be a fool. Stick to what you know best.'

Coward then offered him *Still Life* which he thought might be worth 'having a go at'. He put it no stronger than that and, as originally written, one can see why. It was a one-act stage play, all talk and no action, in a solitary, drab setting. Very un-Cowardlike, dreary and terse from start to finish. When Lean tactfully pointed this out, Coward said, 'But I thought you wanted to escape from comedy. Really, David, you must make up your mind.' It was agreed that Coward would convert *Still Life* into a film script and that other writings would be shelved until the words were ready.

Lean felt certain that the project was a dead duck, but he owed Coward at least the benefit of the doubt until the script was delivered. It was typical of Coward to do the unexpected. When the revised article arrived ten days later, Lean was impressed but continued to harbour doubts, and he said so. A further rewrite was completed by Coward in four days. The theme of forbidden love and guilt had been retained and the story expanded to include visits to a café, a cinema and a boating lake, a drive in the countryside and an attempted seduction in a friend's apartment which goes horribly wrong. The essential ingredients of the film were in place.

Celia Johnson, a particular favourite of Coward's after *In Which We Serve* and *This Happy Breed*, was his first choice to play Laura on the screen. The director and screenwriter shared his enthusiasm for her. Coward had no clear-cut choice of an actor to play Alec but believed that Roger Livesey would do an excellent job. Lean could not visualize Livesey as a persecuted romantic. He also wanted an actor who was, as yet, unknown in films, so that the character could be shaped by the storyline and not by any preconceptions of the actor. Unfortunately he could think of no one suitable and was beginning to feel depressed about it when, by chance, he was invited by Anthony Havelock-Allen, who was to produce *Brief Encounter*, to see a rough cut of *The Way to the Stars*. Howard's playing of the nonchalant but fated RAF flight commander caught Lean's eye.

Afterwards Lean commented, 'He [Trevor] only had one shot on an aerodrome. A plane came in over the field and did a victory roll. Trevor looked up and said, "Lineshoot." It was wonderful. Just that one word, the way he said it and the way he looked. I said to Tony, "That's *him*! That's our Alec!" Havelock-Allen agreed. When they brought the scene to Noel Coward's attention at a private viewing, Coward watched the film in silence, right up to the moment when the Howard character is killed off. He signalled for the projectionist to halt the screening, turned to Lean and said crisply, 'Well done. Don't let's look any further.'

A silly misunderstanding almost cost Howard the role. The script was forwarded to his apartment in Pall Mall by his agent, Eric Goodhead, but it remained unopened and unread. Howard was the world's most reluctant opener of envelopes – letters lay untouched on his hall-mat for days, as Helen has readily confirmed, and on this occasion Goodhead failed to track him down with the good news that the role was his for the asking. After days of hearing nothing, the producer phoned Howard at his apartment to ask if he could attend a meeting at Denham that same afternoon.

'Out of the question, old chap,' said Howard.

'Might I inquire why?' asked Havelock-Allen.

'Certainly,' replied Howard, 'Today I'm taking Helen to see *This Gun for Hire*.'

Havelock-Allen could not understand why watching an Alan Ladd film was more important to Howard than a costume fitting for his first major role, but that was not the case, at all – as the actor ruefully explained when the two men came face to face the following day. The misunderstanding was quickly sorted out, and they both had a laugh about it. 'Blame Eric,' said Howard. He always blamed Eric, whether or not the long-suffering agent was at fault.

With most of the action taking place in and around a railway station, and with the war still on, permission was needed from the

Ministry of War's transport department to film the exteriors. The south of England was ruled out. It remained vulnerable to aerial attacks, particularly from the V2 rockets, seen by many as Hitler's last-ditch attempt to recover the initiative. Carnforth, in Lancashire, on the London Midland and Scottish line, then approaching its first centenary, was one of several stations suggested by the Ministry as being suitable, that is, outside the potential danger zone. One of the reasons why Lean favoured Carnforth was the design of the walkway between the station platforms and the subway that linked them. The walkway had a slope rather than concrete steps. He thought that Laura would look more dignified and composed – 'swan-like' – hurrying between platforms.

He also liked Carnforth because it had long ceased to be a main-line station. The surburban service that used it no longer operated at night, which meant he could work uninterruptedly on those atmospheric night scenes. Seeking to employ local extras, the production company, Independent Film Producers Ltd, contacted the *Morecambe Visitor* which printed a story on 24 January 1945 under the headline 'Chance for Film Fans'. It wrote, 'Those people who have desires to appear in films . . . will have opportunities commencing Monday February 5th onwards . . . the shots will be taken between 10.00 p.m. and 5.00 a.m. and it is stated that meals and good remuneration will be provided. It should be very interesting and perhaps good fun.'

Filming began at the station on that date and continued until the 18th, the final activity being the recording and rerecording of steam engine noises, of trains starting up and braking to a halt and flashing past the platforms at eighty miles an hour. Lean liked the results so much that he used these same effects in his 1962 epic *Lawrence of Arabia*.

The cast's home-from-home while on location was the Low Wood Hotel on the eastern shores of Lake Windermere, where hot food and coal fires were especially welcome when they arrived back after those wearying zero-temperature, all-night shoots. At first, Celia Johnson had hated the idea of being miles from home at 'some horrible station . . . up north' and would certainly have turned down the offer but for the tremendous appeal of the character. Her first glimpse of Carnforth Station, bleak and desolate in the bitter January wind, did nothing to dispel her doubts. Later, when filming got under way and she got to know people, including several locals who had been recruited as extras – and was offered a few small but unexpected courtesies, such as being allowed to pass the time between takes in the warmth of the station-master's office – Celia's dislike for the location mellowed sufficiently for her to concede in a letter home that 'working in the station is far better than I expected . . . there is a very good atmosphere on location'.

Filming was paused at half past one every morning for a brief dinner break. Food was served in two restaurant cars commissioned for the purpose. The cast and senior production staff ate in one of the cars, and the technicians and 'lower orders' had the second one. Celia was unimpressed by the standards of catering and said afterwards, 'Most of it was uneatable – and, goodness, I'm not fussy!' This view would have found little sympathy among the extras and other minions on the set, who were delighted at being rescued, if only for a couple of weeks, from the rigours of wartime rationing. Yet despite the discomforts, the freezing cold, the unsociable hours and catering which Celia felt left a lot to be desired, she remembered it as a contented, well-managed unit. Even David Lean, who lived off his nerves much of the time, seemed calm and relaxed.

The script was opened out so that audiences would see the lovers going to the cinema, together in a rowing boat, taking a drive, lingering over a stone bridge. The 'stone bridge' sequence was the last one filmed in the Lake District, at Middle Fell in Langdale, after the company had already wrapped up at Carnforth. There was a regrettable delay of two days because, being February, the light levels were poor. On the third day, impatient to return south to get on with the boating sequences, which were scheduled to begin on Regent's Park boating lake on 23 February, Lean took a gamble, opened the lens up and filmed on the bridge. Two further locations in the south of England were used to good effect in the film. The fictional town of Milford, where the lovers have tea and go to the pictures, was filmed on the streets of Beaconsfield in Buckinghamshire, and the cinema where they watch *Flames of Passion* was, in reality, the Metropole in Victoria, London, where 'business as usual' meant that the crew could only gain access to the auditorium after the building emptied, usually at around10.30 or 11 p.m. each night.

By late May, when these sequences were shot, Howard had become so used to working on this film during the night that he was in his element when the cameras started turning. Celia, however, had never been much of a night owl and told friends that the whole business was getting her down. Some critics who applauded her tetchiness in the film were unaware that it had its basis in reality.

There was also a slightly incongruous dream interlude in which Laura succumbs to her romantic fantasies and imagines Alec as the perfect lover, sweeping her off her feet to the lush second movement of Rachmaninov's Piano Concerto No. 2, played on the soundtrack by Eileen Joyce, with Muir Matheson conducting the National Symphony Orchestra. To this day the music and the film have become inseparable. These soft-focus images and passionate sounds are counterpointed starkly by the uncosy, unwelcoming apartment where Laura's guilt and Alec's ham-fisted attempts at seduction drive the final wedge between them.

Unlike the two lovers in the film, no visible sparks flew between Celia and Trevor Howard in real life. Both Celia and David Lean formed negative opinions of him at first, although she conceded halfway through filming that he was 'going to be good'. But later, in a letter to her husband Peter Fleming, she called Howard 'pleasant but pretty stupid'. The cause of their impatience may have been that Howard was relatively new to filming, unfamiliar with the techniques and protocols of the industry and perhaps slower on the uptake than she or David Lean would have liked.

Lean never tolerated actors querying explicit directions and became irritated when Howard asked questions. But challenging the director's authority was the last thing he intended. He merely wanted to know what Lean had in mind. In the theatre it was normal behaviour to discuss directions. One flashpoint between them was the scene in which Laura arrives at the borrowed apartment, where their joy at finally being together is marred by the realization that they are about to betray their married partners whom they love. To ease their consciences, they start talking inconsequentially about the weather and the firewood and the rain – everything except what they are about to do.

Coward had employed a similar tactic earlier in the film when the couple's mutual attraction first begins to develop into something serious. Alec talks animatedly about his aspirations as a doctor and his belief in the importance of preventive medicine, but the real cause of his excitement – hers, too – is their deepening mutual attachment, which neither of them can bring themselves to admit.

On the way to the apartment Laura has got soaked by the rain. Alec warns her about catching cold. Howard muttered the lines to himself a few times, then turned to Lean and said, 'If you don't mind me saying so, David, this sounds fucking awful.'

Lean wanted to know why he felt that way.

Howard said, 'I know why she's here. She knows why she's here. What's all this stuff about the rain and the fire not starting and the damp wood? Why doesn't he just get stuck in?' The actor was clearly a lot more certain of his ground than the dithering Alec.

Lean sighed wearily and tried to explain. 'Listen, Trevor,' he said. 'Have you ever been put with a girl, ever been on a dance floor with her, and you know that you're going to make love, whether it's her place or your place, it doesn't matter, but you know it's going to happen. And then when you get there and the door is shut and you are alone, just the two of you, everything has changed and there's a kind of embarrassment that you hadn't got when you were surrounded by people?'

Howard stared at him for a moment, shook his head and said, 'God, you are a funny chap.'

Stung by the remark, Lean replied, 'Funny chap or not, that's how we'll do it.'

Afterwards, Lean observed, 'Trevor was so insensitive he didn't know what we were doing half the time. He later became a wonderful actor, but, oh dear, there were a lot of things that went straight over his head.'

Laura's character was the main focus of the story, in so far as the impact of the affair and later the break-up are viewed entirely from her perspective: it is her family, not Alec's, which comes under the spotlight. After the break-up, when he strides off to catch his train, he's gone, out of the picture. We learn nothing about him from that moment on. There is no information as to whether or not he succeeds in getting his life back into any kind of order or, indeed, if he ever manages to get to Johannesburg. Yet without Alec there is no story, no affair, no drama, nothing to resolve, and Howard was frustrated by what he saw as undue deference to Celia. The huge difference in their salaries also rankled. Howard was paid £500; Celia received £12,000. Even allowing for the fact that she was an established star, paying Howard just 4 per cent of her salary seems, in retrospect, rather mean. Alfred Bergus, a young fireman at the time who helped to put the locomotive through its paces for the cameras, told a reporter that 'Celia Johnson was friendly and spoke to us. She was beautiful, a real lady.'

Howard, by contrast, he remembered as 'a bit reserved . . . unapproachable'. The disparity in their pay-cheques may have had something to do with it.

Everyone agreed that the title of the play, *Still Life*, was completely inappropriate for the film. This was a movie, and the title suggested a bunch of flowers on canvas. Ever the ringmaster, Coward conceded an uncharacteristic lack of inspiration. 'I've been racking my brains. Now it's your turn!' he told his art supervisor Gladys Calthorpe (who designed the eye-catching hat that Celia Johnson wore in the 'grit-in-the-eye' scene). 'Let's not try to be too clever. We need something a bit snappy, something *brief*.'

Gladys thought for a moment and said, 'You want something brief? What about *Brief Encounter*?' Coward repeated the words aloud a couple of times and nodded his head. Later he would jokingly claim to be the author of *half* the title.

Victory for the Allies in Europe was formally confirmed on 8 May 1945, a month before the interiors of *Brief Encounter* were completed at Denham Studios. The two weeks at Carnforth had yielded just over ten minutes of screen time. It took Celia Johnson four days to record the narration, at the end of which she confessed to feeling exhausted and suffering from laryngitis. After seeing the rough cut of the film Noel Coward wrote in his diary: 'Celia quite wonderful. Trevor Howard fine and obviously a new star. Whole thing beautifully played and directed – and, let's face it, most beautifully written.' He told Lean, 'I don't know how you could have done it better.'

More than half a century later Coward's assessment still holds true. Craftsmanship leaps from every frame. The emotions that today would be expressed differently seem fundamentally honest. It is easy to imagine Laura's predicament, having to choose between a loyal but dull husband and the charismatic Alec. It was a dilemma with a national perspective. The war had separated millions of families, but now it was the duty of government – which had split them originally – to reunite husbands and wives and children and keep them together. To rebuild itself into a cohesive nation Britain needed to re-establish family life. It was the recipe for not only stability and progress but for that other important ingredient which had also been missing from people's lives – happiness.

If there was a message in *Brief Encounter* it was a warning against yielding too easily to temptation. Enjoying a bit of slap and tickle between air raids – characterized in the film by the saucy banter between the ticket collector and the buffet manageress – was harmless enough, but serious affairs like the one between Alec and Laura had to be resisted for the sake of the families and for society as a whole. Coward's script, although set just before the war, read in places like a government White Paper on post-war morality. Guilt and hesitancy ran through it like lettering through a stick of rock. And the establishment view triumphed in the end. Conscience got the better of passion, and everyone went back to square one. Laura thought she wanted a dream lover, but when she landed one the only garment she would remove for him was her hat.

Imaginative use of light and shadow created the atmosphere and captured the tension that occupies the core of *Brief Encounter* and which holds the story together. Lean relied heavily on his director of photography Robert Krasker to achieve the effects he wanted. Krasker, who had Austrian and French parents, developed his technical skills in pre-war Germany as an exponent of German expressionism; its stark imagery, menacing shadows, strategic and economic use of lighting and low-angle camerawork later were to become the hallmark of Hollywood *film noir*. As Alec and Laura cross under the subway we see Krasker's skills in action – their shadows on the wall, enlarged and distorted, give advance notice of their appearance; a passing train pumps white-hot steam into the black sky. The mood of tension and alienation created by Krasker extends to the faces of the couple as they walk sadly, wordlessly, to their last goodbye.

Nobody at Cineguild realized that they had a movie classic on their hands, because the first reactions to the film were unpromising. A preview in Rochester, Kent – held there because Lean had already started location work on *Great Expectations* (1946) – went badly wrong when the audience, apparently more street-wise than Alec, guffawed at his lame attempts to get Laura into bed. The hope that its slightly *risqué* theme would appeal to French audiences were dashed when the distributors in France, Gaumont, refused at first to handle it, but they changed their minds when it won the Critics' Prize at the Cannes Film Festival the following year. Its reception was warm but unexceptional. In 1946 Celia Johnson was nominated for Best Actress at the American Academy Awards. She failed to win the ballot. David Lean had a nomination for Best Director, but he, too, was unsuccessful.

While the passage of time has been kind to *Brief Encounter*, its reputation became a millstone round Howard's neck in later years. 'Anyone would think I made nothing else,' he once roared at me across the room after slamming the phone down on yet another caller asking him to talk about Alec Harvey. Right at the tail-end of his career, while filming *White Mischief* in Kenya in 1987 , accompanied by his good friend and occasional 'minder' David Williams, Howard found himself being treated to a showing of *Brief Encounter*. At the end of a day's filming the unit camped on location at Lake Naivasha, miles from the comforts of their Nairobi hotel, were sometimes shown a film in the main dining tent. News that *Brief Encounter* would be screened ensured a bigger audience than usual that night.

Howard acknowledged their applause at the end with his usual courtesy. As they walked outside, Williams said to him, 'I've never understood all the fuss about *Brief Encounter*, Trevor. I think *The Third Man* is a better film.'

Howard went rigid, then launched himself into what Williams called his 'bull moose roar'. 'So do I!' he shouted. '*So do I!*'

Following *Brief Encounter*, Howard was asked by Individual Films, the newly formed Frank Launder–Sidney Gilliat company, to co-star with Deborah Kerr in *I See a Dark Stranger* (1946). This was a romantic thriller set during the Second World War, with Deborah as Bridie Quilty, a spirited Irish girl whose nationalism, fuelled by stories she has heard of British repression and mistreatment of the Irish, makes her an ideal foil for a Nazi spy ring trying to steal plans of a forthcoming Allied invasion. Bridie travels to the Isle of Man to retrieve the plans, but after meeting David Bayne, a British Army lieutenant played by Howard, she realizes her mistake. Her change of heart puts her life in jeopardy. But Bayne is there to round up the bad guys, and it all ends happily.

Some of the exteriors were filmed in County Wexford in Ireland. Howard promptly fell in love with the Irish way of life and on his return home called it his idea of paradise. Ireland, and the Irish, never lost their appeal to him, and the feeling was warmly reciprocated. The interiors were completed at Denham in September 1945. As a new team making their first film, Launder and Gilliat were determined to pare costs to the bone. They instructed everyone on the call sheet to be available on the set at all times. There was to be no sloping off to dressing-rooms or studio bars. Howard thought it was a silly rule and voiced his objections in no uncertain terms to the second assistant director whose job it was round up everybody needed for the day at the start of the morning's shoot.

From inside Howard's room the response would always be 'Fuck off!' It was the same every day. A routine pampering of Howard's ego would follow. After several equally rude responses to the call he would start to feel sorry for the poor assistant director, unlock the door and poke his face out, growling things like 'This is worse than a biscuit factory' or 'You're all completely off your heads!' On one occasion, the assistant, overcome with mock gratitude, grabbed the actor's hand and kissed the back of it. 'Bastard!' roared Howard, snatching back his property.

Since her 1940 film début in *Major Barbara* (1940) Deborah Kerr had made a string of successful movies, including *Love on the Dole* (1941), *Hatter's Castle* (1941), and *The Life and Death of Colonel Blimp* (1943). She was, however, a star with her feet firmly on the ground and extremely easy to get along with. Howard adored her, and Sidney Gilliat attributed her sunny disposition and good humour to satisfaction with her role in the film. The true reason emerged towards the end of shooting, when Deborah announced her plans to get married in November.

I See a Dark Stranger attracted mixed reviews, partly because it was a difficult film to categorize. Some saw it as a light-hearted romance peppered with lively action, others complained that the romantic interludes ruined a cracking good chase movie. *Time* magazine said, 'Some of the comedy is better than the melodrama, while some of it just gets in the melodrama's hair.' Comparison was inevitable with *The Lady Vanishes*, which Launder and Gilliat had written for Alfred Hitchcock in 1938, but the two films were clearly not in the same league. The *Daily Herald* called it 'a lively blend of suspense and comedy with some good acting and excellent lines'.

Launder and Gilliat invited Howard back to Pinewood for their next production, *Green for Danger* (1947). It was a bonus to find that several of the cast were already well known to him. Rosamund John, of whom he had become extremely fond at Stratford in 1936, was in it, as was Alastair Sim, whom Howard knew best from their rivalry on the cricket pitch. He had also known Leo Genn since before the war, but they had not met since 1941 when they shared a taxi in London as both men prepared to report to their army units. James Mason was also in the cab.

'I remember that cab ride quite vividly,' Howard told me. 'Leo was griping about being drafted into the army and wondering what would happen to him next. I said to him, "I know what'll happen next, Leo, old son. An eighteen-mile route march in full kit the day after you arrive." Leo didn't like that idea very much. He sat back and stared out the window. Then James turned to him and said, in that quiet voice of his, "It's your fault for going in. Nobody can force you." James refused to join up. He became a conscientious objector. He stayed at home, made *The Man in Grey* and became a star. Not bad, eh?'

Mason's 'determination not to get involved in the killing of conscripts from their countries' (his words) cost him a leading part in *In Which We Serve* (1942), Noel Coward's flag-waving sea drama. Coward had wanted him but, as Mason recalled in his autobiography, 'he thought that the propaganda value of his film could well be marred by the presence in the cast of such a well-known civilian as myself'.

The action of *Green for Danger*, set in a beleaguered wartime emergency hospital, occurs during a few days in August 1944. An air-raid victim dies during surgery – but not from his injuries, which are fairly minor. He has been murdered. An investigation headed by Inspector Cockrill, played by Sim, identifies the killer. It was a classic whodunit. The theatre staff on duty when the victim dies all conceal dark secrets. A philandering surgeon, played by Genn, and a temperamental anaesthetist, played by Howard, are the chief suspects. But neither of them is the murderer, who is prevented from killing again in the film's tense climax by the quick thinking of the police inspector.

Green for Danger was an engrossing, modestly priced movie, an example of early post-war British film-making at its economic best. To ensure authenticity in the operating-theatre scenes Gilliat made a comprehensive study of surgical procedures and hospital protocols, particularly the difficulties encountered during wartime. A theatre sister was employed to ensure that everything was correct, right down to where the equipment was positioned and how the instruments were laid out. As the anaesthetist, Howard was seen working the equipment during two operations. He prepared for the role by observing real anaesthetists at work, an experience which he told me had put him off operating theatres for life.

The set, built at Pinewood, divided in two so that the cameras could move freely in and out. The walls were constructed on wheels allowing the set to be approached from any angle. According to studio handouts at the time, the hospital interiors were modelled on an old Tudor mansion typical of the kind that would be commandeered for wartime use, with its sturdy oak beams, timber floors, oak-panelled walls and flagged passageways. The main hall, overlooked by a minstrel's gallery in which the party scene, an important piece of the jigsaw, took place, was applauded by Gilliat as 'a triumph by the art department'.

The British Board of Film Censors had tried to stop the film being made. They were afraid that the depiction of doctors and nurses as dangerous neurotics might undermine public confidence in the medical profession. Fortunately the letter explaining all this was never delivered. Told of the Board's concern, Gilliat invited the Censor to lunch at what he later described as 'the best black market restaurant in Soho' and persuaded him to change his mind.

Howard's next film, the second of three he made with John Mills, had the ironic title of *So Well Remembered* (1947) – ironic because it has vanished without trace. The film was jointly produced by the Hollywood studio RKO and J. Arthur Rank, the first to be made in Britain under such an arrangement. It enabled RKO to unfreeze some of its UK assets and gave Rank the benefit of US distribution. It was, as *Time* magazine reported, 'not a very promising start', although its American producer, Adrian Scott, and director, Edward Dymtryk, had previously collaborated on the *film noir* classic *Farewell My Lovely* (1944).

The two imported American stars were Martha Scott, later seen as the mother menaced by Humphrey Bogart in *The Desperate Hours* (1955), and Richard Carlson, who worked mainly in B-movies. *So Well Remembered* was set in a small northern textile town between the war years. Howard played a boozy doctor, and Mills was his friend, an honest local councillor fighting to improve conditions in the town.

The film contained plenty of red herrings, accidental deaths, one disfigurement and a many fiery verbal exchanges before young love, between Mills's stepson and Howard's daughter, finally triumphs. Part of the film's problem was that it tried to incorporate too much. It was too busy. And despite some solid work by the two British stars its view of rural working-class England lacked realism. In the *Observer* C.A. Lejeune commented, 'What Miss Scott and Mr Carlson . . . are doing in a Lancashire mill town passes my understanding.' Howard and Mills shared the top honours. The Americans were simply acted out of the picture. Joan Lester in *Reynolds News* wrote, 'The most brilliant piece of acting comes from Trevor Howard, as the warm-hearted, hard-working, casual-mannered, alcohol-loving medico.' Another critic, John Ross, said, 'Trevor Howard plays Dr Whiteside with a grim bitterness that fits into the dark, rainy streets and the stark moorland countryside.' *The Times* wrote, 'Howard miraculously saves the preposterous part from disaster.'

Howard next starred in a film which had echoes of *film noir*. Directed by Alberto Cavalcanti, it was called *They Made Me a Fugitive* (1947). Howard played Clem Morgan, a disaffected ex-wartime pilot who joins a gang of East End thieves led by a sadistic gang boss named Narcy. When Morgan wants out of their drug-dealing activities, to stop him turning police informer, Narcy, played by Griffith Jones, frames him for murder.

Morgan escapes from Dartmoor high-security prison to clear his name, helped by a former girlfriend of the gang boss. The police bide their time, confident that Morgan will lead them to the gang's secret hideout. The story is a dime novel adventure, a familiar tale of evil-good versus evil-evil but filmed against sleazily realistic backgrounds, the resonant performance from Howard elevates it above run-of-the-mill melodrama.

The grim riverfront wharves at night, cheap rented rooms, dimly lit cobbled streets and alleyways, close-ups of evil, gloating faces: the parade of *noir* images is impressive, but for many critics the sadism, the torturing of gang victims, one of them a defenceless woman, went too far.

The contrasts between the protagonists are as extreme as the violence – Morgan, tight-lipped, wry-humoured, pursuing his nemesis with weary determination, and Narcy, the flashy, effeminate, narcissistic hoodlum. Both Howard and Griffith Jones are effective in their roles, but the film is almost stolen from them by Sally Gray playing a glamorous woman who knows her way around. At one point, while picking individual particles of buckshot out of Morgan's back – put there by an over-zealous gang member – she recites laconically, 'He loves me . . . he loves me not . . . he loves me . . .' With Narcy dead and the gang in handcuffs, Morgan is led away to complete his prison term. His parting line to her – 'Forget about me; it'll be easier than you think' – is straight out of Raymond Chandler.

I asked Howard if he had any recollections of the film. He paused for a second and then said, 'I remember that blasted rooftop scrap with Griff Jones. It was a ground level studio set. Just as well. I kept slipping.' Cavalcanti's original choice to play Morgan had been the alcoholic star Robert Newton, who, having agreed to make it, failed to show up. Howard, who replaced him, later got to know him well. Newton went to Hollywood at the start of the 1950s but was soon reduced to parodying himself – rolling eyes, rustic accent – in a series of second-rate films. When he died in 1956 he was only fifty-one.

Howard told me, 'Bobby had a heart of gold. I met him in Hollywood, when he was supposedly drying out for the fiftieth time. He was drinking ginger beer and throwing triple brandies at me. Bobby was a child, really. He hated Hollywood. It tore his heart out. And he couldn't come back here because he'd burned his bridges. But it wasn't the drink that killed him. What killed him was suddenly taking him off it.'

After *They Made Me a Fugitive* was completed, Sally Gray confessed that she found Howard's 'perfect English charm a refreshing contrast to the boys of the slug-'em-and-leave-'em brigade, even though some of the latter are better-looking'. She went on, 'Women are fed up with violence of all kinds. What they want now is more permanent romance and tender understanding which makes every girl feel that she is the one. That's much more potent than all that caveman stuff, and Trevor ideally personifies that appeal.'

6

PLAYAWAY

I hate a successful run in the theatre . . .

I prefer a play to be a flop, with fresh work looming ahead.

– Trevor Howard

HOWARD returned to Cineguild, and to David Lean, to make *The Passionate Friends* (1947) in which he again loves and loses a married woman. Ann Todd and Claude Rains played the wife and husband. Neither Howard nor Lean were in the original line-up for this film, which Lean's partner at Cineguild, Ronald Neame, had directed until it ran into scripting and other difficulties.

J. Arthur Rank halted the production after three weeks and asked Lean to take over. When Lean hesitated, Rank declared bluntly, 'We've done a lot for you. I think you owe it to us.' Lean did not agree, but he wanted to keep on good terms with the most powerful man in British films, so reluctantly he took charge of the film. Lean recalled, 'I sat down with a friend of mine, Stanley Haynes, who had worked on *Oliver Twist* with me. We worked day and night, and we rewrote the script, sharpened it up, and after two weeks I was ready to start shooting.' Eric Ambler, who drafted the original screenplay, kept his writing credit. Lean's and Haynes' writing contribution was listed as an 'adaptation'.

One of Lean's first decisions was to replace Marius Goring with Trevor Howard as the woman's lover. Goring later complained that it was because Lean did not like him. The observation may have been true, for Lean disliked all actors, but, with hindsight, Goring would have been less than ideal for the part. It needed someone with plenty of charisma, and charm on the screen was never Goring's strong point.

The original story, written by H.G. Wells and published in 1913, was set in the 1890s and dealt with the conflicts that arise when a woman has to choose between a man who loves her who isn't very wealthy and another one who is. According to Wells's son Anthony

West (whose mother was Rebecca West), the novel had its roots in Wells's love for Amber Reeves, whom many years later West described as 'the embodiment of my father's ideal of what a liberated woman should be'. A silent film version of the book, starring Milton Rosner and directed by Maurice Elvey, watered down the passions to appease the censor, but after the Second World War infidelity and divorce were no longer taboo subjects as long as they were dealt with sensitively.

In Lean's film, Mary, the Ann Todd character, marries a wealthy older man, Justin (Claude Rains) after rejecting a marriage proposal from Steven, a university lecturer, played by Trevor Howard. Steven is everything that Mary admires in a man; he's romantic, caring, honest, but he isn't rich. Justin, a top-notch London barrister, is cold, manipulative, devious and has stacks of money. Mary likes the good life, so she marries Justin. Nine years later a chance meeting with Steven while she waits in a Swiss holiday resort for Justin to join her convinces her that the embers are not dead, but Steven is happily married and has no interest in turning back the clock.

By the evening the husband has arrived, but before he can say hello to her he sees her kissing Steven. It is all quite innocent, but Justin suspects the worst and returns to London to initiate divorce proceedings. Mary tries desperately to patch things up – a scandal could wreck Steven's career – and when this fails she attempts to commit suicide by throwing herself under a tube train. Justin, by then aware that he was in the wrong and feeling remorseful, arrives beside her in the nick of time, saving her life and their marriage.

One of Ronald Neame's many problems from the outset was Ann Todd, with whom he had a poor rapport. His mistake, which he admitted afterwards, was being too soft with her. He had been too willing to accommodate her moods and tantrums, and she had taken advantage of it. Lean's brusque approach with actors was what was needed. He was the only one permitted to have a tantrum on his films. And it was not long before he was laying down the law to Ann Todd. Once when she was late for a run-through on camera he dismissed her excuse that she had not been called. 'You have an obligation to be here when you are needed,' he said.

When she complained to Claude Rains, who occupied an adjacent dressing-room to hers, she found the imperturbable Rains as unsympathetic as Lean had been. Rains had been for many years a stalwart at Warner Brothers, a studio in Hollywood noted for its no-nonsense treatment of star egos. Rains told her, 'We're in a factory, dear girl. You get to the job at eight and you are paid for it. Now trot along and don't make a fuss.'

During the first week of filming Howard cut his right wrist while trying to open his dressing-room window which had got stuck. He was due to film a crowd scene at the end of a New Year's Eve dance. One of the crew told Lean that Howard was delayed because he was in the sick bay having stitches put in the wound. Lean was his usual compassionate self. 'Hope he isn't long,' he grumbled. Howard eventually appeared with his hand and arm encased in a large bandage, but Lean was determined to minimize the delay. He simply draped a scarf over the affected part and called, 'OK, everyone, let's go!'

Location filming took place at two French resorts close to the Swiss border. The first was at the Hôtel de l'Abbaye, on the shores of Lake Annecy. At one point, the former lovers cross the lake in a powerboat. Lean was so taken with the idea of skimming across the water at the wheel of the craft that he doubled for the boatman. He is clearly visible in freeze-frame. While filming at the lake, despite being married at the time to the actress Kay Walsh, Lean found himself falling in love with Ann Todd. The experience certainly had a mellowing effect on him. Delays caused by bad weather usually exasperated him, but at Annecy, after several stoppages, he showed not a trace of a bad temper. It was so uncharacteristic that it began to irritate everyone. They missed his bloody-mindedness. More than once he took the powerboat and disappeared with Ann to the other side of the lake, just like the lovers in the film. By the time they arrived at their second location, at Chamonix, twenty-six miles from the lake, the affair was serious on both sides.

For Howard it was almost a reprise of his experience on *Brief Encounter*, when Lean had favoured the female star. This time it was worse. Lean was in love. Norman Spencer has said that because of this Howard was treated unfairly, that Ann Todd was 'the great thing' and that Howard was angry but kept calm, knowing that he would be treading on sensitive toes if he said anything. Watching the film closely, I didn't share Spencer's viewpoint that Howard had been boxed out in any way. It is true that Ann Todd got the lion's share of the close-ups, but she was the centrepiece of the drama.

Other comparisons with *Brief Encounter* were inevitable, given that both movies had the same director and male star, that it was the story of an unhappy love triangle told in a series of flashbacks from the woman's point of view and that at the emotional climax of both films the woman thinks about throwing herself under a train. One of the strengths of the earlier film had been its everyday, unglamorous locations, the drab railway buffet, the rail underpass at night, the rain-soaked streets and the cinema showing terrible B-movies. Early post-war audiences lived in these kind of settings, not the luxury hotels and Alpine retreats of *The Passionate Friends*. Here was a world beyond their experience and a vain, pampered, deceitful heroine for whom it was difficult to feel sympathy.

The Howard character differed little in the two films – he was a doctor in one, a university don in the other – and in both he was decent, hard-working and a good citizen. You wanted him to wrest this awful woman from her cold moneybags of a husband, not so that he could make love to her but to throw her down a ravine. Both films dealt with sexual repression, but in *The Passionate Friends* it has a sinister, even cruel edge. A flashback scene in the couple's luxury apartment in London has wonderful Hitchcockian overtones: Justin has returned unexpectedly; Steven is with Mary – all perfectly innocent, of course – but they haven't gone to the theatre where she said they would be because the tickets have been left behind on a table. Justin stares at the tickets, inflamed by his wife's apparent deceit.

When Steven drops her off at the apartment Justin invites him in for a drink. The trap is set. Justin inquires about the show which he knows they haven't seen and asks whether they had good seats. Mary and Stephen behave normally until she realizes that Justin knows the truth. At that moment he is pouring her drink. 'Ice?' he inquires with a lifted eyebrow. Behind the bland question you can see there is murder in his heart, but he hasn't the guts to carry it out. Rains was outstanding, and utterly believable, as the jealous husband. Howard told me, 'Claude Rains was my kind of actor. Calm and natural and no conceit whatever. His technique was so good you couldn't see it.' During the dozens of interviews I arranged while researching this book, the same comment was made to me about Howard many times over.

After *The Passionate Friends* Howard began to survey the direction that his career was taking with a growing sense of unease. Despite a succession of favourable reviews, top-level directors and co-stars and a widening of his public recognition, he wanted greater artistic challenges. None of the films completed up till that time rated highly in his estimation, except perhaps *Brief Encounter*, but that, as he quickly reminded me, was Celia Johnson's film, not his.

Films afforded him a lifestyle the theatre had never been able to provide and for which he was grateful. However, film-making, with its stop-start technique and fragmented method of production, shooting bits and pieces out of sequence, could be exasperating. But so, too – although in a different way – could a long run in the theatre, and his memories of *French Without Tears* never left him. He told reporter James Langham, 'I hate a successful run in the theatre. In rehearsal an actor learns to know and act his part. But when the lights go up on the first night, he's had it. His work is over. For month after month he's nothing more than a gramophone record. I prefer a play to be a flop, with fresh work looming ahead.'

Quality was what he wanted, and in his next film quality was what he got, boosting not simply his own career but putting him in the centre of a classic movie. *The Third Man* (1949) began as a scribbled outline on the back of an envelope and ended up a screen landmark. When Graham Greene, whose idea it was, and the director Carol Reed discussed with Alexander Korda, the flamboyant head of London Films, the storyline, which involved an author's search to find out who killed his long-time friend in the ruins of a war-torn city, Korda was impressed. As a Hungarian, he thought Vienna would be an ideal location. It was a city then under four-power occupation, which he suggested could be exploited to widen the dramatic effect.

In fact little widening was necessary. The situation was dramatic enough without resorting to fiction. However, Korda wanted a US distribution deal, for which a major American star was essential and, with the USA one of the four major powers in Vienna after the war, inserting an American actor into the action was logical. Korda also wanted the story developed as a lightweight comedy thriller, along the lines of a post-war *Night Train to Munich*, and even suggested reviving the Naunton Wayne and Basil Radford characters from Hitchcock's *The Lady Vanishes*, whom Reed had included in his *Night Train to Munich*. He was granted only the first item on his wish-list, but it exceeded his wildest dreams: he ended up with not one but two highly rated American stars.

In February 1948, responding to Korda's desire for the film to have a Viennese location, Greene spent two weeks scouting round the city for ideas. He was shown the large web of underground sewers and heard tales of racketeering in stolen penicillin that made his hair stand on end. Gradually the story took shape, but it was a far cry from the satirical jollities of *Night Train to Munich*.

It followed the experiences of an American writer of cowboy novels called Holly Martins, who travels to Europe at the invitation of his old chum Harry Lime. When Martins arrives he discovers that Lime has been killed. Attending the funeral, he is approached by a British Army officer, Calloway, who shocks an already dazed Martins by telling him that Lime was a ruthless racketeer who deserved to die.

Martins does not believe him and decides to remain in Vienna to prove his friend's innocence, but the deeper he digs the more he realizes that Calloway has told the truth – Lime was a drug trafficker. Of course, he isn't dead. Someone else's body occupies his coffin, and it's a simple guess who put it there. But it is not the trade itself which turns Martins against him, it is the human tragedies that result from Lime's cynical dilution of the drugs. Martins agrees to help Calloway, and the climax is played out in the cavernous sewer tunnels beneath the city, with Lime trapped and urging Martins to finish him off, which he does.

By midsummer 1948 the script was ready, and Korda, who had agreed to produce it, roped in the influential Hollywood producer David O. Selznick to handle the US distribution. The original stars were going to be Cary Grant as Martins and Noel Coward as Lime, but Grant's insistence on too large a fee and Reed's opposition to Coward caused a rethink. Film buffs are grateful that it did. Reed dined in London with Orson Welles, who showed interest in playing Harry Lime but who would not commit himself. He was halfway through making *Othello* but had run into serious financial problems. Welles spent most of the evening puzzling aloud how he could save his project. With less than half a promise from Welles, Reed flew to Hollywood to consult Selznick and inferred during their conversation that Welles was sold on the idea. This secured Selznick's agreement. The American mogul also proposed Joseph Cotten to play Martins, and to play Lime's love interest, the central female role in the film, he suggested the Italian actress Alida Valli – both of whom Selznick had under contract. Reed approved his casting choices without a murmur and returned to England in a jubilant mood.

Welles and Cotten were old friends, having worked together in Welles's Mercury Theater Company before the war. It was Welles who brought Cotten to Hollywood to co-star with him in *Citizen Kane* (1941) and *The Magnificent Ambersons* (1946). Cotten and Welles created electricity together on the screen, but Selznick, who knew both men well, had hinted to Reed that they might prove to be a handful; he thought they might misbehave and make up their own dialogue. But Reed was a contented man as he made the return flight to London. Not only had he the best actor that he could think of to play Martins, he sensed that Cotten was the perfect bait to finally land Welles, and this proved to be the case.

There was a huge sense of anticipation among the cast and crew on the day Welles was scheduled to arrive in Vienna. He was a big man in every sense of the word – independent-minded, multi-talented, buoyant, bullish and a great story-teller. It was inevitably Welles's film, although his entrance is delayed until an hour into the action. That hour supplied him with a magnificent build-up – the other characters spend most of it talking about him. His presence is everywhere, long before that first, tantalizing glimpse of him standing in a doorway at night, lit only long enough for us to see the mocking grin; and, after all the speculation and the background music hinting at a shock to come, finally there he is, smug and sleek, well fed, immaculately dressed in the deserted streets of starving Vienna. It is a dazzling moment which, no matter how often you see the film, never loses its power.

Howard was Reed's first and only choice to play Calloway, and to give the character additional gravitas, to make him look more like a high-ranking officer, it was suggested that he grow a moustache. The contrast between Lime, the master criminal who uses charm like a scalpel, and Calloway, his blunt, methodical nemesis, is memorably achieved by both actors. Even physically their contrasts appear striking – the stocky, swaggering Lime and the hunched, sober Calloway. Howard was in superb form. He lets you see how badly he hates Lime, but the hatred is inside him. On the surface he gives nothing away. That is acting of a high order.

Welles was full of admiration for the largely British crew, declaring them the best he had known. Selznick's initial fears that he and Cotten might hijack the film, or, at least, play around with parts of it, came to nothing. The two Americans appeared tamed by the quality of the material, and not once did they query Reed's direction or cause trouble. Welles had a few ideas of his own, but his suggestions were designed to improve, not sabotage, the film. Sometimes they were incorporated, at other times not.

The original concept of the Ferris-wheel sequence, for example, was modified after Welles and Reed got talking. Although some background shots had been undertaken in Vienna, it proved impossible – and would have been highly dangerous – to mount a camera outside the Ferris-wheel carriage in which Lime warns Martins against getting involved with the police. Reed therefore shot the scene in the studio and back-projected the view the characters would see during the ride.

Welles suggested that Lime's cruelty behind his charming manner could be brought to the surface with a few additional lines of dialogue. Reed had no objection. Lime worries about the poor children of Vienna being unable to afford to ride on the big wheel, yet he doesn't care that they are dying because of his watered-down drugs. Against that, his complaint about his indigestion – 'I wish I could throw off this thing' – seems self-centred and callous. Welles also added a bitter joke, a swipe at the US Treasury, which rightly or wrongly he blamed for his financial difficulties on *Othello*. From the carriage, high in the air, Lime wonders if Martins would object so strongly if he was to get £20,000 for every person, or 'dot', on the ground who stopped breathing – 'Would you really, old man, tell me to keep my money – or would you calculate how many dots you could have? Free of income tax, old man. Free of income tax. It's the only way to save nowadays.'

Welles requested one further script addition, a piece of dialogue to be spoken by Lime at the end of the ride, as he dons his gloves and strides off across the fairground. Lime needs Martins on his side. Calloway is gaining ground, but Martins is the key to his survival. Lime can be caught only if Martins deserts him. So at the end of the ride Lime has to make sure they part as friends, even though he has threatened him. The famous 'cuckoo-clock' speech was Welles's invention to lighten the tension between the two characters. Millions of cinemagoers still joyfully recite the lines from memory.

He thought, however, that for Martins to turn against Lime he would have to be shown something truly stomach-churning. The trick was to show it to Martins without showing the audience. The scene where Calloway takes him on a tour of the children's hospital was added. The shocked expression on his face, and the matter-of-fact discarding of yet another teddy bear into a waste basket, subtly conveys the horror Martins is feeling.

Selznick was unsure about Greene's original ending in which Martins and Anna resolve their differences. He suggested that Anna would never forgive Martins for helping to destroy the man she loved. Her grief for Lime immediately after his funeral would rule out any reconciliation. Reed and Greene were persuaded to change the ending to one in which Anna ignores him after her long walk between the poplar trees. This is another scene cherished by movie buffs.

A few adjustments had to be made to satisfy the censors. They objected to Martins's mercy killing of Lime because only the police were licensed to have guns. Greene was obliged to give Calloway an additional line of dialogue – 'If you see him, shoot!' – which authorized Martins to go after him. Welles filmed a few days in Vienna and a few in London. He wore no make-up and looked no different on the screen from the globe-hopping bon viveur he was in real life.

The script called for Lime to have 'on his face a look of cheerful rascality'. Welles was born with that look. All that was required of him was to be himself. Great actor though he was, Welles had no head for business. He was offered the choice of a straight fee of $100,000 cash or 20 per cent of the profits, and he chose the money. It was sufficient to rescue *Othello*, but it proved to be the worst financial decision of his life. A percentage of the profits would have netted him a much larger sum. But Welles had no time to dwell on past mistakes; he was too busy getting ready for the next one.

Reed made four films with cinematographer Robert Krasker, of which *Odd Man Out* (1947) and *The Third Man* are the most visually striking. In the latter film, his low-angle shots of Vienna after dark, with its deserted, cobbled streets and bomb-damaged buildings, create an atmosphere of silent menace. The sequences filmed in the sewers, with their huge interconnecting tunnels large enough in places for tube trains to pass through, the cascading water and the white-suited guards make the place look awesome and futuristic.

Reed described the thinking behind the camerawork: 'I shot most of the film with a wide-angle lens that distorted the buildings and emphasized the wet cobblestone streets which had to be hosed down constantly while we were filming. The angle of vision was just to suggest that something crooked was going on.' Krasker also repeated the technique he had employed in *Brief Encounter* and in *Odd Man Out* of tilting the camera to emphasize peaks of tension.

These images were bold enough, memorable enough and were repeated often enough to give Reed the status of an auteur. They became his trademark, although he never acknowledged that he had one. Nevertheless the claustrophobic, expressionist feel of many of Reed's Krasker-shot night sequences contain a distinctive signature.

The tilted camera, however, irritated some film critics. C.A. Lejeune in the *Observer* described Reed's 'habit of printing his scenes askew, with floors sloping at a diagonal and close-ups deliriously tilted' as 'most distracting'. Even members of his own profession complained that he overdid it. William Wyler, a close friend of Reed's, sent him a spirit level, with a note saying, 'Carol, next time you make a picture, just put it on top of the camera, will you?'

Finding the right theme music for *The Third Man* was not easy, despite Vienna having been home at one time or other to Mozart, Schubert, Beethoven and the Strauss family. Reed felt that these composers were all unsuitable for a modern-day story about narcotics and betrayal. There are several versions of the tale of how Anton Karas came to be the composer and soloist on the soundtrack. I am most familiar with Trevor Howard's version, so that is the one I shall retell.

One night Howard and a friend – he didn't say who – went for a quiet drink in a tiny beer-and-sausage café in Sievering, a suburb of Vienna. Anton Karas was strumming the zither, but nobody took any notice of him. The music could scarcely be heard above the chatter of the customers, but, as the night wore on and people started leaving, the zither-playing caught Howard's attention. He loved jazz and the folk music of many countries and was quite taken with the exciting sounds that Karas was creating.

Several nights later he took Reed to the café. The director also liked the music, but Karas spoke no English and could not understand the compliments of the two Britons as they left the place at around midnight. Reed had noticed that, as well as sounding soft and romantic and mournful, the zither could produce harsh and vibrant sounds, like the contrasting moods of his film. He revisited the café with an interpreter and was told that Karas composed many tunes, some with simple melody lines for playing to customers, others more complicated for his own amusement. Karas agreed to record some of them on a reel-to-reel tape machine that Reed set up in the bedroom of his hotel.

One of them was a piece that Karas had not played for about fifteen years because it was quite complicated. Karas explained, through the interpreter, 'This tune takes a lot out of my fingers. In the café nobody bothers to listen. They like easy tunes, the sort one can hear while at the same time eat sausages.' Reed brought the tape to London and played it to Korda, who was impressed by Karas's musicianship. Reed returned the following day to Vienna and invited him to compose and play the score for the film. A recording of the segment played behind the opening credits, called the 'Harry Lime Theme', was to become a popular hit all over the world.

At the time of its release (in August 1949 in Britain and the following February in the United States) *The Third Man* attracted mixed reviews. With some critics it struck an immediate chord. Quentin Crisp described it as 'the only good picture ever to come out of Britain'. A.E. Wilson wrote, 'I am inclined to use the word genius sparingly, but there is no other word that adequately suggests the power, the thrill, the mystery and the suspense.' *Time* magazine deemed it 'the work of a craftsman so skilled that he [Reed] has earned the right to be judged as an artist'. The *New York Daily News* called it 'enthralling . . . with the quality of a symphonic movement'. The respected American critic Bosley Crowther viewed it as 'essentially a first-rate contrivance in the way of melodrama and that's all . . . It doesn't present any message. It hasn't a point of view. It is just a bang-up melodrama designed to excite and entertain.' Cyril Ray was among the least impressed. He wrote, 'There is little in the story that would seem to matter. Whether it was all worth doing with so much care and talent and wit can only be a minority's murmured query.' Yet, like good wine and violins, and possibly zithers, *The Third Man* has improved with age. Today we are less likely to notice flaws or share Dilys Powell's 'disappointment'. We feast our senses instead on the near-perfect performances, particularly from Welles and Howard, the fluent black-and-white photography, the unusual score and the compelling narrative, and not for the first time are we driven to ignore the carping critics.

7
SETTING STANDARDS

He has the ability to create an atmosphere of helplessness and sadness and misery without it showing on his face.
– Dilys Powell speaking about Trevor Howard in 1986

THE difficulties Ronald Neame encountered at the beginning of *The Passionate Friends* were quickly forgotten when Rank offered him *The Golden Salamander* (1950), a pedestrian thriller with Howard in the lead role. He played an archaeologist sent to Tunisia by the British Museum to bring back Greek antiquities. On a lonely stretch of mountain road, late at night, he sees some gun-runners, but they do not see him. His attempts to put a stop to it are thwarted by the slimy crook who controls the town. However, with the help of Anna, played by Anouk Aimée, who runs the hotel where he is staying, he defeats the smugglers after a lively chase across the Tunisian countryside.

The plot could have come from any one of a dozen scripts seen by the story editor that month. Howard looked the part of the dour, pipe-smoking archaeologist, but it is a one-dimensional character and he is offered no room to expand. He comes visibly alive in his love scenes with his teenage French co-star, and you begin to wish there was more of that and less of everything else – a view apparently shared by the two stars. They were seen in a hotel late at night, evidently not rehearsing their lines. It was not the first time, and wouldn't be the last, that a reporter had caught Howard in a delicate situation. Fortunately, he had time to rehearse his explanations before returning home to Helen.

Reports of Howard's carryings on were nothing new, but the Aimée episode was more public, and more damaging to his good-guy image, than any of his previous involvements. The press had known for years that he played around, but these were mostly brief flings that came to nothing. But with Anouk Aimée the columnists sensed that things were different, that Howard's feelings for her ran deep. When I asked him to own up, he just shrugged and said that he could not remember much, that it all happened a long time ago, which was his well-worn response to questions he preferred not to be asked.

But he could not escape the consequences of what he had done. For the first time his relationship with Helen came under intense pressure, not because he had been caught in the middle of an affair (which he made no attempt to deny) but because he did not shield his wife from the fall-out of the affair becoming public. Helen read about it while staying in Switzerland. Humiliated, she caught an early flight home. When the film unit returned to Denham, Anouk came too. She attempted to keep their affair alive, but it was doomed from the minute they landed on British soil. Anouk was hurt and bewildered. Helen had got him back without lifting an eyebrow.

To my knowledge, Helen had never spoken of the affair, but she admitted to me that it had been 'serious'. She added, 'After it was over, the papers wrote about this "sad little girl" he had abandoned. She wanted to keep it going. Tried desperately, in fact. Kept trying to see him. It was a difficult time.' Those were her only comments, and wild horses wouldn't drag another word from her on that subject. She stood by him of course. And she was shrewd enough to recognize that a major change in their lives was needed to safeguard their marriage in the future. She decided it was time they moved out of London. Meanwhile, he had work to do, in a film that went a long way towards repairing his prestige, as the real-life resistance hero and husband of the equally courageous Odette Churchill.

Anna Neagle starred in the story of her dangerous missions behind enemy lines in the film *Odette* (1950), which was produced by Anna's husband Herbert Wilcox. In a career that had alternated between frothy romances and solid but glamorized biopics, most notably Queen Victoria, this was Anna's meatiest subject by far. The film was based on Jerrard Tickell's graphic account of the events before and after her capture by the Germans and her refusal, under torture, to give the enemy any information that might endanger fellow agents.

The film signalled a departure from Wilcox's, and Anna Neagle's, familiar style. The brutal interrogation and torture scenes were a long way from their breezy collaborations such as *Spring in Park Lane* (1948) and *Maytime in Mayfair* (1949). It was strong stuff for audiences at the start of the 1950s. Anna had not been Wilcox's first choice for the part. She came third after Michèle Morgan and Ingrid Bergman and took the part only after Wilcox had threatened to shelve the project. She wanted the film made because she thought it was a magnificent story. 'If you're really stuck, I'll do it for you,' she told him. 'But it'll take a huge stretch of the audience's imagination to accept me as Odette.'

The film starts with the French-born heroine volunteering to help the resistance in France in 1942 and ends with her repatriation after the war. Her first mission, sending back information on the layout of the Marseilles docklands, sets the German military intelligence on her trail. Marius Goring is the officer given the job of trapping her, which he does with the help of an unpleasant double-agent. Howard played her field commander whom she marries after the war. She avoids the firing squad by fooling her captors into believing that she and Churchill are already married and that he is a relative of the British Prime Minister. He is not, but the subterfuge saves her life. With the German army in full retreat and her captors hoping for clemency when the war ends, none of them wants to be accused of killing someone called Churchill.

The Clouded Yellow (1950) was a rather pointless slice of hokum which demanded little of its stars beyond an ability to scamper across rugged landscapes. It was one of those films with no engine power, so it stands lamely on the ground, unable to take off in any direction. Howard played David Somers, a government agent recalled to London to be sacked for bungling a sensitive mission. Down on his luck, he accepts a job cataloguing butterflies in a large country house in the New Forest. A clouded yellow, we are told by David's eccentric boss, is a rare species of butterfly, hence the film's title.

It turns out to be a nonsense job in a weirdly dysfunctional household, where David meets the beautiful but disturbed Sophie – played by Jean Simmons – a house guest who believes that her father murdered her mother and then committed suicide. This proves not to have been the case; they were both murdered. David finds out who did it and restores Sophie's peace of mind.

The Clouded Yellow is essentially a chase movie, as David and the girl skip across the Lake District trying to shake off their pursuers, who include the police and MI5. It contains passable moments of minor drama but suffers through not being able to make up its mind what it is. It starts off like a spy movie but has nothing to do with spying. It switches to being a whodunit, then becomes a chase movie, then briefly a kidnap thriller and ends up with the hero and the villain slugging it out on a warehouse roof. A lot of energy went into making *The Clouded Yellow*, but regrettably nothing very watchable came out at the other end. Except, of course, the Lake District, which never disappoints.

An Outcast of the Islands (1951), based on a story by Joseph Conrad, gave Howard his juiciest role for years. He played Willems, a dissolute shipping manager working in Macassar in Borneo, who robs his boss, Hudig, played by Frederick Valk, at every opportunity. With the police chasing him, and thrown out of his home by his long-suffering wife, Willems persuades his wealthy, influential father-in-law, Captain Lingard, played by Ralph Richardson, to give him another chance. Lingard moves Willems up-river to Sambir, a remote village with a trading-post managed by his commercial partner, Almayer, played by Robert Morley. Lingard is alone in having navigated a route into Sambir, and on that rests his commercial superiority.

Removed from the temptations that previously he could not resist, this is Willems's last chance to redeem himself. But he cannot settle to the harsh, colourless life on the river's edge. He develops an infatuation for Aissa, the daughter of a local chief – played by the Algerian actress Kerima – whose family wish to destroy Lingard. Willems plays into their hands, but in the end it is he, not Lingard, who is destroyed, by his greed and his vanity. Lingard makes him pay dearly for his weakness and his treachery.

One of the interesting aspects of *An Outcast of the Islands*, in addition to Howard's adrenalin-packed performance, was that Conrad wrote mostly about people whom he knew, sometimes only slightly changing the spelling of their names and other times not even bothering to do that. Almayer, for example, was based on a William Charles Olmeijer, a Dutch trader living up-river from Singapore, whose cargoes of gutta-percha and rubber were shipped by a real-life Captain Tom Lingard. The fictional Almayer of his novel remained true to Conrad's impressions of the trader's character and behaviour. There is no record of a character called Willems, but Conrad could have met any number of misfits and drifters on whom to base the character. For example, a Dutch sailor called de Veer had apparently lived for a short while with Olmeijer and had caused trouble because he drank too much.

An Outcast of the Islands was an excellently made film, but it is flawed in a number of ways. In the film people do not talk to each other. Instead, they stand back and make short speeches, as if still auditioning for their roles. The Dutch origins of the characters are lost in the solidly English portrayals of the actors. Ralph Richardson was curiously wooden as Lingard, and Robert Morley's fussy, bourgeois

Almayer seems hopelessly out of place in this murky backwater. Wendy Hiller, as Almayer's wife, was another curious piece of casting. In the book Almayer was married to a native woman. Wendy Hiller could never be anything but a native of Tunbridge Wells, with her prim manners and trays of tea. The two of them flap around in their roles like stuffy English tourists left stranded when their cruise ship sailed away without them.

By contrast, Howard seized the role of Willems by the scruff of the neck and fashioned him into something both tragic and poetic. At the beginning of the film he swaggers around in a white suit with a floral shirt and matching tie, the very essence of swampland chic. Soon he is sacked, booted out of his house and scrounging for hand-outs. Howard captures the abrupt reversal of Willems's fortunes, and his eventual disintegration, without shifting the gearstick. His work in this film is character-acting of impeccable quality. Not including *The Way Ahead*, he had taken twelve films to attain the peak of his powers.

Lawrence Shaffer wrote, in *Films & Filming*, 'In *An Outcast of the Islands*, Trevor Howard is not exactly identical with the shifty, opportunistic Willems, but he is so close that the character's traits seem almost second nature to Howard. It's as if Howard's analyst, if he had one, might discover that Willems embodies for Howard aspects of his personality that Howard could have liked to surrender to if a socially fostered Puritan ethic hadn't restrained him.'

Robert F. Moss, in *The Films of Carol Reed*, wrote, 'Trevor Howard, an actor of such consummate professionalism that he may never have given a less than competent performance, is at the top of his form in *Outcast*, which may be his best work as a film actor. It is most striking for the intensity of passion that Howard was able to exhibit, a rare accomplishment from an actor whose countrymen are so noted for their sang-froid and emotional reserve. The spectrum of feelings through which Willems passes includes haughty smugness, disdain, *ennui*, cackling triumph, feverish love, rage, frenzy and morbid despair. His realization of these emotions never misses by a flicker.'

That, perhaps, summarizes as well as any words can the difference between being a good actor and a good technician. Ralph Richardson, in virtually every film that he appears, is an accomplished, if not expert, technician. He recites his lines with a cold, clinical exactness that makes you think he is more obsessed with the poetry of the lines than with being the character. This is certainly the case in *An Outcast of the Islands*, where his denunciation of Willems, at the end, sounds like an extract from *King Lear*. In the film we see too much of Richardson and too little of Lingard to be able to judge what, if anything, lurks inside the captain's soul.

As good a yardstick as any by which an actor's versatility can be measured is to visualize the lead actors in any film swapping roles. In *An Outcast of the Islands* one can imagine Howard slipping comfortably inside the skin of Lingard, but Richardson as Willems would be a disaster. There was no other actor I can think of, except Howard, who in 1950 could have taken on Willems and given him that resonance of character, that explosive mixture of vanity, folly, anger and weakness, and carried it off so convincingly.

The Gift Horse (1952) was the film that linked him in the public's mind with Jack Hawkins. 'That *Cruel Sea* was a great film you made,' they told Howard endlessly. He would smile tolerantly and reply, 'I'm *so* glad you liked it.' The confusion was caused by the similarities in the plot to both films, and on their respective performances, between which at times you could barely slide a credit card.

Howard played Fraser, the captain of a wartime destroyer, one of fifty fighting ships given to the British Navy by the United States early in the war to patrol the Western approaches, rather like the SS *Compass Rose* did in *The Cruel Sea*. Unlike Ericson of the *Compass Rose*, Fraser has been court-martialled for causing a collision at sea.

He appears at first to be like the ship that he commands – long in the tooth and a bit temperamental – but as the story unfolds a nicer side emerges. He takes the blame for a mistake by junior officer and saves him from a court-martial. Later, when a brawl between his crew and rival sailors wrecks a dockside pub and the publican demands financial recompense, Fraser has a night on the tiles with him and the claim is dropped. The ship's last mission, a kamikaze ramming of a harbour to delay enemy ships getting out, is successfully accomplished, but Fraser and the surviving crew members are taken prisoner.

The Gift Horse was an excellent example of the kind of tight, economical movie-making of the period, and it kept audiences involved in every twist of the action. Fraser and Ericson (from *The Cruel Sea*) were chipped from the same block of old English oak, strong men masking their emotions. Their crews were interchangeable, too. They both had a First Officer in love with a Wren in the telegraph office, both First Officers stayed with their captains despite being offered ships of their own, and they both had Meredith Edwards as a crew member.

Howard's unshowy performance draws you into the character of Fraser. One scene in particular demonstrates his remarkable skill. His son, played by James Kenney, joins the Navy against Fraser's wishes, but his father is proud, naturally, of the boy's initiative and gives him his blessing. Enlistment quickly leads to combat, during which the boy is killed. Fraser is informed by telegram as the officers begin their pre-Christmas party drinks to celebrate the First Officer's engagement. Unaware of Fraser's bad news, they continue celebrating, laughing and wishing each other 'Merry Christmas'.

The camera films Fraser from the back, with the others in mid-shot. Without his face on screen, Howard conveys the extreme contrast between his emotions and theirs. The body language, the drooping shoulders, are as eloquent as any line of dialogue. Afterwards, at the party for all the crew, he says, 'To all those who can't be with us today, our wives, our parents, our . . . absent friends, whoever they may be, God bless them.' The slight pause when he can't bring himself to say 'our children' and the crack in his voice when he substitutes 'absent friends' is a powerful, poignant moment delivered with immense subtlety.

Richard Attenborough, a supporting actor in *The Gift Horse*, told me that he remembered the film for one reason: Trevor Howard. He said, 'His generation of actors were theatre-trained. Central to that training was an obsession with the text, often to the detriment of the performance. Then along came Trevor after the war, relatively unfettered by that form of technique, and suddenly, in a small part in *The Way to the Stars*, he created a character of almost documentary reality. He set a standard of reality and truth in British films which was quite unheard of before he did it and which was thrilling to watch.'

This reality that ran through all his performances and the sorts of characters he played – strong, resilient, level-headed – had made him, by 1952, a symbol of quintessential Britishness. In *The Way to the Stars* he had been terribly matter-of-fact about life and death. As Jeffrey Richards has remarked, the procession of deaths produced 'no flag-waving, no soupy soundtrack music, no over-the-top emotionalism'. Howard was a decent chap, helping his country to get out of a mess, one of millions doing the same thing without making a fuss or expecting any thanks. And when the war was won – a different result was unthinkable – you knew that he would stick around, thoughtful, good-humoured and courteous as always, helping to sort out the peace.

Howard's Britishness was in greater evidence in *Brief Encounter*. The film is awash with decency, guilt and self-denial. Alec and Laura were not fantasy figures throttling their passions for the hell of it. That was how English people of that era behaved. It was all very well for the French or the Italians to give in to desire, but the English weren't supposed to do that. The English turned their backs on temptation. And the few who succumbed to it never enjoyed it. Guilt, remorse and the fear of being found out saw to that.

Decency and how to preserve it were the twin themes of *The Heart of the Matter* (1953), adapted from a novel by Graham Greene. Howard played Harry Scobie, a deputy police commissioner based in Sierra Leone in 1942, whose failure to be promoted when his boss retires is one of a procession of disappointments. His fourteen-year marriage to Louise, played by Elizabeth Allen, is in difficulties, partly because his love for her has worn down to edgy tolerance. Louise is a weak woman living on her nerves the whole time. She blames her state of mind on him, an accusation which has more to do with keeping him on a chain than being truthful. Unable to raise a bank loan – policemen are a poor risk in Sierra Leone – which would buy for Louise the comforts that might stop her going completely round the bend, he foolishly accepts a bribe from a shady Arab businessman who later blackmails him. Scobie's life is further complicated when he falls for a younger but equally troubled woman, Helen Rolt, played by Maria Schell. Their brief affair dooms not only his marriage but his entire future. The emotional avarice of both these highly strung, unstable women suck him dry and, to make matters worse, his superiors are on to him for having aided and abetted criminals.

It all becomes too much for Scobie, and he decides to commit suicide, but just as he is about to shoot himself in a parked car a commotion outside the vehicle reminds him that he is first and foremost a policeman. He rushes to investigate, and the armed bandits finish the job he had been interrupted in the course of doing. They shoot him dead and toss his body into a sluice channel, and it is washed out to sea.

The Heart of the Matter was about a decent man trying unsuccessfully to keep his head above failure. Scobie fails everyone including, in the end, himself. His marriage is a sham. Louise's instability suggests that he has failed as a husband. More than once she bitterly makes that assertion. His inability to get a bank loan confirms his failure as a provider. The law is broken with his connivance, thus he has failed in his duty. Even his attempt to find happiness with Helen fails when she becomes as possessive and demanding as Louise. For Scobie, love, like everything else, is doomed to end in failure.

We learn that his only daughter Catherine died in England at the age of three, while he was serving abroad. The telegram containing the news overtook an earlier one that said that the girl was merely ill. Scobie learned that she was dead before being told she was sick. It was one more cruel irony in a life already submerged and struggling under the weight of many others.

This was a film that relied totally on Howard to pull it through. The way he played it determined its success or failure. His scenes with Elizabeth Allen crackle with suppressed tension. Howard conveys this inner turmoil with a marvellous economy of expression, and his movements around the house, when Louise is there, are almost in slow motion, like a man rehearsing a funeral march – his own, as it turns out.

In his early scenes with Helen he comes alive in a wholly different way, sharing with us an all-too-brief reawakening of desire. He achieves this change of mood without the slightest deflection of character. The change comes from within. We cannot see it, but we know that something exciting, something out of the ordinary, has happened to him. In his farewell to Helen, when he admits that he has 'given up hope', again he takes us inside his head without resorting to an actor's tricks. Every note is finely tuned, every gesture pared to the bone. He shows once again what a fine, cerebral actor he was.

Although nobody knew it at the time, *The Heart of the Matter* was in fact a thinly disguised account of Graham Greene's unhappy love life during the period when he was writing the book. The setting was authentic too. Greene had spent several years in Freetown, Sierra Leone, as an intelligence officer working for MI5. The central characters have their parallels in real life. Greene was Scobie; Louise Scobie was based on the character of Greene's wife Vivien, with whom, by 1942, relations had stretched to breaking point; Helen, the younger woman for whom Scobie falls, was Greene's mistress, Dorothy Glover. The first part of Greene's novel focuses on his problems at home, the second on his troubles with his mistress. The film follows the novel's basic narrative structure.

In October 1942 Greene confessed in a letter to his sister Elizabeth that for the previous four years he had been in love with two women 'as equally as makes no difference' and that he was tormented 'by the awful struggle to have your cake and eat it, the inability to throw over one for the other'. Scobie faces an identical dilemma. When Greene described Scobie as having 'never been so alone before' he was describing his own feelings. He simply fictionalized his own traumatic love life in the same setting it had all taken place.

The bitterness between Scobie and Louise mirrored the widening rift between Greene and his wife. Louise's 'holiday' in the film is separation by another name, an expression of Greene's desire to be alone so that he can work things out for himself. One has the impression that he poured his troubled thoughts into the novel, sparing nothing, in an attempt to offload his burden of guilt. For this to work – and I have no idea whether or not it achieved the desired effect – true feelings and past events would need to described as honestly as the dramatic development of the book would allow. This appears to have been the case. For example, Vivien gave Greene the nickname of 'Ticki'. It was one of many names she called him, supposedly playful but equally wounding in arguments because she knew that he disliked it. In *The Heart of the Matter* Louise has the same nickname for Scobie.

But perhaps the clearest evidence that Greene was exorcizing painful memories through the pages of the novel – and repeated in the film – was where Scobie describes how the news of the death of his daughter arrived in two telegrams delivered in reverse order so that he learns of her death before he reads that she is ill. That was precisely how Greene was informed about the death of his father. Reviewers who praised the film for the accuracy of the fictional relationships did not realize at the time that it had been based on a book that was essentially autobiographical with just a few of the names changed.

Howard's performance earned him another long-term admirer, Dilys Powell. She said, 'Perhaps it wasn't such a marvellous film, but his was a marvellous performance. I found it deeply moving, and I thought, this is a real actor, not just a film actor. It was absolutely beautiful. Somehow it captured the very best of him.' On another occasion, in a direct reference to *The Heart of the Matter*, she said, 'I think he has certain qualities which the actors we call in this country the greatest haven't got. He has the ability to create an atmosphere of helplessness and sadness and misery without showing it on his face, without that contortion of the face which even the greatest actors perform.'

8
LORD'S ALMIGHTY

Trevor was so illogical. I was a member of the MCC so, naturally, I had to be the best translator of Strindberg who ever lived.
– Michael Meyer

TREVOR Howard loved his cricket. Correction. He loved everybody's cricket. He loved playing it, watching it, loved the smell of the changing-rooms, the camaraderie between players, the pies and the pints afterwards. He thought that anyone who shared his passion for cricket was a tiny bit special. I have always found the game enjoyable to watch on television, and knew enough of the game's finer points to hold a sensible conversation with him, but I am a relatively late convert to cricket. It was not my favourite sport when Howard and I began our collaboration on this book, and when he got tanked up he would express his disapproval of this in characteristically robust language.

Cricket brought out the best and the worst in Howard. He cheered up when he started talking about it, but if England were in trouble, which they were for much of his lifetime, he became grouchy and hadn't a kind word for anything. As we have seen, his affinity for cricket took shape at Clifton College. There he also played rugby and boxed, but it was cricket that captured his attention, and it gripped him like a wheel-clamp for the remainder of his life.

I found him extraordinarily knowledgeable about the game but never boring. He knew so much about cricket because he had watched from a front-row seat many of the century's great cricketing occasions. A few of the sport's legendary names had been personal friends. The game had transformed his life at an early age, and his favourite recollections were not the eulogies written about his acting or the exotic places he had visited; they were mostly to do with cricket.

Howard had opinions on everything. The famous 'Bodyline' controversy of 1932–3, where British bowlers caused a sensation by aiming the ball at their opponents' heads – something nobody takes any notice of today – was just 'the Australians being bloody silly', he said. Douglas

Jardine, England's captain, was later censured and sacked for bad sportsmanship, so somebody must have taken it seriously. 'Listen,' Howard thundered, waving his finger like an umpire giving somebody out, 'Lillee or Thomson [Australian fast bowlers of the 1970s] were lethal compared with the likes of Larwood.' I mentioned the famous story of Lillee getting LBW off an unnamed player who stayed at the crease longer than Lillee thought he should. 'Move your fucking arse,' snarled one of the fastest bowling arms and mouths in history. 'I can't move anything,' replied the batsman. 'You've just broken my leg.' Howard thought the story was probably apocryphal but disapproved of intimidation that got out of hand. 'No harm in taking people on, but I think Lillee overdid it at times. If he wanted to kill people, I'm sure the SAS would have had him.'

Why did he think the rivalry with Australia got so built up at times? 'John Arlott used to say, "Never feel sorry for an Australian cricketer." Too right, I never have! But, to answer your question, the national identity of Australia is cricket. Yes, they have tennis and rugby, but cricket is number one. When they don't win, their pride goes down the fucking toilet. And an Australian without pride is like manure without the shit!' Howard clearly relished the metaphor. Yet off the field he enjoyed friendly relations with many famous Australian players. 'I knew Bradman, although not very well. He was a shy man. A kind of Australian Will Rogers, if you remember him. That's how I remember Bradman. He had an amazing career. Amazing.'

When I mentioned Keith Miller, he roared again. 'Keith was a joyful man. And very sporting. When Compton was injured, at Old Trafford in '48, after edging a ball from Lindwall on to his own brow, Keith ran forward and kept Denis on his feet till he could be helped off the field. And later led the applause for Denis when he came back on. And, typical of Denis, he expressed his appreciation by knocking up a hundred and something. But, yes, Keith and I got up to a few things. He liked a drink after the game.

'After he stopped playing, he used to go round the world commentating and writing articles. They all do it. We'd go to Lord's together from my house, but he didn't like the discipline of having to be there. Any excuse, anything livelier happening that day, he'd be off. One time, the Derby or some big race was on the same day that Keith should have been at Lord's. He said to me, "Fuck it, let's watch the gee-gees." So we buggered off to Epsom instead. He just phoned someone up afterwards and they told him how the game had gone. He spent half an hour writing it up, wired it off, and that was that.'

Keith Miller was an honorary guest of the Australian team at the Ashes game at Lord's in June 1997. He looked very frail and walked with the aid of a stick and, really, was not up to giving an interview. Afterwards he left a message on my answering-machine apologizing once again for not being able to help, repeating that 'Trevor was a great chum' and wishing me every success with the book.

And what did Howard think of Miller's old adversary Denis Compton? 'Ran like a fart between the stumps – he wouldn't mind me saying that – but it didn't matter. He and Bill [Edrich] were great openers. Denis didn't take himself seriously, but when it came to doing the business, no, he didn't mess around. I'd be waiting to do my stuff at Pinewood, and the phone would ring and it would be Denis, out of the blue, and he'd say "I'm at the Rose and Crown (or wherever). Stop whatever you're doing. Your beer is on the bar and it's getting warm!" And, of course, I would go. With the powder and paint still on my face. It was the only civilized thing to do. Denis had spoken!'

At Stratford in 1939 Howard's cricketing ambitions took a leap forward. Lodging at the Dower House, he met John McCallum, an Australian-born actor destined for stardom. McCallum had played cricket in his native Queensland at roughly English minor county league level. He was tall and sturdy and knew how to swing a bat. With McCallum effectively his Number Two, Howard started to build a Memorial Theatre team he hoped would make its mark in the town. Ernest Green remembered, 'When Frank Benson was there, to be a member of the company you had to play cricket. He had a strong passion for the game. Iden Payne, who followed him, wasn't that affected by it.' Consequently the Iden Payne years saw a decline in the team's abilities, but, with McCallum's skill and enthusiasm to complement his own, Howard set his mind to stopping the rot.

I met John McCallum backstage at Her Majesty's Theatre, London. The strong face and brawny physique which had made him both a romantic star and photogenic villain in films had not deserted him. He had put on a few pounds but was still in good shape. During the 1950s he had returned to his native Australia and in the intervening years had become a leading theatre producer. However, he still enjoyed acting and made frequent visits to London. He told me, 'We're here a lot because our daughter Joanna lives here. When there's a play to do as well, that's a bonus.' He is married to the actress Googie Withers.

'Yes, Trevor and I started the Memorial team in 1939,' he recalled. 'He was a useful cricketer. We decided that since we got the team started – he mainly, by the way – that he'd captain the side and I would be vice-captain. We also opened the batting. Rather selfish of us, now I think of it.' Theirs was a successful opening partnership, leading the fight-back and restoring the team's pride. As early in the season as 15 June 1939 the *Banbury Guardian* reported, 'Onlookers who have watched the Festival cricket teams since Benson's day say they have never seen an actors' side so strong in all departments – batting, bowling and fielding. This year's captain is Trevor Howard, who is now busy arranging fixtures with teams of varying strengths.'

According to McCallum, those fixtures included local teams and schools and other theatre companies which could be reached easily on wheels. Ernest Green remembered 'a game at Sibford Ferris in Oxfordshire, about halfway between Shipston-on-Stour and Banbury, played against the first co-educational school in the country. It was actually a Quaker school that accepted girls as well as boys.'

Green thought he was probably in the team because he was Howard's flatmate and drinking partner. However, he proved the hero of a game against the Malvern Players. A long-standing rivalry between the two acting sides gave their battles a tremendous edge. Before the coin was tossed, Howard gave his lads what Green remembered as a 'rattling good team talk'. The message was brief and unambiguous. His exact words were: 'Get out there and give them fucking hell!'

The match, at Malvern College, in strong sunshine, was finely balanced. The Malvern side, captained by Anthony Bushell, included Ernest Thesiger, Alastair Sim and Kenneth More. Bushell scored 112 runs in a low-scoring game. The last man to bat for the Memorial side was Ernest Green, who, in the excitement of the game, had drunk more than was sensible for a player who had yet to face the bowler. When it was his turn to pad up he discovered, to his horror, that Howard was still at the crease. His captain had survived everything the Malvern team had thrown at him, but if victory was to be snatched Green would have to run with his captain, make sure that Howard kept the strike and, importantly, avoid being bowled or run out. It was a tall order for a player who scored in single figures when sober. Considerably the worse for wear, and seeing not one bowler running towards him but two, throwing identical balls, Green closed one eye and opened his innings. Howard's frantic hand signals made no sense to him at all. He was in a world of his own, using his bat to steady himself and regretting not having gone to the lavatory before swaying on to the field.

Green told me, 'They'd gone on their bended knees to me, including Alec Clunes, saying "For Christ's sake, Greenie, don't try anything. Don't attempt to score. Let Trevor take the strike." That's what Trevor was probably signalling to me. I don't know how I did it, but I must've stayed in long enough for Trevor to get the runs we needed to win. Don't remember much about it except that my bladder was full and I was the hero. Yes, me, not Trevor. They knew he'd be all right, but everyone expected me to be out first ball. When I wasn't, they couldn't believe their eyes!'

When war was declared, on 3 September 1939, the Memorial Theatre closed, as did most theatres and cinemas across the country, and the company dispersed. Howard went to help a friend from RADA, Bob Digby, set up Colchester repertory company. Ernest Green decided to go back to his home town of Altrincham and took a job at Avro, the aircraft manufacturer. It was to lead to one of the most unlikely cricket matches of the war years and to Howard playing opposite Guy Gibson, who led the famous Dambusters raid.

Lancaster bombers were built by the Avro company at Woodford near Wilmslow. A special order for nineteen Lancasters with substantial modifications to the fuselage and bomb bays was rushed through. Nobody at the firm knew why these planes had to be different from the standard production Lancaster. It was only after 617 Squadron had completed its bombing raid on the Mohne and Eder dams in the Ruhr valley in 1943 that the mystery was solved. The custom-built Lancasters had carried Barnes Wallis's famously effective bouncing bombs to their targets.

To help take his mind off the war, Ernest Green formed a works cricket team. Sir Learie Constantine, who later captained the West Indies, began his career there. Green persuaded a local vicar to let them practise on a field owned by the Church of England at nearby Lindow End. It became the ground on which they also played matches.

The Dambusters raid had been wonderful for British morale, at a stage in the war when pessimism could so easily have become the national mood. The breach in the Mohne dam had been a hundred yards long. During an extended visit to Germany in the late 1950s I had an opportunity to see the repaired dam. The new brickwork was clearly visible.

In 1943 the Eder dam was the largest in Europe, the burly neck of a seventeen-mile reservoir. When its massive wall collapsed, a tidal wave almost impossible to imagine, comprising an estimated 300 million gallons, swept through the enemy's industrial heartland. It poured into coal mines, swamped ironworks and delivered the knock-out punch to scores of power stations. Crowded trains were swept like plastic toys down crumbling embankments. Germany's war machine had been severely damaged, but for the British who took part in the raid the price was high. Eight of the nineteen Lancasters did not return.

Reports of the raid caused jubilation in Britain, and, to maximize the effect it had on the public mood, the War Office arranged for the surviving flyers to visit a number of sites where essential war work was in progress. Gibson expressed a particular desire to meet the employees at Woodford. He had been greatly impressed by their workmanship and wished to thank them personally.

When Green heard about the Gibson visit he telephoned the office of 617 Squadron and asked if the Wing Commander liked cricket. 'He's mad on it,' was the reply. Green then told the squadron leader, a man called Scampton, 'Look, I have Roy Chadwick, who designed the plane, and Dobson, the head man here. If you send a cricket team over, we'll play you. It would be great for morale. But I should warn you. We have a bloody good team here. Our wicket won't be as easy to hit as those blessed dams were!' Scampton loved the sound of fighting talk. He told Green, 'You're on! I'm sure I'll get clearance. Leave it with me.'

Green told me, 'I thought immediately of roping Trevor into our team if it could be done. We had lost contact, but it was possible to trace him. He was in a camp at Watford waiting to become a civilian. When he heard what I was planning, he leaped at the chance. It was a tremendous game. At Lindow Cricket Club there is a plaque on the wall to this day commemorating the Dambusters match in September 1943. I've seen it.'

When the match had finished, Avro organized a dinner for the two teams and other guests at a pub called the Good Companions, which is near Winsford in Cheshire, close to what is now Junction 18 on the M6 Motorway. Howard was there and was seen having a long conversation at the bar with Gibson before dinner. Later in the evening Gibson told Green that it had been 'the happiest day I've had during the war'. Gibson, a private man, did not enjoy the spotlight under which the raid on the dams had placed him. He did not see himself as a hero but as an operational flyer who had a job to do, and he wanted to get on with it.

However, the War Office saw things differently. His value as a morale-booster outshone anything else he could achieve thereafter for them in the air, and they barred him from taking part in any further operations. Gibson argued and pleaded with them. It was several months before the top brass relented. Gibson was killed in action in 1944 and was awarded a posthumous Victoria Cross.

After the war, with his screen career burgeoning, Howard applied to join the Marylebone Cricket Club. He was told that he would have to wait several years; there was a long waiting-list. Patience was never his strong point. He fumed at the authorities and was shown the door. However, there was a fast-track for applicants who played the game to an acceptable standard – acceptable to the MCC, that is. Howard submitted another application to become a player-member and went through the qualifying procedures, which meant entering a schedule of tournaments approved by the Membership Committee. His scores in a number of previous games were also taken into account. After playing to the best of his ability on several occasions he was accepted. It was a thrilling moment, he told me, that first morning when he put on the famous ham-and-egg tie and sank into a chair at the window of the Long Room.

Just a few wicket-lengths from the north-east corner of Regent's Park, Lord's is quite different from any other cricket ground in the world. It is the ancestral home of cricket. People travel thousands of miles to watch cricket at Lord's, and I can understand why. As a regular visitor these days I, too, have fallen under the spell of this unique ground and its exceptional atmosphere.

Lord's was Howard's favourite place on earth, and he was arguably its most frequent celebrity visitor. His preferred seat was in the upper tier of the Warner's stand. Sometimes he would be surrounded by friends, other times he preferred to be alone, peering through his binoculars. When it was cold or overcast he would retreat to the Long

Room where there would be no shortage of members willing to offer him a seat. It was a gentle, predictable routine, but everything at Lord's tends to be gentle and predictable. That is part of the timeless charm of the place.

No cricketing nation in the world sparks as much emotion in the English breast as Australia. They are the old enemy, the feared 'soft green caps', and their arrival in England at the start of a test series brings a rush of blood to the heads of MCC members – a dangerous experience for most of them, given their advanced years. Howard, as we know already, loved to see Australia beaten. Sadly, it happened only once at Lord's during his lifetime. And, since he was only twenty at the time, he was compelled to travel the world to be there in case it happened again.

Michael Meyer is one of Britain's foremost translators of Scandinavian classical drama. He is also a cricket enthusiast and a member of the MCC. His first meeting with Howard led to the actor's return to the West End stage. They found themselves side by side during the West Indies versus England test match at Lords in 1963. Meyer told me, 'I rather timidly began talking to him, and he was very friendly, and we spent a lot of the day in conversation. Next morning I looked out for him, and he did the same for me.'

At the time Meyer was collaborating with Caspar Wrede, a Finnish stage director, on a stage production of Strindberg's *The Father*. Casting the central role of the officer driven crazy by his vindictive wife was causing them a few headaches. The problem was resolved on the last day of the test match. It was *the* match of the series, thought by many to be the most thrilling ever played at Lord's. Certainly, the climax put years on everyone who attended, and, as they returned to the Pavilion at the end of the final day, several players appeared visibly affected by the drama in which they had taken part.

The match was played between 20 and 25 June, excluding Sunday the 23rd. England's openers were Mickey Stewart, father of Alec, and John Edrich, and the home eleven included Ted Dexter, Colin Cowdrey, Brian Close, Fred Trueman and David Allen. The West Indies side included Garfield Sobers, Frank Worrall, Wes Hall and Laurie Gibbs. From the start the omens were not good for England. The Windies had won the first test at Old Trafford by ten wickets. They came to Lord's full of confidence. Each day the balance of advantage swung back and forth, favouring one side then the other but at no time decisively. At the end of the fourth day England were 116 for three. They needed 234 runs to win.

Everything depended on the final day. Rain delayed the start of play until 2.20 in the afternoon. The vital hours of the morning had been lost. England had only 200 minutes to knock up 118. They began to fall behind the clock. With nineteen minutes left, fifteen runs were still needed. With eight wickets gone, at the start of the final over, the deficit had been reduced to six runs. Off the fourth ball of the over Shackleton was run out. Nine wickets down. The two teams were all square. Pandemonium erupted. It meant that for the final over Colin Cowdrey, who was off the field nursing a broken right arm, would have to be brought in to start off at the non-striker's end. He would already be out of the game for twelve weeks; another blow on the arm could finish his career completely.

These were agonizing moments for both teams and for the packed stands. A win for England was still possible, but if the batsman on strike, David Allen, only got a single it would expose Cowdrey to the formidable bowling of Wes Hall. They conferred and decided not to risk it. Allen kept strike, and the match was drawn. Meyer recalled, 'Trevor was upset for Cowdrey, and at times he could barely look. I glanced at him, and saw that magnificent profile looking so agonized, so persecuted. I thought right away: That's who we're looking for! That's the *Father*.'

Wrede responded enthusiastically when Meyer proposed Howard for the part. When the director phoned the actor, he found him slightly daunted by the prospect of taking on a role previously associated with his great idol Wilfrid Lawson, whom he thought had given 'one of the greatest ever performances of that part'. Howard told Wrede, 'It's a damn shame there aren't any decent translations around.'

Wrede replied, 'There's a new translator called Michael Meyer who is bloody good.'

Howard grumbled, 'Huh, never heard of him.'

Wrede said, 'No, but you've met him. In fact, you've just spent five days at Lord's with him.'

Howard laughed. 'In that case, he'll be splendid!'

Meyer told me, 'Trevor could be so illogical. I was a member of the MCC, so, naturally, I had to be the best translator of Strindberg who ever lived! But he wasn't disappointed when the script was sent to him. He loved it.' Meyer went on, 'What did we talk about at Lord's? Cricket, naturally. Now and then, the theatre. It was always a joy to see him. He was someone with whom you could pick up a conversation from the year before, and it would always seem no longer than a week. Conversation was effortless. It just flowed. I never heard anyone say a bad word about him.'

Howard also played in matches at Lord's, and when he got older, and would appear fairly low in the batting order, he had plenty of time before strapping on his pads to have a drink or two or maybe five or six. In one game, against a team from Ireland, Howard failed to understand a signal from his playing partner to stay where he was and found himself stranded when his bails were sent flying. This delighted the Irishmen because their movie-star victim had not made a single run. The following day, strolling along St Martin's Lane in London with his wife, Howard bumped into several members of the Irish team whose celebrations had stretched into the early hours. Loud greetings and back-slappings ensued. Helen said to one of the Irishmen, 'I understand you got my husband out for nought.'

'Well, missus,' he replied, 'I'd put it this way. Yer man was the victim of a dastardly run-out.'

Another time, after a more successful day's play, Howard met a few friends in the Pavilion bar, where they downed a few pints together. Outside the Grace gate they caught a taxi to the West End, to an exclusive drinking club where one of them was a member. It was after midnight when a taxi began the long-drawn-out process of delivering the celebrants to their respective homes. Howard lived the furthest from the West End, so he was the last one to arrive. By then it was gone two in the morning. He might have been drunk, but at least he was a considerate drunk and let himself into the house with as little noise as possible.

In the hallway suddenly the light went on, which puzzled him because he had not touched anything. Drunks are always confused by events that happen quicker than their thought processes. When the inside of the house swam into focus he saw Helen, her arms folded, looking decidedly fed up. 'Gosh, you are home early, darling,' she trilled. 'What happened? Did bad light stop play?' The hall light went out as suddenly as it had come on, and he was left swaying in the dark.

But despite the occasional spat when he behaved atrociously, Helen did not object to her husband's trips to Lord's. He was safe there from the attentions of other women, although that bolt-hole no longer exists, as ladies are now admitted into the members' areas. A story attributed to the actor Kenneth Haigh – although he denies it – reached me through Mike Johnson, a friend of Howard's. It appears that Howard and the playwright Terence Rattigan were watching the first day's play of a test match at Lord's when they were joined by Haigh, who starred in the original Royal Court production of John Osborne's *Look Back in Anger* in 1956. When the stumps were drawn at the end of the first day they agreed to meet the following day, Friday, and when Friday drew to a close the same 'see-you-tomorrow' arrangements were made.

As the teams left the field to have lunch on the third day Rattigan glanced at his watch and said, 'Excuse me. I have to meet someone. Shan't be long.' At the end of the first over of the afternoon session a somewhat breathless Rattigan returned to his seat. He had only missed the first couple of minutes' play. According to Mike Johnson, Howard leaned across to Haigh and sniffed, 'See that? I told you. He doesn't give a shit about cricket!'

Lord's was, in effect, Howard's second home. He loved everything about the place except the no-nonsense rules on correct attire that apply to all members and visitors. Anybody not wearing a jacket and tie is turned away from the Pavilion. The stewards are courteous but inflexible. I have never been able to talk my way past any one of them. Nor to my knowledge has anybody else.

Leslie Bradbrook, who lived in Finchley Road, used to drink frequently in the Star, a pub not far from Lord's to which Howard went regularly. They got to know each other and often exchanged greetings. Another nearby pub in which Howard was often seen was the Knights of St John, in Queens Terrace, managed by Ron Reeder, whose cuisine was more ambitious than that of the Star. The clientele drifted back and forth between the two, squeezing into the Star for a drink but preferring the Knights when they were hungry. Bradbrook also considered the Knights one of his local pubs, and sometimes when he popped in there he would run into Howard, who was always ready to exchange a few words.

Later, Bradbrook moved to a house in Mill Hill and began drinking at the Gate in Arkley. It was not long before his and Howard's paths crossed once again. Howard said to him, 'Have you got fed up with the Star?'

Bradbook explained that he had moved to Mill Hill.

Howard said, 'That's a relief. I thought you were following me.'

Bradbrook told me, 'I saw quite a lot of him at Lord's, and we'd chat, perhaps for a few minutes at a time, nothing longer. I was never one to push my company on to famous people. He usually had someone with him, anyway.' One time during a test match at Lord's during the late 1960s, Bradbrook could scarcely believe his eyes. Walking up the stairs towards him, inside the Pavilion, was Howard, wearing instead of the obligatory jacket and tie a pink short-sleeved casual shirt half tucked into a pair of badly creased lime-green trousers. He looked a mess. Bradbrook was astonished. He told me, 'I wasn't the only one who did a double-take. Trevor didn't just break the dress code. He drove a coach and horses through it. In forty-five years of going to Lord's regularly I had never seen anything like it. Trevor was the only one who could get away with it. I remember thinking at the time: Bloody good luck to him.'

9
MUTINY

If Mr Brando would care to tell me beforehand what he's planning to say, then I might know when he's going to finish!
– Trevor Howard on location during the filming of *Mutiny on the Bounty* (1962)

BETWEEN *The Men* (1950) and *The Godfather* (1969) Marlon Brando was arguably the brightest and most original star in movies. He put method acting on the map and gave it respectability. Howard's involvement with Brando began one day when the director Carol Reed telephoned him to ask if playing Captain Bligh in a remake of *Mutiny on the Bounty* appealed to him and what changes he would make to Charles Laughton's 1935 portrayal.

Howard, who knew Laughton well, thought that Hollywood had ruined the story of the mutiny by trying to depict the conflict between Bligh and Fletcher Christian, the mutineers' leader, as a simple black-and-white struggle between good and evil. Bligh had been less evil than portrayed by Laughton, and the real-life Christian, played by Clark Gable, had been no saint.

Howard felt that there was sufficient meat in the true story to make fictionalization unnecessary. It could be dramatized for the screen without jettisoning the facts. Although he and Reed had no previous discussion of the subject, their views were similar. Howard thought nothing more about the conversation until Reed phoned him two months later with the news that the green light had been given, that Metro-Goldwyn-Mayer would produce it and that the role of Captain Bligh was his. Howard was told that he was everyone's first choice for the role, including Brando's, who would play Christian. Howard accepted immediately, elated at the thought of working again with Reed and for the first time with Brando. What he did not know at the time was that, in order to attract the moody star, MGM had caved in to several of Brando's demands which would stretch relationships beyond breaking-point and send the production costs spiralling.

Desperate to repeat the success of its remake of *Ben Hur* (1959), which scooped up eight Oscars, the studio decided to film the exteriors in Tahiti where the *Bounty* collected its cargo and where the sun and the sand and the tropical vegetation would provide an authentic backdrop. The cast and crew thus assembled on Tahiti in readiness for the arrival of a full-size replica of the *Bounty*, built in Lunenburg, Nova Scotia, at a cost of $700,000. Work began on the three-masted ship in February 1960. It was as faithful a replica of the original as circumstances would allow, although additional space was needed for securing and moving the cameras during filming. The total height from the deck to the top of the mainmast was 103 feet. More than 10,000 square feet of canvas was used for the sails. Severe weather delayed the delivery of large quantities of oak from New Jersey which were needed for the planking.

Careful planning failed to avert costly delays and disappointments. From the beginning, one disaster followed another. The design modifications and extra weight (of a diesel engine, camera mounts and so on) seriously affected the buoyancy and steerability of the ship, which meant that it not only took longer than planned to reach the South Seas from Nova Scotia via the Panama Canal but that it almost capsized several times and caught fire twice during the 7,327-mile voyage. It finally reached Tahiti on 4 December 1960, two months after the film's planned starting date.

Tahiti is the largest of a group of islands known as the Society Island group, which include Moorea and Bora Bora. Scenes were filmed on all three islands. The total population of Tahiti is around fifty thousand, more than half of whom live in the only town of any size on the island, Papeete, which became headquarters for the unit. The interior of the island is rugged and beautiful, with lots of crags and peaks, palm trees and plunging waterfalls, but hardly any inhabitants. The bulk of the population hugs the coastline.

The first scene that Reed filmed was the stone fishing sequence, in which hundreds of native women wade offshore and, beating the water with their hands, drive the fish towards their menfolk in canoes. Almost every inhabitant of the island appeared in the shot, each of whom was paid $10 a day. The eight hundred who used their canoes to catch the fish earned a further $10, and they were allowed to keep whatever they caught. The scene depicting the arrival of the *Bounty* at Matavaii Bay was filmed with more than six thousand Tahitians milling around on the sea and on the shoreline. These scenes were not only spectacular to watch; they recreated the original event with uncanny accuracy.

The true story of the *Bounty* is well documented. It set sail from Spithead in England on 23 December 1787 under orders to proceed to Otaheite (later renamed Tahiti) to collect breadfruit for transport to the West Indies. Early explorers such as Captain Cook had reported that breadfruit, the staple diet of the South Seas, produced strong, healthy islanders. Colonists in the British West Indies wanted an inexpensive, nourishing food for their African slaves, and they petitioned the King, George III, to have it introduced to the colonies. The *Bounty*, under Captain Bligh, was commissioned to transport a cargo of young breadfruit samples to Jamaica, where they were to be replanted, grown to full size and harvested.

While passing through Endeavour Strait, off the island of Torfua, *en route* for Jamaica, the mutiny erupted. Its leader was Fletcher Christian. The trigger was Bligh's curtailment of drinking water for his crew, because the plants needed more of it than he had allowed for. There was only so much to share around, and if the choice was between saving the men or the cargo Bligh was under orders to safeguard the breadfruit first and foremost. Every drop of water had to be rationed. Not surprisingly, the crew mutinied and seized control of the ship.

Bligh and eighteen crew members who remained loyal to him were set adrift in an open boat no more than twenty-three feet long. They were expected not to survive. But forty-one days later, against overwhelming odds, they waded ashore at Timor in the Dutch East Indies, having rowed a distance of 3,618 miles with the loss of only one life. And that man had not been lost at sea. He had been killed by hostile natives on a small island after the boat had pulled up on the beach for an overnight rest.

In an effort to keep their whereabouts secret from the Admiralty, Christian and his followers left Tahiti and sailed 1,300 miles southwards to the uninhabited island of Pitcairn, which is only two miles long and a mile wide. They burned the *Bounty* so that it could not be seen from a passing ship. The island became their home, and also their prison, since they had destroyed their only means of getting away from the island.

It was a story that lent itself to numerous interpretations. Brando disagreed with the slant British screenwriter Eric Ambler had put on the story. He wanted something 'more meaningful'. Ambler endured the star's moody criticisms for several weeks and then quit. With replacement writers the same arguments persisted, and while this was going on filming ground to a halt. Papeete became a transit camp for the hundred-strong disgruntled unit, although it was generally felt that being paid regularly for taking life easy was nothing to grumble about.

Reed was wary of upsetting Brando unnecessarily, but he wanted the story told truthfully, and what emerged from Brando's daily tinkering with the script was a storyline that departed from the truth at several critical points. Reed was also annoyed at the ease with which Brando subverted the procession of screenwriters who displaced each other with clockwork precision. Charles Lederer, for example, incorporated all Brando's impromptu mutterings into the script, whether or not they made narrative sense. Mostly they did not. Between them they turned Bligh into a one-dimensional bad guy, a scowling ogre better suited to a B-movie. The real-life Bligh was bull-headed and had a notorious bad temper, but he was not a sadistic megalomaniac, and the sailors under his command, while treated harshly, suffered no worse than others in naval service during the eighteenth century. When Reed pointed this out Brando went into one of his prolonged sulks, and the atmosphere between them which had begun so promisingly took an abrupt nose-dive.

Howard and Richard Harris, who was playing a character called John Mills, promptly took Reed's side, and, gradually, a split emerged. It was not serious to begin with, but, as views became entrenched and professional pride entered the equation, the divisions widened. One faction comprised Brando, Lederer, the producer Aaron Rosenberg, a front office executive called J.J. Cohn and the cinematographer Bob Surtees. The rival group that formed behind Reed included most of the British and Irish actors on the film. Howard promptly emerged as their most articulate and respected spokesperson. He also had the most to lose among the British and Irish contingent if the film turned out to be a flop.

While genuinely in awe of Brando's talent, this group were puzzled by his wilful conduct. He had hijacked the production and appeared accountable to nobody. With a growing sense of helplessness Reed's supporters retreated to their favourite bar in Papeete, Quinn's, and briefly contemplated a mutiny of their own.

Then, suddenly, a new problem swept in from the sea: heavy rain.

Solid, unrelenting rain. In MGM's eagerness to get started, nobody had considered how bad the weather can be in the South Seas at the end of the year. Cloudbursts forced everyone to dash for cover, strong winds put the small boats out of action and, at times, almost toppled the replica of the *Bounty* where it rested, top-heavy, in shallow water. Illness was another delaying factor. One by one key members of the unit collapsed with dysentery and other debilitating tropical conditions. Finally, demoralized after four months of relative inactivity, and with the bills mounting at the rate of $50,000 a day, the studio was forced to switch production to Hollywood where the sound stages were equipped and waiting.

Back in Hollywood Brando and Reed continued their disagreements. Rumours that a vast amount of money had been squandered with barely anything to show for it caused shares in MGM to plunge several points. Panic and gloom engulfed Culver City. The press stopped believing it would be 'Ben Hur Part Two' and began calling it 'Cleopatra on Water'. Brando, of course, could not be sacked, but Reed had no safety-net. Before the director had unpacked his suitcase the knives were out for him.

The head of production, Sol Siegel, accused Reed of mishandling the Tahitian shoot and insisted that every effort be made to catch up with the original schedule. The director agreed but could not give Siegel a completion date. Siegel lost his temper at Reed's refusal to provide the answers he wanted to hear. 'You have a hundred days to finish the job,' said Siegel flatly.

Reed shook his head. 'I won't say "yes" because I know I can't do it in that time,' he said. 'One hundred and fifty days, maybe.'

This statement fell on deafer ears than Reed's earlier plea to keep the story factual – a request that had Siegel on his feet shouting, 'Nobody goes to the movies to watch history! We have museums for that!' Siegel and MGM's vice-president Ray Klune decided that the only solution was to cut their losses, and, reluctantly, they told Reed that his services were no longer required. Honesty, bad weather and a star actor who would not behave had cost Reed his job.

Howard and Richard Harris were angry when they heard the news. Harris groaned, 'We're in the hands of bloody philistines.' They wanted Siegel to reconsider.

By then Siegel was sick of all of them. He told them, 'Gentlemen, before you say anything, I want you to understand one thing. A star is a star. Everyone else is expendable. Reed doesn't want the job, and I don't want him doing the job. Now what was it you wanted?'

Howard told me, 'Carol's departure, for reasons that I quite understand, was a terrible shock. Without him, they made a different film.' Earlier he had told Cecil Wilson of the *Daily Mail*: 'When Carol offered me the part, the idea was that we should bring out the good side of Bligh as well as the bad. We had talked this over. But the Americans thought that the public wouldn't be interested.' He went on, 'They wanted as big a villain as Charles Laughton had been in the old picture. It's wrong to show a real person like Bligh in a false light.' But the studio was not interested in historical accuracy. It was desperate for a box-office smash hit. It really did seem to think it was making 'Ben Hur Part Two'. It was the same basic formula. Swap the chariots for a galleon and roll the cameras.

Reed's replacement was Lewis Milestone, a veteran director who had made the granddaddy of all anti-war movies, *All Quiet on the Western Front* (1930). Brando nodded through his appointment, because by then it scarcely mattered to him who picked up the reins after Reed. He would film it the way that he wanted, and a director nearing seventy with the same recent track record as Greta Garbo – in that he hadn't made a film for thirty years – suited his plan perfectly.

After several weeks in Hollywood, filming the departure of the *Bounty* from Spithead at the start of the voyage, Bligh recounting his misfortunes to the Admiralty and the subsequent court martial of the captured mutineers (which was cut in the final edit because Brando wanted the film to end with Christian's death), the unit returned to Tahiti on 22 April 1961 to restart location work in improved, although less than ideal weather conditions. Filming the mutiny on board the *Bounty*, when Christian and Bligh have their violent confrontation, took most of the month of June. Half of the cast and crew became seasick as the ship was battered by strong offshore winds. Howard told me that every evening, after he had returned to dry land, he continued to feel the ground heaving beneath his feet. 'And that was *before* I'd had a fucking drink!' he joked.

Lewis Milestone was on a completely different wavelength to Brando. While Carol Reed had been receptive to the star's constant revisions to the script, Milestone wanted none of it. He had no patience with method actors. He distrusted their preoccupation with meaning and motivation. The only meaning that an actor needed was in the script. Milestone expected them to learn it, perform it and not ask questions about it. But Brando was too sharp for him. Within days he had circumvented the veteran director and was giving the orders. Milestone battled on for a while, growing more and more exasperated, but the writing was on the wall or, in this case, on a fresh batch of script pages which Brando distributed each morning. Before long Milestone was pointedly omitted from the circulation list. Nobody was sure why Brando decided to play Christian as a laughable fop; but nobody had the authority to stop him.

Brando's bizarre performance did not go down well with Harris. In the scene in which Christian slaps Mills, the sailor played by Harris, to show his opposition to the idea of a mutiny, Brando merely brushed Harris's face with the back of his hand. It was an effete, almost girlish slap. Harris responded with a mock curtsy and waggled a limp wrist in the air. Everybody saw the joke except Brando. They tried the scene once more, and again Brando's blow was almost non-existent. Everybody waited to see how Harris would react. He did not fail them. He thrust his chin forward and said, 'Come on, big boy. Why don't you fucking kiss me and be done with it!' Brando stared at him, white with rage. The Irishman decided that he had had enough. He turned his back on Brando and marched off the set.

The next day they returned to the scene, but despite further barracking from Harris Brando would not change the way that he landed the blow. When the shot was completed to his satisfaction he calmly walked off the set. Harris had to be restrained from going after him. According to Peter Manso, Harris told an American reporter that when he returned, three days later, Brando approached him and said, 'Dick, you shouldn't have done that. I'd like you to know this. I'm the star of this picture and you're opposing me. Remember that, please.'

Brando's insistence on multiple takes was a further irritation for the British actors, who were used to working much faster. In another scene with Harris, after a dozen or more takes Brando appeared suddenly to lose interest and walked away muttering, 'I don't know if it's going to work or not.' Harris was left standing with his mouth open, without any hint of an acknowledgement from Brando. The anger boiled up inside him again. 'Damn you! Look at me! Act! Who the hell do you think you are?' he shouted at the retreating star.

Howard, less truculent than Harris but equally disenchanted, griped about his co-star's demands to rewrite everything just before a take. The rewriting, of course, was intended for everyone except Brando, who never took the trouble to learn lines because it drained energies which he preferred to disperse off the set. He had words chalked on large boards from which he read whenever he felt like it and ignored at other times. A dispassionate observer would deduce that Brando saw other actors' lines as merely convenient spaces for him to think up what he would say or do next. Howard complained, 'You never know were the hell you are. You don't know for ten minutes what you're playing because the next scene contradicts it.'

After one disagreement with him, Howard began to call him '*Mr* Brando', partly to mock the fact that Brando had taken charge but also because of the continuous references made throughout the script to 'Mr Christian'. When Milestone tackled Howard for being slow to respond to Brando's lines, Howard's impatient roar echoed around the set. Milestone said, 'Trevor, I'm just trying to get to the root of the problem.' Howard pointed a baleful finger at Brando. 'There's your fucking problem,' he roared. 'If Mr Brando would care to tell me beforehand what he's planning to say, then I *might* know when he's going to finish!'

Most of the time, though, he managed to keep a lid on his frustration. Sometimes he paid Brando back in his own currency. One stiflingly hot day a scene had been set up on the shoreline at Bora Bora showing the natives' welcome for the sailors off the *Bounty*. It was a massive scene, with thousands of extras spread around the beach and waiting in the shallow water. Howard took his place in the baking sunshine, clad in a heavy ceremonial uniform and hat. Brando could be seen twenty or so yards along the beach, shaded by a palm tree, chatting with three Polynesian girls.

Ridgeway ('Reggie') Callow, the assistant director, called everyone to order through a loud-hailer. Brando made no movement. He continued to talk to his lady friends. Once more Callow called out, 'Mr Brando, we're ready for you.' The amplified voice carried easily to where Brando stood, but again he pretended not to hear. Howard, meanwhile, continued to sweat under a hat which grew hotter by the minute. A further call to Brando got no response. Had there been water in Howard's headgear by this time he could have brewed himself a coffee. At the fourth invitation Brando broke off his conversation and strolled towards Howard as if he had all the time in the world. When he arrived at his marks, there was no sign of Howard. The British actor had disappeared and was cooling off, in more ways than one. Callow put the loud-hailer to his lips again and announced, wearily, 'Mr Howard, if you wouldn't mind, we're ready for you . . .'

As filming progressed, Harris learned that the most effective way to deal with Brando was not to be drawn into a confrontation with him. The star seemed to relish confrontation, which from his position of absolute authority was a form of bullying. The simplest way to turn the tables on him was to ignore him. If you didn't react, there was little he could do. On one occasion Brando moved the marks where Harris, an onlooker during a tense scene on deck, was supposed to be standing. Three times the cameras began turning, and three times Brando halted them to move the Irishman to a fresh spot. But Harris had learned his lesson well. He refused to be provoked into the angry response Brando expected. Taking his latest position, Harris turned to the other actors and said with a tolerant smile, 'Forget your grand ideas, lads. We're just cabbages in this man's cabbage patch.'

But the star ultimately got his revenge. In a scene before the mutiny Mills accompanies another crew member to the Captain's cabin to spell out their grievances. In his cabin Christian overhears their conversation. As written, the scene belonged to Howard and Harris. Brando had no lines. He had nothing to do except lie back and look thoughtful.

But expecting Brando not to steal a scene is like expecting the Pope to change the Vatican into a five-star hotel. When the camera picks him up he is dressed in a silk night-gown and matching night-cap, with a huge clay pipe clenched between his teeth. While the audience wonders why suddenly he looks like a cross between Sherlock Holmes and something out of a mail order catalogue, they miss the explanation as to why the mutiny is about to erupt. Whether Brando was playing power politics, relieving boredom or just being plain cussed is anybody's guess. But it demonstrated again what a power he was in the industry. Few other actors could hijack a key scene, cynically drain its dramatic potential and knock a hole in its narrative structure by just lying back and looking silly.

The film was completed during October 1961. Clifton College had taught Howard that grievances should be left behind on the playing field, but the goings-on in Tahiti had affected him so profoundly that for once he lowered his guard while talking to American journalist Bill Davidson. He called Brando 'unprofessional and absolutely ridiculous'. But his criticisms were mild compared with those of Lewis Milestone, who accused Brando of costing the production at least $6 million and months of extra work. He is quoted as having said, 'The movie industry has come to a sorry state when a thing like this can happen, but maybe the experience will bring the executives back to their senses. They deserve what they get when they give a ham actor, a petulant child, complete control over an expensive picture.'

The article appeared in New York's *Saturday Evening Post* under the headline 'Six Million Dollars Down the Drain: The Mutiny of Marlon Brando'. The subhead read, 'A petulant superstar turns paradise into a movie maker's nightmare. How Brando broke the budget in a marathon remake of *Mutiny on the Bounty*.' It accused him of making outrageous demands, of colossal self-indulgence, of squandering vast sums of MGM revenue, of lacking professional judgement and of putting on forty pounds in weight between the start and completion of the film. Brando and Elizabeth Taylor, following the disastrously overpriced and delayed *Cleopatra* (1962), were accused of jeopardizing the future of the entire industry. The article suggested that a suitable penalty might be to send them both to Tahiti to make 'epic pictures of each other'. If Tahiti would not tolerate them they should try 'nearby Bora Bora, an island whose very name onomatopoeically suggests our reaction to both stars'.

Brando was outraged. He flew to New York to confront Joseph Vogel, head of MGM, who backed down and issued a statement on 25 June to the Screen Actors' Guild as well as to the press that Brando had cost the studio no extra money and that the production problems were not of his making. Instead, Vogel blamed the delay in receiving the *Bounty* replica, the weather, the script, the clashes between directors and cast, the abrupt departure of Carol Reed – everyone and everything, it seemed, had conspired to create the mess except Brando, whom he said had 'performed throughout the entire production in a professional manner and to the fullest limit of his capabilities, resulting . . . in the finest portrayal of his brilliant career'. Handed this giant tub of whitewash, Brando promptly filed a libel suit against the *Saturday Evening Post*, demanding $4 million in general and special damages and $1 million in exemplary and punitive damages. Howard did not escape his wrath either. Brando wrote him a personal letter describing his anger and sorrow at being labelled 'unprofessional' by someone whom he had trusted, a 'fellow-professional, of all people'. He also claimed that for him, too, making the *Bounty* film had been an exhausting and frustrating experience, although he did not expect anyone to believe him. Howard certainly did not. 'Damn fool,' he growled, two decades later. 'Kicks up an almighty bloody stink and then he's the first to complain about the smell!'

Helen flew to Papeete for short holiday with Howard at the start of the production before the tempers became frayed. She told me, 'Driving from the airport I saw Hugh Griffith in a lurid-coloured shirt. He had gone native.' She recalled the *Bounty* moored in a picturesque bay and her meeting with Brando. 'Trevor introduced us,' she said. 'They were both in costume. I didn't recognize Brando at first. He was a lot shorter than I'd imagined.'

Brando switched on the charm for her, and it worked. 'He was very nice to me,' she said. 'He wanted to learn about our aristocracy. He wanted to know how the peerage in Britain was created and who were allowed to wear coronets. He seemed fascinated by English protocol.' Helen was aware that there was a less charming side to Brando, too. She told me, 'Trevor was sure that he got Carol [Reed] sacked. He always denied it, but Trevor wasn't convinced. Brando had the power to get rid of anybody. Even Trevor would have been sacked if Brando decided that he didn't want him, although as time went on it would have been more difficult to explain, after they had done a lot of scenes together.'

When filming was completed, the replica ship was promptly dispatched on a world trip to publicize the forthcoming epic and also to allow audiences to see for themselves the craftsmanship that had gone into its construction. It sailed from Tahiti to California, to the port of San Pedro near Los Angeles, where thousands of spectators lined the wharves to greet it. Then it went northwards to Vancouver and Victoria in British Columbia where, once again, the well-wishers turned out in their thousands. At Seattle it became the centre of attention at the 1962 World Fair, and from there the route taking it to Britain and Europe was via San Francisco, the Panama Canal, New Orleans, Miami, then northwards up the Atlantic Seaboard and finally across the Atlantic itself.

When the *Bounty* reached London Howard was the guest of honour at a reception hosted by MGM officials. The sight of the ship arriving between the elevated bascules of Tower Bridge dragged him back, momentarily, to the broken promises, personal slights and tetchy arguments of the previous year, but these were easy to set aside, because Howard had a fondness for the ship that dwarfed the bad memories. As it sailed past their vantage point, an MGM publicity officer noticed Howard looking a bit misty-eyed, savouring the moment. He approached the actor and said to him, 'Beautiful, isn't it?'

Howard nodded. 'Yes, it is,' he said. 'And it was once mine!'

After brief stop-overs in Europe the *Bounty* sailed back across the Atlantic, and its arrival in New York was scheduled to coincide with the joint première of the film in New York and California. In Hollywood the opening at the Egyptian Theater was a star-studded occasion, with tickets nominally priced at $100, and many of the cast and their guests and other celebrities attended, including Brando and Howard. The New York showing, at Loew's State Theater, was comparatively low-key. Brando also put an appearance in at Loew's and probably wished that he hadn't. The audience did not know what to make of his performance and booed the film.

The reviews displayed puzzlement and disappointment in almost equal measures. Critic after critic wondered what Brando was playing at. Bosely Crowther, the *New York Times*'s respected critic, wrote, 'There is so much in this picture that is stirring and beautiful that it is painful to note and call attention to the fact that it also has faults. The most obvious of them is the way that Marlon Brando makes Fletcher Christian an eccentric . . . Brando puts tinsel and cold cream into Christian's oddly foppish frame.' Crowther added that Howard's Bligh was 'really quite a fearful and unassailable martinet'. The *New Republic*'s Stanley Kauffmann asked, 'Is it all a talented actor's revenge on a big studio for snaring him inside an empty, spectacular film? Only in a few moments of fury does life touch the part and Brando burn through. The rest is like an all-American half-back imitating Leslie Howard as the Scarlet Pimpernel.'

In the year following its release *Mutiny on the Bounty* earned only about $10 million in the United States and the same amount abroad – a disastrous take given the fact that it needed to make $60 million to recoup the $30 million it cost. As a result, in April 1963 MGM reported a drop of $3.39 per share on the stock market. A clean sweep of the executive offices followed. Studio head Sol Siegel, who had fired Carol Reed, lost his job along with Joseph Vogel, the chairman who had been browbeaten into praising Brando's part in the fiasco. Furious stockholders cited the letter of exoneration as sufficient reason for getting rid of him.

Richard Harris's fears proved well founded – the film did nothing at all for his international career. But at least he had the satisfaction of knowing that although Brando made money out of it, following closely on the heels of two other flops – *The Fugitive Kind* (1959) and *One-Eyed Jacks* – his damaged reputation would ensure that never again would he have the authority, or the freedom to misuse it, that he had enjoyed on *Mutiny on the Bounty*.

Despite a cautious mellowing of his feelings as time passed, Howard resolved never to put himself through that kind of experience again, imagining that it was a safe enough bet after his public row with Brando. But fate has a habit of sneaking up on you, and everybody in the industry knows that Hollywood is where people say 'Never' when what they mean is 'Ask me again in an hour's time'.

In the town to complete *Von Ryan's Express* in 1964, Howard had a run-in with several expensive limousines. At a lavish party attended by Howard and his wife Helen, it appears that their hired car got hemmed in on the driveway by later arrivals. Halfway through the evening they decided to leave. Howard went outside to extricate their car, not realizing he was very drunk. He accelerated forwards, ramming the vehicle parked in front, which in turn rammed the one ahead. He then reversed gently, or so he thought, but the car thudded into the one behind him, which shunted and damaged the one behind that. The noise brought other guests spilling out of the house. In the centre of the mayhem was a British actor, unsteady on his feet, making foolish noises. It all took place inside private gates, so the police weren't involved, but the costs of replacing the damaged limousines made it the most expensive night out of Howard's entire life.

Shortly afterwards he received a phone call from Aaron Rosenberg, the producer of *Mutiny on the Bounty*, offering him a guest role in Brando's latest movie, a wartime thriller entitled *The Saboteur: Code Name Morituri*. 'Good God,' said Howard, 'You haven't tied in with him again, have you?' Rosenberg briefly explained the situation. He and Brando were collaborating again. Brando wanted money for a development on a coral island in the South Seas named Teti'aroa which he had recently bought. 'He's a changed man since *Mutiny*,' Rosenberg declared. 'The island has got to him. Now all he wants is to be earning again and do a good job.' With this in mind, Brando had agreed to co-star in the film with Yul Brynner.

Rosenberg went on, 'Marlon's right for this picture, and so are you. It'll mean staying over for a short while, but you'll be well paid, Trevor. I do mean well paid. He really wants you, and so do I.' The words 'well paid' were especially welcome to hear after writing off the limousines, leaving his earnings from *Von Ryan's Express* more or less intact. The stuff about Brando waving an olive branch could be taken with a pinch of salt. If the star was genuinely seeking to make amends, that was a bonus, but frankly Howard doubted it. A brief phone call to his agent the following morning got the deal moving, and by mid-afternoon he was in Rosenberg's office putting his signature on the contract.

Brando's character in *Morituri* (1965), as it came to be called, was a middle-aged German pacifist who defects to Nepal when war breaks out. There he builds a luxurious hideaway stocked with his favourite books and art treasures and recordings. Into his life strides a plain-clothes intelligence officer, played by Howard, who blackmails him into spying for the Allies by threatening to turn him over to the Nazis. They had one scene together, straight after the opening credits, in which Howard had most of the dialogue and controls the pace of the narrative. Brando's job was to react, at first dismissively, followed by sullen insolence.

Howard should have remembered that Brando could never allow a scene in which he appeared to be anyone's but his. Generosity has no currency in method acting. James Dean stole scene after scene from Rock Hudson in *Giant* (1955) by fiddling with a variety of props, including a lariat, with devastating effect. Steve McQueen added so many quirky mannerisms to his screen character in *The Magnificent Seven* (1960) that Yul Brynner complained bitterly about his conduct to the director, John Sturges, who restored harmony to the set by telling McQueen, 'For Christ's sake, Steve, do nothing. Just stand still!'

Brando could never just stand still. If a scene was being filmed he had to steal it. He understood no other rule. And naturally he drove Howard crazy on *Morituri*, contriving to look the picture of innocence while he mischievously reduced the British actor's impact to zero. While Howard got on with the speech, bowling it straight down the pitch as he always did, Brando countered with camera-hogging tricks which, in a fairer world, would have got him arrested. He got a large dog to feed out of his hand. He ordered tea. He put a scratchy old record on a gramophone. He gazed fixedly at a collection of paintings. While Howard talked, Brando play-acted. He was in the world that he knew best. He was both tormentor and tutor, dishing out a lesson in one-upmanship at which he had become the grand master. A critic once wrote that Brando could 'chew on a matchstick with more skill than many actors can summon up to create a whole character'. At the end of the scene Howard felt as if he had been fed into a grinding-machine. He could only shake his head and curse the man's audacity. After returning home Howard read an item about Brando's libel action against the *Saturday Evening Post*, which was still dragging on. As well as Joseph Vogel's letter of exoneration, Brando could now say that his producer and co-star on *Mutiny on the Bounty* had worked with him again, which substantially weakened the magazine's claim that everybody who had worked on that film held him in contempt. Yet, despite having victory in his grasp, Brando, ever the unpredictable, withdrew the suit. He had won a significant moral victory, and that appeared to satisfy him.

The encounter between Ol' Blues Eyes and Ol' Red Eyes was an astonishing disappointment. Yet from a casting director's point of view it looked like a dream coupling. Frank Sinatra was the world's Number One post-war singer, at the height of his fame and influence, whose versatility as an actor was equally acknowledged. No challenge in the entertainment field had fazed him. Crooner, musical star, Oscar-winning actor, tycoon, Rat Pack leader – everything, it seems, had succumbed to his drive and charm. Sinatra made everything that he did appear effortless and enjoyable. That was the public perception, at any rate. Behind the scenes, we were to learn later, it was a different story.

Although opposites in intellect and temperament, Howard and Sinatra were two honchos who knew how to party. There were parallels in their relationships with their wives, too – in Sinatra's case, with his first wife, Nancy. Both women had married their husbands before fame and fortune came their way, and both had taken a back seat, calmly, loyally, while their partners fooled around. Nancy had been discarded, but she was the mother of the singer's three children, which kept her permanently to the forefront of his life. She once told her friend Phyllis McGuire, one of the singing McGuire Sisters, 'Despite all the women he's had, I'm the only one who gave him children.'

The Howards had no children, yet Helen's grip on Trevor was as secure as if she had had half a dozen. He adored her in his clumsy, wayward, maverick way, but he would say, laughingly, 'A standing prick has no conscience', as though it was a command which had to be obeyed even when he didn't feel like it. Yet however silly and ill-judged his antics away from Arkley, Howard desperately needed someone constant in his life, someone who would smarten him up for a public appearance and ensure he got there on time, who would smooth his pillows and tuck him up after a night or a week out on the tiles, who would tolerate his moodiness and his maddening ways. He needed a steady, reliable wind beneath his wings, and there was no woman in his life more steady, more constant, more reliable than Helen.

The film that Howard made with Sinatra, *Von Ryan's Express* (1965), was conceived as a vehicle for its star. That was the limit of its ambition. Few concessions were made to inject realism into the story. Sinatra played Colonel Ryan, an American flyer captured by the Germans during the Second World War who leads an escape while a group of prisoners are being transferred by train from their prisoner-of-war camp in Italy to one in Germany. The escape succeeds, but Ryan is killed while shepherding the others to freedom. 'It was, I think, the beginning of the trend of big names wanting to die before the end of the picture,' Howard said afterwards.

The Sinatra character was a sharp, street-wise kid from New York – in other words, the familiar Sinatra stereotype, Pal Joey in a sleek, black flying-jacket, a pearl in the quagmire of creased tunics, unshaven faces and hopelessly negative clowns who make up the British prisoners. Until Ryan arrives to teach the British how to fight a war, they slouch around the prison camp, defeated, demoralized, dressed in rags. No escape plan of any kind has entered their heads. The British officer, Major Fincham, played by Howard, comes across as a grumpy old-school traditionalist, a relic left over from the Crimean campaign. In their battle for screen honours, everything was geared to ensure that Sinatra smelled of roses and Howard, to put it bluntly, just smelled.

The main location camp was at Cortina D'Ampezzo, high in the Dolomite Alps, which was an hour's drive from where the cast – with the exception of Sinatra – and the crew were staying. Howard's co-star status was a nominal arrangement, a cynical device for boosting the film's sales outside the United States. It quickly became clear that Howard would be given none of the privileges ordinarily accorded to an actor whose name went above the title. In a Sinatra picture only one person matters and, true to form, that person ruled completely. It made for erratic film-making, to say the least. Sinatra would work only when he felt like it, sometimes for no longer than two hours a day. At the snap of his fingers he would be helicoptered to his luxury villa, still in his US Air Force flying-jacket.

To avoid hanging around, Sinatra ordered that his scenes be shot end-to-tail, although the budget made no allowance for that. Watching these shenanigans, Howard was reminded of Marlon Brando and muttered to John Leyton, one of the other British actors, 'Why is it, the bigger they get, the more they fucking annoy?'

The largely English and Italian crew had never experienced film-making like it. When everything was ready to roll in the morning, occasionally the star was ready, but mostly he wasn't. Sometimes, after arriving an hour or two late, instead of getting on with the job he would disappear to his trailer to confer with an assortment of cronies and bodyguards who shadowed him everywhere and went to extraordinary lengths to feed Sinatra's ego.

One incident amused Howard so much that he constantly referred to it afterwards. He told me, 'I was in Cortina before Frank arrived, and, d'you know, his staff, or "gorillas" as the press called them, emptied all the jukeboxes in all the cafés and filled them with Sinatra records. Nobody else's songs could be played. I said to Johnnie Leyton, who sang a bit, "D'you think they're trying to tell Frank that he's the only singer in the world worth listening to?" and Johnnie said, "I'm sure he thinks that already."'

Howard was disappointed when his relationship with Sinatra failed to get off the ground. He couldn't understand why. The singer who appeared to be such a regular guy in his movies was unapproachable in real life. No discussion of any kind was tolerated before filming their scenes. Sinatra did not speak to Howard other than delivering his lines, and he was shielded day and night from the world beyond his trusted entourage.

On one occasion Howard decided he needed to clarify with Sinatra something in the script that seemed wrong. He started to walk towards the cluster of trailers occupied by Sinatra and his friends, but before he had taken many steps inside the studio compound two shadowy figures in snap-brim hats persuaded him to turn round.

Helen flew out to spend a few days with Howard halfway through the location shoot. The trip involved a scheduled flight from Heathrow to Venice and then a smaller plane on to Cortina. At Venice airport a mix-up over her luggage meant she had to fly on to Cortina without her suitcases. She arrived at her hotel feeling angry and miserable. As she sat in the lounge waiting for Howard, who was on the set, a stranger walked up to her, said, 'Hey, you look depressed. Don't be like that', and offered to get her a drink. But Helen had had a gruelling day and was in no mood to be chatted up by a man whom she described to me as 'on the short side and balding'. With great effort she managed to smile and be civil. As she began to plan her escape from him, 'because it was a terribly ordinary conversation, really dreary', Howard suddenly appeared behind them and said to Helen, 'Darling, I see you've already met Frank!' She hadn't recognized her husband's co-star. She was too busy thinking of her lost luggage.

When filming finished in Italy, the unit moved on to Spain and finally to Hollywood for the interiors. Even on his home territory Sinatra's off-hand attitude persisted. Howard received no invitation to have a drink with the Rat Pack. Many years later, when he talked about it, he still couldn't understand Sinatra's extraordinary behaviour.

'As an actor Frank is remarkably good,' he told me. 'He liked to wrap things up quickly, which is how I prefer to work, too, so there was never any dissent between us on that score. He's not a trained actor, of course. He plays himself all the time, which is all he needs to do, because that's what the people want to see. Things were done his way because he was top dog. The director, Mark Robson, had a miserable time, always being overruled. Money is power, you see. If Frank hadn't liked the picture at the end he'd have burned it. He could afford to. But one thing I will say. I can't think of one actor whose career has been damaged by being in a film with Frank Sinatra. It's always the other way around.'

10

TO IRELAND WITH SMILES

I loved his innocence, his bravura and his kindness, just his whole aura of total humanity. I was always seeking his company. He gave me such joy. – Sarah Miles

THE idea for *Ryan's Daughter* came from Robert Bolt, the celebrated English playwright and long-term collaborator with David Lean. Holidaying in Italy in 1968, Lean read the first draft, which was a reworking of Flaubert's romantic novel *Madame Bovary*. It promised a comparable visual style to their earlier films together, *Lawrence of Arabia* (1962) and *Doctor Zhivago* (1965). Bolt was excited by its possibilities, and the two of them worked energetically on the script for the next nine months, at the end of which they discussed it with Anthony Havelock-Allen, the producer of *Brief Encounter* and several other Lean movies.

Although the location and period Flaubert had described were abandoned in favour of Ireland during the Troubles of 1916, their script owed much to the flavour and central characters of the nineteenth-century French novel. The saga of an unsatisfied young wife exchanging a dull husband for an ardent lover was familiar territory for Lean. Subsidiary characters in the Flaubert novel, such as the girl's father and a rumbustuous priest, were retained in a modified form, and the leafy woodlands where the lovers meet were re-created in Ireland for the notorious 'ride-in-the-woods' scene.

The film story was set in a tiny seaside village, Kirraray. The local publican's daughter, Rosy Ryan, played by Sarah Miles (then Bolt's wife) is infatuated with Charles Shaughnessy, a mild-mannered schoolteacher played by Robert Mitchum. She coaxes him into marrying her, but their wedding night and the ones that follow shatter her romantic illusions. The village priest, Father Collins, played by Howard, is outraged when Rosy insists there must be more to marriage than what she can find in hers. 'Why must there be? Because Rosy Ryan wants it?' he roars at her.

She has a brief but tragic affair with a handsome British Army officer,

Major Doryan, played by Christopher Jones, whose time in the trenches has left him morose and shell-shocked. Her husband has a different kind of shock when he discovers what she's up to. As their marriage heads for the rocks, so does Shaughnessy, but only to sit on them and stare out to sea while he struggles to come to terms with Rosy's infidelity.

When a shipment of weapons intended for Republican activists is intercepted by British troops, everyone in the village suspects that Rosy has tipped off her lover. They swarm around the schoolhouse, drag her outside, rip off her outer clothes and crop her long hair. The informer was actually her cowardly father, played by Leo McKern, who diverts suspicion from himself by joining in the condemnation of Rosy, although he hasn't the stomach to stay and witness her humiliation. Later that night on the beach, a distracted Doryan blows himself to pieces with some IRA explosives discovered there. The Shaughnessys leave Kirraray for good, hoping to put the tragic events behind them.

The actress who would play the central role of Rosy was always going to be Sarah Miles. The writer had created the role with his wife in mind. Although she was twenty-five years old at the time playing someone much younger, Bolt and David Lean were unanimous in their choice. It had not always been that way. When they had collaborated on *Doctor Zhivago* Lean had wanted Sarah in the role of Lara, because, he said, she was the only actress he could name, apart from Celia Johnson, who 'acts with her eyes'. However, Robert Bolt, who at the time had not met her and knew of her only through her films *Term of Trial* (1962) and *The Servant* (1963), protested to Lean, 'You can't cast her. She's working class!' Later, when they met, Bolt realized that he had made a terrible gaffe. Roedean-educated Sarah had deceived him by the quality of her acting.

Luring Robert Mitchum, their choice to play Shaughnessy, to Ireland for the location shooting was not an easy task. The rationale behind his selection never ceased to puzzle the American star. Arriving in Ireland, he told reporters, 'Dunno why I'm playing an Irish schoolteacher. For a fraction of what they're paying me, they could have a real one.' Sarah's first meeting with Mitchum was enough to accelerate any girl's heartbeat. He strolled into the production office wearing large sunglasses and carrying a red rose. 'For you, my rose, with all my love,' he said, without the merest hint of mockery. The man had style.

Most members of the cast, and much of the crew, were housed

around Dingle, a small coastal village in County Kerry, with a picturesque harbour where rows of tiny fishing boats rode the tide. Mainly as a result of the film, the place became a thriving tourist attraction and in economic terms it has never looked back. Bolt and Sarah rented Fermoyle House, a spacious property twenty miles to the north along a rugged road. While Bolt worked at the house on a new project most days, its distance from the film location added extra hours to Sarah's already long day. She told me, 'We were, in a sense, lord and lady of the manor, occupying this gracious house, but being so far from the location I had to leave the house at four every morning! I would have preferred a hotel nearer.'

Lean defended his choice of Mitchum, saying that 'a quiet, smooth-sweet character actor in the part would have been totally wrong and, even worse, deadly boring. Whatever one thinks of Bob Mitchum, he has never been boring.' Another reason might have been the large quantity of US finance behind the film, for which an American star would have been mandatory. Mitchum was a heavyweight, a safe name, a crowd-pleaser with an enviable track record. But if he imagined that this was just another rapid-shoot movie he could stroll through without touching the sides, he was heading for a big surprise.

Howard was not Lean's first choice to play the rough-and-ready parish priest. Alec Guinness turned it down before Howard was considered. When Lean phoned him to inquire if he'd do another film with him, remembering that his two previous roles for Lean had been as a marriage wrecker, Howard said to him, 'Tell me one thing, David. Whose wife do you want me to fuck this time?'

After he read the script he began to understand why Guinness had not liked the part. The priest seemed on the fringes of the drama, always arriving after things had happened, but it was a take-it-or-leave-it offer and Lean wouldn't hear of expanding the role. In Ireland, Howard said to Lean one day, 'You know, David, I'm only doing this because of you.'

Lean was a bit taken aback, figuring that if there was any charity in their relationship it had always come from his side. He said, 'Oh, come on, Trevor. It's a bloody good part.'

Howard replied, 'It's a terrible part.'

Lean explained to Howard what he and Bolt wanted of the character and that he was not peripheral but right at the centre of things, the strident voice of sanity and moral reason raging against infidelity, bigotry and armed rebellion. For a canny director Lean was also a fine salesman, and Howard went for the bait. Twenty years afterwards the hook was still embedded in his mouth. He told me, 'David gives all the characters, not just the main ones, a job to do. The size of the part isn't everything. Where it fits in the jigsaw also counts.' One could almost hear Lean applauding in the background.

The arrival of the film crew delighted those in the town with goods to sell or hire – rooms, drinks, transport and so on – at often triple or quadruple their normal prices. One of the most popular bars in Dingle is Paddy Bawn's (it has since been renamed Paddy Bawn Brosnan's). On the inside it looks like a giant dog kennel, with dark wood as far as the eye can see. The lighting is just bright enough to let you see that you're not drinking someone else's beer.

Another murky alehouse is Dick Mack's on Green Street, which heads north out of the village. Dick has decorated the flagstones outside his pub with the names of his many famous clientele, among them three of the stars of *Ryan's Daughter* – Mitchum, John Mills and Christopher Jones. On one of the days I was there a funeral was taking place in the church directly opposite Dick's place. It was barely three in the afternoon, yet the drinking and chattering classes were already three deep at Dick's solid wood bar. The arrival of the hearse drew a few solemn-faced drinkers to the doorway of the pub, where they stood silently, impassively, blinking against the strong sunlight.

Lean chose the coastline around the peninsula for its combination of picturesque beaches and jagged mountains which in places drop almost vertically into the sea. The village of Kirrary was built on a hill called Maoilinn na Ceathrun, behind the village of Carhoo in Dunquin, a parish whose only claim to fame before *Ryan's Daughter* was that it was the most westward parish in the whole of Ireland. I have disappointing news for film buffs thinking of visiting the remains of Lean's purpose-built village. It is, sadly, no more. The fronts of the houses had been built of bricks and mortar and might have survived had a group of local residents, fearful of an endless invasion of tourists, not insisted that the structures be demolished when the film was finished.

The rugged locations have changed little since the film was made. Shaughnessy is met by Rosy on his return from Dublin and later traces her and Doryan's footprints in the sand, on Inch Strand, a wide stretch of beach at right-angles to the snake-like coastal road between Dingle and Slea Head, the most westerly point of the peninsula. Sometimes the cameras skip several miles without the audience suspecting. The opening sequence shows Rosy losing her parasol on a cliff top and it being scooped out of the water below by two figures in a curragh, a flat-bottomed boat used by Irish fishermen. She is actually standing on the cliffs at Moher in County Clare when she loses the parasol, and it is returned to her at Coumeenoole Cove in County Kerry, a distance of forty miles.

The recovery of the arms shipment from the sea was also filmed on Coumeenoole Cove, above which rises a steep, spiral stone road. Here, too, the film-makers cheated. The sequence featuring the big storm, which batters the crowds as they retrieve the arms from the sea, was filmed at the Bridges of Ross, County Clare, an area famous for its extraordinary rock formations, sixty miles from where the shipment came ashore. Comparing these locations then with now is an interesting exercise. Coumeenoole Cove is the same today as it appears in the film. Huge breakers pound the sand strip below the rocks exactly as they did when Rosy poured her heart out to Father Collins. Where Slea Head, another location in the film, slopes down to the sea, the rocky shoreline today matches its celluloid image groove for groove.

Filming began in March 1969, in the sea off Coumeenoole Cove. Almost immediately the unit experienced its first near disaster. Howard and John Mills had climbed aboard a curragh. It is a small, nimble craft designed to skim over the water with comparatively little oar-power. The problem is that a curragh without a cargo of fish is tremendously unstable because, when empty, the hull barely dips below the waterline. Even an experienced oarsman can have problems manoeuvring an empty curragh in choppy seas. By his own admission, Mills was 'a fair-weather sailor', but with no dialogue in the scene he hoped it would take only a few minutes to capture the shot, and he felt confident that, with a bit of practice beforehand, he would be able to manage it. Any longer and he would have had serious reservations.

While Mills rehearsed, the weather deteriorated. Lean was determined to complete the scene before conditions became too adverse. Six handlers in frogmen's suits hauled the curragh, with Mills and Howard squatting inside it, beyond the point where the waves broke and waited for Lean's signal to release it. Howard peered at the churning water and said to Mills, 'I hope you know what you're doing,

Johnnie. This cassock weighs a bloody ton.' By this time the winds coming in from the Atlantic whipped up the surf, blinding the actors and stinging their faces, but having taken hours to set up the shot Lean insisted on a take.

Howard told me, 'I didn't like it, but one doesn't argue with David Lean. The man said, "Get in the boat," so I got in the bloody boat!' When the frogmen released the curragh, it rocked uncontrollably. The actors could do nothing but hang on grimly and hope that the cameras were rolling.

Lean's behaviour shocked Sarah Miles. She told me, 'I was right there, beside the camera. Trevor's sense of balance is not his strong point. It was a dangerous thing to ask them to do in normal conditions, but with a storm roaring in from the Atlantic it was madness. Johnnie was in the front, scrambling to keep it balanced. He is an athletic chap, very coordinated. Trevor was sitting in the back, in his black robe, looking grimly at the huge swell. He wasn't giving and taking with each wave that came. He seemed to be just sitting there, not moving at all, like a statue. Then, suddenly, this great big wave came over and the boat tipped up. The divers wanted to go in, but David said, "No, you'll ruin the sand. We mustn't have footprints on the sand!" So all of us just stood there, gawping both at David, who was holding the divers back from rescuing them, and at the sea, for Johnnie and Trevor had disappeared. There was no sign of them in the water.'

She went on, 'I was frightened. Really frightened. I won't ever forget it. Trevor appeared first. About then David decided he had to stop the camera. So the guys went in to get Trevor. But there was no sign of Johnnie for quite a time. The poor man had been knocked unconscious.'

Mills recalled the incident in his autobiography: 'I caught sight of an enormous wave coming towards me on my left. I pulled hard on my right oar to try to face it, but it came at us too fast and hit us with a crash. The curragh went up in the air and turned over. I felt a sharp blow on the back of my neck and blacked out.' The frogmen reached Mills in time and he was rushed to hospital, wrapped in a blanket, in the back of a unit car. Fortunately, there was no serious injury, just a mild concussion, and he was back at work within two days.

Both Mills and Howard had worked with Lean more than once before and were prepared for a long haul. Mills said, 'First and foremost, you have to surrender your time, because it doesn't exist, period.

If you accept that, which you should, then you will be presented in the best possible way. There won't be one bad shot.'

Sarah Miles agreed: 'Genius often comes wrapped in ruthlessness and bolshieness. That's the price we have to pay.'

Mitchum, however, was unfamiliar with Lean's tortoise ways, and it was a rude awakening for him. 'After ten days on the film we were already seven days behind,' he grumbled. Bad weather contributed to many of the delays. Mitchum began to hate overcast skies. 'Ireland makes the rain a national monument,' he said. 'I think it's deliberate. They do it so they can make the tourist season last twelve months a year.' He later described his time in Ireland as the least joyful period of his life and compared it with working in the Lockheed manufacturing plant in California and with being in the US Army.

He escaped boredom by throwing parties at the Mill House Hotel outside Dingle, which he had taken over. Sarah Miles recalled, 'It was on the waterside, a bit further on from the Skellig Hotel, between Dingle and Dunquin. It was situated down a track, on a sort of cliff beside the shoreline. It had about fourteen rooms with numbers on the doors. Girls would come and go from time to time. They were all given keys and room numbers. Make of that what you will. Mitchum's wife Dorothy visited him periodically but not enough, in my opinion. I think she should have been there all the time. If wives want husbands like him to behave, they should be there to make sure that they do.'

Unlike Howard, Mitchum was a long-time marijuana user. He had spent sixty days in Honor Farm Prison in California for possession back in 1948. While in Ireland Mitchum passed him a few joints, but Howard preferred alcohol to loosen up. However, too much alcohol had the opposite effect on him, and on one fact you could always rely. When Howard started drinking he would carry on until he had too much of it. Sarah told me, 'If Trevor had been on marijuana instead of drink while we were in Dingle he would have been a lot happier. You could tell immediately if Trevor was on dope or alcohol. He was so divinely easy and joyful on marijuana and so cantankerous on drink. I could always tell what Trevor had been taking. Marijuana suited him in a way that booze never did.'

As the film progressed it became the norm rather than the exception to have weeks of inactivity between shooting one half of a scene and completing it. The love scene in the woods was typical of this. Rosy and her lover, Doryan, meet on horseback, ride slowly through a bluebell wood, dismount in a clearing and make love. In the film it lasts a matter of minutes. Shooting it took several months, more than one location and a bundle of headaches for everyone involved.

Lean began filming the sequence in an area of woodland on the Kenmare Estate, at the edge of the Ring of Kerry, which looked absolutely stunning in the sunshine. He got lots of excellent 'establishing' shots of sunlight through the trees, the carpet of bluebells – reminiscent of the sea of daffodils in *Doctor Zhivago* – and tracking shots of the lovers on horseback threading their way through the trees.

The intention had been to film the entire sequence at Kenmare, but the weather changed abruptly and it became impossible to continue for several weeks. When they returned, in September 1969, the leaves were a different colour, but the art director Roy Walker and his assistant Derek Irvine were able to match the original and the later close-ups with a few licks of paint and clever use of lighting. However, Doryan got no further than unbuttoning Rosy's blouse when the heavens opened again and turned the woods into a bog.

By the time everything dried out scarcely a leaf could be seen on any of the trees. They had been dislodged by the heavy rain. Restoring the backgrounds was no longer practicable, so the unit had no alternative but to continue the scene indoors. Locations manager Eddie Fowlie chose a dance hall in Murreigh, a nearby village, which was equipped to replicate the Kenmare woods. The earlier footage was matched leaf for leaf, colour for colour. The birds released on to the set had the time of their lives. It was their second spring in less than six months.

In June Howard got permission to return home for a couple of days 'to sort a few things out'. What he had in mind were the test match at Lord's, the Wimbledon finals and downing a few jars at the Gate. He saw Ray Illingworth captain England against a West Indies side led by Garfield Sobers. Wimbledon was subdued that summer, after the news that Maureen Connolly, who had won the singles title on two consecutive visits in 1953 and 1954 and who had been a great favourite with the crowds, had died of cancer at the age of thirty-five.

As his days at home stretched into weeks, Howard began to worry that he might have unintentionally broken his contract. He had been given permission to leave the location but not for anything like the time he had taken. He decided to return to Ireland and face the consequences. On the return, however, Lean greeted him warmly – 'Ah,

Trevor, there you are. Good man. Be with you in a jiffy' – and nothing was mentioned about his absence. Howard told me, 'David didn't say anything, because he hadn't missed me at all. He was too bloody preoccupied with the sand and the seagulls and those blasted cloud formations to notice that I'd been gone for three fucking weeks.'

Accidents caused several delays, and Howard was responsible for one of them. He had wanted to go on a donkey ride along the beach for weeks before mentioning it to the production manager. He had a thing about donkey rides, possibly a legacy from those seaside school holidays, enviously watching other children riding on donkeys when he hadn't the price of a ride for himself. For insurance reasons stars of the film were not permitted to do anything out of the ordinary. Donkey rides were forbidden, although activities such as riding motor cycles and getting stoned out of their skulls every night were permitted. Smarting from their refusal to give in to him, Howard enlisted Sarah Miles's help: 'Go on, Smiles. Tell 'em I want that bloody donkey ride.' She spoke up on his behalf, but again they refused.

Howard wouldn't back off. Sarah told me, 'After a month of him banging on about this damn donkey ride, I went back to the producers and said, "Look, it's driving him crazy. Let him do it. I'll stay with him. I'll see to it that he doesn't fall off. Trust me." They had a discussion about it. They weren't happy, but eventually they said "OK". So Trevor and I went out for his donkey ride. We were just walking along the beach, and he was like a big, joyful child. It was a lovely morning, the sand was soft, everything was perfect. We got half a mile or so, then turned to come back. Something happened at that moment. I saw daylight between him and his donkey. He fell with a thump and shattered his collarbone. The production team were furious. They said, "Now you understand why we said no, Sarah. But you knew better, didn't you, Sarah? Now look what you've done, Sarah." It's actually quite difficult to fall off a donkey at a slow walk, but, yes, Trevs managed it.'

He was rushed to hospital, strapped up and placed in a private room. Helen was working in a play, so she couldn't join him till the end of the week. On the Sunday morning she hired a small aircraft from Elstree Flying Club, the nearest airstrip to their home in Arkley, and flew to Killarney where the pilot managed to land the plane on the racecourse, and from there she was driven to the hospital in a taxi. A nurse ushered her into the room where Howard was being taken good care of, allegedly, by a young woman from the publicity unit.

A couple of weeks later, when her theatre contract ended, Helen decided to make her presence felt more sharply. This time she brought with her their pet poodle Mathieu. Everything went smoothly until they attended a party at Mitchum's hotel on 6 August to celebrate the actor's fifty-second birthday. It was Dingle's biggest social event for years. Dorothy Mitchum was there, as was Mary Hayley Bell (John Mills's wife), together with people from the film unit and one or two regulars from Paddy Bawn's bar. The party was noisy and good-natured, and everybody enjoyed themselves. Mitchum and Sarah danced in the living-room, as did a number of the other guests. Mills, Bolt and Howard played darts in a back room. Howard drank heavily and worked himself into a dark mood.

Helen began to feel ignored and decided she would join her husband in the darts room. After a couple of minutes Howard's raised voice could be heard. Helen's attempt to lift his mood had achieved the opposite effect. He was overheard shouting at her, 'Go home then. Take the fucking plane home if you want to!' Helen ran, red-faced, from the room. She scooped up the dog, reattached its lead, muttered, 'We're off now, Matty. I can't take any more of this', and swept out the front door. Sarah Miles's elder brother Martin remembered Helen brushing past him, clearly distressed and close to tears.

The party quickly got under way again, the music from the radiogram once more drowned by the chatter of voices. Mitchum and Sarah resumed their dance. She lost track of the time, but it was probably no more than ten or fifteen minutes later when, out of corner of her eye, she noticed Martin waving his arms at her from the hallway. She thought: Oh no, he can't want to go home yet; she called out, above the noise of the record player, 'What is it?' He beckoned to her again, and she shouted, 'No, you come to me. I'm dancing.'

Martin threaded his way between the couples on the floor, and when he reached her he said, 'That lady who just left – she has fallen in through the door.'

Sure enough, Helen was lying on the hallway floor, unconscious, her hair spattered with blood. Mitchum and Sarah rushed to her side while someone went to find Howard. Helen drifted in and out of consciousness, weakly calling the poodle's name. She had fallen badly outside the hotel and almost toppled into the bay. Howard was mortified by what had happened. She was hospitalized for a few days – at the same hospital in Killarney where Howard had been treated for his fall – and as soon as she had recovered sufficiently to travel home she packed her bags and left, announcing that she was glad to see the back of Dingle for the last time.

Sarah said to me, 'Trevor was never intentionally cruel or anything like that, but he could appear uncaring. He did have a dark side. We all have it. If you have a light side, you must have a dark side too. One goes with the other. It's his light side that I always think about. That was captivating.'

The casting of moody American method actor Christopher Jones as Major Doryan was a mistake. His lean face, quirky body language and soulful eyes looked right for the part, but he made little impact on the film or on his co-stars, and he seemed to be weighed down with personal problems. Also he couldn't arouse Sarah Miles to anything but annoyance. Their romp-in-the-swamp scene was cinematically a disaster. Sarah believes that Lean intercut the scene with treetops and close-ups of spiders' webs to spare the audience from having to watch the phoney antics on the ground. Here was a man acting out a million male fantasies, lying on top of a scantily clad Sarah Miles, and making it look about as much fun as returning a book to the library. Sarah said afterwards, 'I kept smelling my armpits, wondering what the hell was wrong with me. I've never felt so unwanted in my whole life!' She told me, 'David had no patience with him. He wanted to sack him, but by then we were well into the film, so he couldn't.'

Jones had a red Ferrari sports car in Ireland, but he was forbidden to drive it, for the same reason that they hadn't wanted Howard to ride a donkey. One morning Jones asked the director, 'David, can I go for a drive in the Ferrari?' Lean replied, almost jovially, 'By all means. Go ahead.' Jones had expected a blunt refusal and repeated the question to make sure that he had heard correctly. He said, 'Really? Are you saying that I can?' Again, Lean nodded, doing his best to appear chummy and tolerant. 'Yes, Chris, I'm saying that you can.' When Jones was out of earshot Lean turned to Sarah who was standing near by and said, 'With luck, he'll break his bloody neck!'

Ryan's Daughter was premièred at New York's Ziegfeld Theater on 9 November 1970. The US critics hated it and savaged Lean, who became depressed by the severity of the onslaught. Pauline Kael, doyenne of American movie reviewers, wrote a particularly vicious critique. She called it 'gush made respectable by millions of dollars tastefully wasted', adding, 'the emptiness shows in every frame'. She called the main characters 'stereotypes worked up to fit the big screen'. For Lean and Bolt she reserved her most acid comments, saying, 'They don't have it in them to create Irish characters; there isn't a joke in [it] except maybe the idea that an Irish girl needs a half-dead Englishman to arouse her.' She condemned the film as 'an awe-inspiringly tedious lump of soggy romanticism'.

Although *Ryan's Daughter*'s reception in Britain was generally warmer than it had been in the United States, only a minority of critics came down in favour of it. Dilys Powell was one of them. She encouraged us to 'sit back, enjoy and for the most part accept the story . . . set out with the professional skill one expects of Mr Bolt and Mr Lean.' She singled out Howard for praise, adding, 'His playing of the village priest dominates the cast. It is his image which I see when I recall the film; and the command and humanity with which he invests the role does much to counter the sour view (not mine) which in general the film offers of Irish rural character.'

In a sense, it was as unfair to compare *Ryan's Daughter* with Lean's earlier epics as it would be to compare one director with another. Were the critics really expecting him to go on making the same film for the rest of his life? Did *Oliver Twist* and *Great Expectations* have to be the standards by which he would be always be judged? This seemed to be the lines on which the critics were thinking. Howard had called him a visionary, and visionaries tend to be ahead of their time. Lean's affinity for nature, and his ability to capture on film nature at its most awesome, was quite unique. The storm sequence, for example, is a powerful visual experience, and one is left wondering how it was achieved.

Lean crammed the film with elegant imagery, potent symbolism and clever counterpoint, but praise for all this invention was largely denied him. The scenes on the beach, where the husband finally has his worst suspicions confirmed, is stark in its intimacy, despite the vastness of the open spaces around him. The increasing estrangement between the married couple, the British officer's mental disintegration and the tension between Church and State are all delicately understated, yet the critics seemed obsessed with the narrative. Yes, the plot is slim for a film lasting three hours, and some of the set-pieces are arranged too neatly, but in telling his story Lean has provided a glorious feast for the eyes which, for my money, could hardly be improved upon. It may be the fate of visionaries to have their talents derided in their lifetimes and not truly be appreciated until after they are dead. I suspect that one day *Ryan's Daughter* will be seen as a masterpiece of the cinema and Lean's extremely diligent form of artistry will finally be acknowledged.

I asked Sarah Miles if her memories of making *Ryan's Daughter* were on the whole good or bad? She said, 'My main memory is of sitting on a hilltop in a caravan at six in the morning in the pissing rain wondering what the hell I was doing there, because there was no other actor or member of the crew around me. I would sit there getting mad, waiting for either the rain to stop or someone to arrive. Film acting is so horrifically belittling. It's hurry-wait, hurry-wait all day. I don't really have happy memories of anything that I have ever done in films.'

Happy memories of Howard, however, persist. Sarah told me, 'I loved that man. My God, yes. I loved his innocence, his bravura and his kindness, just his whole aura of total humanity, which is very rare. And of course one does always seek that out. I think we are all aiming to get back to that state from whence we came, and Trevor was nearer to that state than almost anybody I've ever known. I was always seeking his company and going up to him to see if he was all right in his little cottage, because he gave me such joy.'

11

HOT WATER

It is alleged that this ex-officer, who is thought to be mentally unstable, has posed as a person who is entitled to wear the decoration of the Military Cross. – Vincent Evans, Assistant Director of Public Prosecutions

By October 1943 the war in Europe had reached a critical phase. The desert victory at El Alamein the year before had given Britain its first real taste of success after three horrific years of being fought into a corner. D-Day was under discussion, but the landings were eight months into the future. However, the Eighth Army victory in North Africa prompted Winston Churchill to slip a note of optimism into his speeches. At the Mansion House in London he declared that we had reached 'perhaps, the end of the beginning'.

The message was clear and unequivocal. Everyone must knuckle down and do his or her duty. It was therefore an odd time for a trained officer who had yet to see combat to be asked to resign his commission and leave the service. But that was the decision reached by senior War Office personnel when they reviewed the case of Second Lieutenant Trevor Wallace Howard-Smith of the Staffordshire Regiment. He was told to pack his bags and leave the Army. Not just his regiment. The Army. The reasons why they took this action remain locked away in their files, the contents of which will remain secret until the year 2018, to comply with the 75-year confidentiality rule which keeps out of the public domain the career records all military personnel.

That should have been the end of the story. Not everyone is cut out for soldiering. So what? Other vital jobs needed doing to help the war effort. Howard was in his late twenties, more fit after his training than he had ever been, and nobody has ever questioned his patriotism. So, what went wrong?

It is not an easy story to piece together. His service in the Army started off badly. He made no secret of not wanting to be in uniform. The idea of killing another human being, for patriotic or any other reasons, was abhorrent to him. The prospect of being killed was equally unattractive. He had had no life up till then. He had achieved nothing, and there was much that he wanted to do.

Orders to report for army training reached him at Harrogate, while he was with the White Rose Players. He realized that if he ignored the instruction it could only be a matter of time before they caught up with him, but the letter stunned him nevertheless. He did not tell anyone. He stuffed the unwelcome documents back into their brown envelope and hid them. He simply wanted to put the whole thing out of his mind. That was not easy. When the curtain went up later that evening he felt so agitated that he fluffed his lines several times. A second demand to report for duty went the same way as the first one. After that his name was added to a growing list of draftees who failed to report for service as ordered. But, unlike many of them, Howard did not go into hiding, change his address or make a determined effort to keep out of their clutches. He simply wanted to put off the dreaded day for as long as he could without appearing to be a fifth columnist or a coward.

When the long arm of the law eventually encircled his neck, Howard told them there had been a dreadful misunderstanding. The two ladies who ran the White Rose Players were responsible, he said. They had, he said, destroyed the documents without realizing their importance. There had probably been a certain amount of collusion between Howard and the women, for they certainly would not have wished to lose him, and who better to have covering his tracks than two eccentric females whose explanation, that they couldn't tell call-up papers from a street map of Singapore, would seem too bizarre to be anything but the truth.

The public, perhaps misguidedly, had their heads stuffed full of heroes. Not the louche heroes of 1930s fiction but real ones. The Royal Marines, newly formed in 1942; the famous Few; individuals whose memoirs would, when the war ended, become household names when they published their stories. During a war heroes occupy the centre stage. People want to read about them. They are the stuff of propaganda. It is difficult to understand today how obsessed with heroes the general public had become during the middle years of the war. This may explain why some movie heroes signed up as soon as the recruiting offices opened in 1939. A 'good war' would safeguard, possibly increase, their popularity. One could therefore reasonably assume that a 'bad war' would have the opposite effect.

For Howard, his departure from the Army in 1943 in less than heroic circumstances must have been humiliating – another entry in a lengthening catalogue of rejections, begun when his parents sent him to Clifton College in 1921. But this was far more serious for him than anything that had occurred previously. He had his sights set on a career in the movies. The chances of this happening would disappear in a puff of smoke the minute it became known that his Army career had ended badly. And being booted out at that particular time was about as bad as it could get.

Nobody can be certain whether it was bitterness or envy or fear of rejection that prompted him to reinvent himself after his return to civilian life. Even Howard had no answer when I asked him about it. It may have started as straightforward commercial expediency, a feeling that he had to conceal the past to be given a fair chance to demonstrate his acting skills to the people who would make up his audiences of the future. Of course casualty levels within every walk of life – servicemen, the Merchant Navy, civilians – were so great that by the time the war ended almost everybody had lost someone, neighbours, friends, members of their family. Being thrown out of the Army must have been deeply upsetting for Howard. But it wasn't his act of concealing the truth that landed him in trouble with the police. It was what he substituted in its place.

An article appeared in the *Tatler*, dated 15 November 1944, which described Howard as the holder of the Military Cross, a former paratroops captain who had been 'invalided out of the Army and is now rehearsing at the Arts Theatre in *Anna Christie*'. Several weeks later, on 27 January 1945, the London *Evening News* carried an article headed 'My Friends the Stars' by Jympson Harman who wrote, 'Leading man of the next Noel Coward film *Brief Encounter*, which begins shortly, is to be an actor back from the wars who has run into luck after waiting ten years. He is Captain Trevor Howard, MC, Airborne Division. He joined up in 1940, was invalided out last year.'

Harman, an experienced columnist, had got his facts muddled. Howard had not been a captain, he had been a second lieutenant. He hadn't been awarded the Military Cross or any other decoration; he hadn't joined up, he had been compelled to join up; he was not invalided out, he was ordered to resign his commission and had suffered no physical injury; and, finally, he returned to civilian life in 1943, not the following year as reported.

The two articles came to the notice of Vincent Evans, Assistant

Director of Public Prosecutions, based at Mayfair House in Piccadilly, who wrote to the Commissioner of Police at New Scotland Yard on 28 March 1945 requesting 'the services of one of your officers for the purpose of making inquiries . . . it is alleged that this ex-officer, who is thought to be mentally unstable, has posed as a person who is entitled to wear the decoration of the Military Cross.'

Sergeant William Mogford was assigned to the case. He interviewed Howard at his flat in Pall Mall, and on 2 May communicated his findings to his chief inspector. Mogford wrote: 'War Office documents show this ex-officer's name to be Trevor Wallace Howard-Smith and that he enlisted in the Royal Corps of Signals in October 1940, later being granted a commission as Second Lieutenant in the South Staffordshire Regiment. On the 2nd October 1943, he had to relinquish his commission on the grounds of ill health as he was found to be suffering from psychopathic personality and considered unfit for further military service. He did not serve out of this country and was not awarded the Military Cross or any other decoration.'

Mogford told Howard that he could be prosecuted for claiming to have a war decoration when it was untrue. It was a criminal offence under Section 156a of the Army Act of 1881. He also warned him that any further attempt to pose as a decorated war hero would be treated with the utmost seriousness. That should have been the end of the matter. But the story would not go away. In an *Evening News* follow-up article on Howard on 23 November 1945, Jympson Harman wrote, 'Perhaps the outstanding individual achievement of the picture [*Brief Encounter*] is that of Trevor Howard, who plays the doctor. Two years ago he was winning the MC with the Red Devils Airborne Forces, risking a life which is now clear the British Cinema needs very much.'

As a result of the second article repeating the inaccuracies of the earlier one, Mogford talked to Harman, who told him that Howard and a Rank film company publicist had given him the information. Harman was angry, suspecting that he had been used rather cynically to give readers of the *Evening News* the false impression that Howard had risked his life in the service of his country and had been in combat. The relationship between press agents and newspaper columnists is one of mutual dependence. It can only flourish in an atmosphere of trust. Harman felt that his trust had been betrayed and made no further reference to Howard's military service. But, as any journalist knows, correcting a wrong impression is a bit like trying to get a genie back into the lamp. Printed stories are archived where they can be raided by other reporters, who may innocently perpetuate the lie. The bigger the story, the less chance there is that it will ever be satisfactorily corrected, particularly when the source of the lie does not want anybody to get to the truth.

The police were certain that Howard was being two-faced with them – protesting that he could not stop the fictions appearing about him while behind the scenes encouraging the recycling of the potted biographies. But they could not prove anything. All that they could do was express their dissatisfaction in the strongest possible terms.

Howard was summoned to New Scotland Yard two days after Christmas 1946. The warnings were repeated, and he was asked to provide a signed written statement which said, 'I am not in possession of the Military Cross.' He followed this with an implausible – and, to police ears, risible – explanation that the reporters were confusing him with other holders of the Military Cross in his old regiment. It was all a misunderstanding, he said. An obvious case of mistaken identity. His statement went on: 'I know there were two Howards who had won the MC whilst serving in the same Airborne Division as myself,' he said. 'The Press must have mistaken me for one of the other Howards . . . The situation is very embarrassing for me. Since I was cautioned by Detective Sergeant Mogford about eight months ago, I have taken every step I can think of to have this kind of publicity concerning myself stopped.'

But it didn't stop. A press release issued to publicize *I See a Dark Stranger* (1946) described him as 'very reticent. In this he resembles many other servicemen who have distinguished themselves in action. All we know is that he was in the Red Devils Airborne Division, and was awarded the Military Cross . . . Trevor saw action in Norway and in the invasion of Sicily, where his ardour was slightly dampened by his being accidentally dropped into the sea.' Another story had him clinging to a glider that had been shot down over the sea, holding on for eleven hours while several of his platoon drowned or died of exposure during the night. He was beginning to sound like Pimpernel Smith, Audie Murphy and GI Joe all rolled into one. And this about a man who, throughout his time in the Army, had never been outside Britain.

The Criminal Investigation Department lost patience with him and wanted to press charges, claiming that the publicity would frighten other fraudsters. However, the Director of Public Prosecutions advised them against it, because there was nothing that connected Howard personally with the stories. Accordingly, an instruction was issued to stop the investigation.

With the prospect of proceedings removed, press releases about his films trumpeted his war-hero image at every opportunity. His biographical notes press pack for *The Long Duel* (1967) repeated the lie thus: 'When World War Two came, he volunteered for Army service but after two years' active duty requested a transfer to the 6th Airborne Division. "I was bored," Howard explains, "and I just wanted a little excitement." He won the Military Cross in the Norway and Sicily campaigns before being invalided out in 1943.' The hand-out for *The Offence* (1972) stated, 'After rooting about in the ranks, he was commissioned in the 6th Airborne "for a little excitement", saw action in Norway, got decorated, dropped in the sea at the invasion of Sicily, and was finally invalided out, as a Captain, in '43.' I need not quote from other releases I have seen except to confirm that in most of them the Military Cross story was highlighted in a separate paragraph.

There is no doubt in my mind that Howard wanted people to believe the lie. He had no difficulty finding journalists willing to roll over and have their tummies tickled. On 3 May 1959, he was quoted in the *Sunday Dispatch* saying, 'Really one does not want to talk about the war . . . That's all in the past, you know.' When asked about his Military Cross, Howard replied, 'I just don't want anybody to know about it. I hate people who wear their laundry marks, or talk about them. I just want to forget the war.' But not enough, it seemed, to stop fuelling the robust fictions.

Profiling Howard at the première of *The Charge of the Light Brigade* (1968), James Thomas wrote, ' Howard had some things in common with Lord Cardigan – they both had a hard war. Howard took part in three airborne landings and won the MC.' That any journalist could imagine a parallel between Howard and Lord Cardigan is bizarre, but it shows how deeply the lie had its roots. They had absolutely nothing in common.

Similarly, in an article to publicize *Scorpion Tales* (1980), Janet Watts quoted Howard as saying, 'I treated war as a form of theatre.' She wrote, admiringly, 'In the Sicily campaign he spent eleven hours in the ocean, hanging on to a glider. Most of his friends died. That was his war.' It most certainly wasn't.

In the *Sunday Telegraph* magazine dated 26 January 1986 – thirty

Rowley Green House
Arkley. Herts

Terence Pettigrew is researching my biography with my permission, and I would be very grateful if you could help him in any way.

Sincerely

Trevor Howard

(TREVOR HOWARD)

Trevor Howard's letter of authorization for this book, 1980

Top: Clifton College, Bristol © Terence Pettigrew, 1998

Bottom: Rugby Team, Clifton College, 1931. Howard, aged eighteen, is third from left, back row

© Reproduced by kind permission of Norman Travis

Top: Hockey Team, Clifton College, 1931. Howard is third from left, front row, and Norman Travis is fourth from right, back row

Bottom: Fives Team, Clifton College, 1931. Howard is second from right and Norman Travis is third from right

Top: Cricket Team, Clifton College, 1931. Howard is second from left and Norman Travis is fifth from right

Bottom: Stratford production of *Julius Caesar*, 1936; Trevor Howard as Cinna is second from right

Stratford production of *Romeo and Juliet*, 1936, with Trevor Howard as Benvolio. Inset: Howard (left) as Benvolio and James Dale as Mercutio

Stratford production of *Romeo and Juliet*, 1936; with Rosamund John as Lady Montague (fifth from left, in the cape) and Trevor Howard as Benvolio (left of centre in the foreground, with pouch on his belt)

Top: Stratford production of *Twelfth Night*, 1936; with Trevor Howard as Fabian (fourth from right)

Bottom: Stratford production of *The Taming of the Shrew*, 1936; Trevor Howard is the Lord second from right.
Inset: Rosamund John as Bianca in the same production

Top: Stratford production of *Troilus and Cressida*, 1936; with Trevor Howard (fourth from left) as Paris and Pamela Brown (far right) as Cressida © The Shakespeare Centre, 1936

Bottom: Stratford production of *The Merchant of Venice*, 1936; with Trevor Howard as Salanio (far left) and Donald Wolfit as Graziano (second from right) © The Shakespeare Centre, 1936

Top: Stratford production of *Richard III*, 1939; with Trevor Howard as Hastings (second from left) and John Laurie as Richard III (centre, pointing) © The Shakespeare Centre, 1939

Bottom: Stratford production of *Othello*, 1939; with Alec Clunes as Iago (third from left behind Othello), John Laurie as Othello, and Trevor Howard as Montano (third from right) © The Shakespeare Centre, 1939

Top: Stratford production of *As You Like It*, 1939; with Trevor Howard (centre) as Charles the Wrestler and Geoffrey Keen (centre) as Orlando © The Shakespeare Centre, 1939

Bottom: Trevor Howard and Celia Johnson in *Brief Encounter*, 1945 © The Rank Organisation

Left: Celia Johnson and Trevor Howard in *Brief Encounter*, 1945
© The Rank Organisation

Above: Pipe dreams: Trevor Howard during the 1940s © The Rank Organisation

Dressed to kill: Trevor Howard, *c*. 1946 © Rank Organisation

Left to right: Trevor Howard, Wilfrid Hyde White, Herbert Lom and Jacques Sernas in *The Golden Salamander*, 1950

Top: Trevor Howard and his wife Helen Cherry (third and fourth from left) relax at a cricket match in 1950 with *Clouded Yellow* co-stars Jean Simmons (second from left) and Kenneth More (far right). Also present was US actor Dane Clark (far left)

Bottom: Trevor Howard filling up his Alvis car at Arkley Garage, Hertfordshire, 1954 Reproduced by kind permission of Helen Howard

Top: Yul Brynner and Trevor Howard on poster shot for *The Long Duel*, 1967 © The Rank Organisation

Bottom: Trevor Howard with Harry Andrews (right) in *The Long Duel* © The Rank Organisation

Right: Howard preparing for a scene in *The Long Duel* © The Rank Organisation

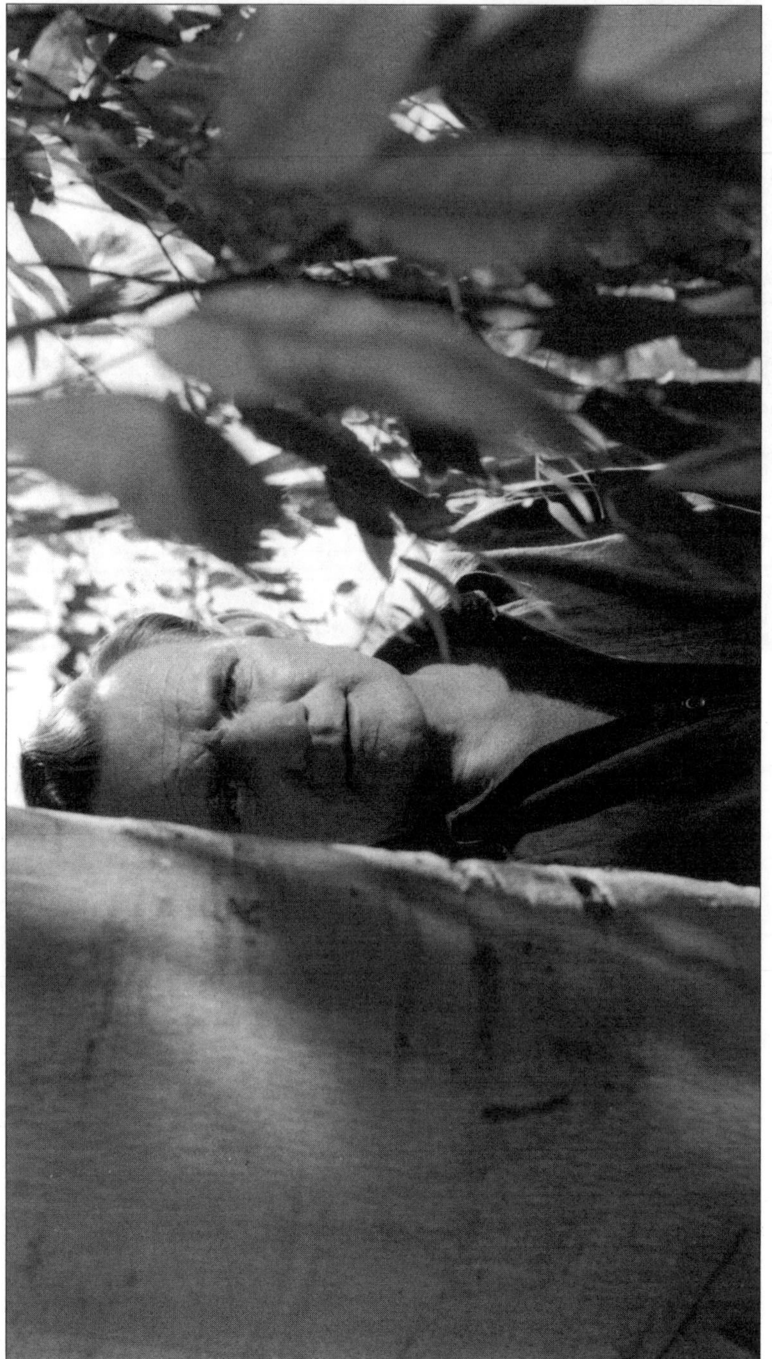

Left: Late 1950s publicity shot of Trevor Howard

Above: Trevor Howard relaxes with a cigarette in the late 1950s

Above: Trevor Howard as Father Collins in *Ryan's Daughter*, 1970

© Metro-Goldwyn-Mayer

Right: The Dingle peninsula where some of the film was shot

© Debbi Pettigrew, 1996

Above: Trevor Howard (left) with Roger Moore in *The Sea Wolves*, 1980

© The Rank Organisation; picture provided by Euan Lloyd

Right: Howard in *The Sea Wolves*

© The Rank Organisation; picture provided by Euan Lloyd

Above left: Trevor Howard (left) with Dennis Waterman in *Words on War*, ATV, 1980 © Associated Television

Bottom left: Trevor Howard as Inspector Mavor (right) with Patrick Allen in *Scorpion Tales*, ATV, 1980 © Associated Television

Above: Trevor and Helen Howard's home, Rowley Green House, in Hertfordshire Reproduced by kind permission of Helen Howard

Portrait of Trevor Howard, 1982 Reproduced by kind permission of Ian Vickery

Taking it easy: Trevor Howard at home, 1985

Trevor Howard in his last role, as the grandfather in *The Dawning*, ITV, 1988 © Reproduced by kind permission of David Williams

years after the story had first appeared – Patrick Skene Catling wrote, 'It is a matter of public record that, as an officer of the 1st Airborne Division, he spent eleven hours clinging to the wreckage of a glider which ditched off Sicily, and was awarded the Military Cross.' A matter of public record? More likely a press release from a film company. Or perhaps something Catling was told by an old codger who, by that time, two years before turning up his toes, had completely lost touch with reality?

Howard had become so comfortable with his imaginary war medal that he could poke fun at naval officers who, unlike himself, had spent time in combat zones. About his imagined rescue from the waters off Sicily Howard told Catling, 'It would have been funny if Alec Guinness had been in the landing craft which picked me up.' Guinness had been a serving officer in Sicily. One wonders if he would have seen the funny side, too.

Until Howard's death in 1988 newspapers and magazines kept trumpeting about his heroism and his Military Cross. The columns were full of references to it the morning after he died. The *Daily Mirror* wrote, 'Former colleagues last night paid tribute to the actor who was awarded the Military Cross. But he didn't really talk very much about that.' The *Today* newspaper said, 'Trevor Howard has been a war hero himself. He was a parachutist in the Sixth Airborne Division before being invalided out as an acting captain in 1943 with a Military Cross for bravery. It was later revealed that he had taken part in a raid on a heavy water plant in Norway.' Even the normally reliable *Times* declared, 'From 1940 to 1943 he served in the Army's 1st Airborne Division and won the Military Cross after parachuting into Nazi-occupied Norway and taking part in the invasion of Sicily.'

When Howard went to his grave only a handful of people knew for certain that he had not won a Military Cross. It took ten more years for the truth to hit the headlines. The release of the original police inquiry documents by the Public Records Office in August 1998 confirmed the whole messy saga. But within a week of the documents being released the old apologists for Howard's conduct were dreaming up fresh excuses. New villains were being blamed for the lie, among them Howard's mother Mabel, according to the *Daily Mail*. On 22 August 1998 columnist Peter Lewis reported that earlier that week Helen had told him, 'The MC wasn't Trevor's doing. He never said a word to me about his war service or the MC. His mother told me. She made up a story about his being in the Sicily landings and winning the MC . . . His mother talked to everybody. That's how the story got out.' The report went on, 'His mother's claims about her war hero son left Howard in an impossible position. Should he contradict her publicly and reveal her as a liar? He could not, so he simply maintained a rigid silence.'

Several questions are raised by this article. Because of their long separations Howard's relationship with his mother was fragile to say the least. He told me so, on at least three occasions. 'I hardly knew either of my parents. They were never there for me,' he said, and it was a considered remark, made slowly, with evident sadness. It is of course possible that his mother could have dreamed up such a story. But why would she want to? If she sought to get close to him after all their long years of separation, both geographically and emotionally, this was hardly the way to go about it. Neither is it plausible, in my view, that Howard would play along with the deception simply to please her, knowing it was why the police were pursuing him and that the case they wanted to bring against him, were it to come to court, could have appalling consequences for his civilian career. I have not been persuaded that Howard would put himself in that position to satisfy a whim of his mother's.

Peter Lewis called it 'a falsehood concealed for honourable reasons'. Perhaps so, but others were less accommodating, among them Robert Flemyng, a genuine MC holder, who told me that he thought Howard's conduct 'very stupid . . . he betrayed those who got their MCs the hard way'. I once asked Howard, who never showed interest in any aspect of filming other than acting, why he got such a buzz out of the job. He replied, 'I enjoy being somebody else. Directing a film is no fun. You have to be yourself.' A clue to his odd behaviour might be contained in that answer.

But anyone imagining that the Military Cross controversy was a solitary instance of Howard attempting to reinvent himself should think again. Howard had done such a thing before, with equal success, as I discovered when I visited Clifton College to examine his academic and sporting records. The archives paint a different portrait from the one contained in his press hand-outs, which, not once it seems, did newspaper editors question. The hand-out for *I See a Dark Stranger* (1946) states, '. . . at Clifton College he captained the rugby and cricket teams'. Hand-outs for later films repeated the claim. Everyone knows that Howard loved cricket and played it competently as an adult. But sporting performances at Clifton are meticulously archived, and there is no record of Howard having been captain of anything during his years there.

He entered Clifton in 1922. As we have seen, it was 1931 before his name first appeared on a cricketing record, when he played for his house, Dakyn's, and also for the college's Second XI. Nine years had passed before he was selected by his house. He was promoted to the First XI during the summer of 1932, his final year. He batted at eighth or ninth position, and his total number of runs for the year, gained during twelve innings, was an unimpressive sixty-three – an average of less than six runs per innings. The highest score he managed to get in a single innings was nineteen runs.

Tom Gover, the Chairman of the Old Cliftonians' Society and a keen cricketer himself, told me, 'As a batsman, Howard-Smith – as he was known here – was the sort of player, batting quite low down the order, who made the occasional run. Pretty undistinguished stuff. Barely average, I'd say. He fared better as a bowler. He got seventeen wickets at an average of sixteen runs. I'd say that he justified his selection more on his bowling than on his batting. He was a respectable member of the side, nothing more.'

The rugby archives reveal a similar story. He never captained any squad and, as with cricket, he was in his final year before being selected. Rugby would have been confined to the autumn term, that is, September to December. Howard was the tenth member of the squad, so he only just scraped into the team. Because of his weight and build he would most likely have been in the forwards. Gover suspects that he might have been on the wing. He was not mentioned in any match report except in the team listing, which, contrary to claims that he captained the team, suggests an unremarkable, virtually anonymous, season for him – a verdict with which Gover agreed.

While journalists might be forgiven for getting it wrong, it is harder to excuse the magazine of the Old Cliftonians for propagating the fiction. In the college's Centenary Annual Report published in 1997, Howard was quoted as saying, 'I wasn't much of a scholar but I was captain of pretty much everything that wasn't academic.' This fiction went unchallenged. Gover commented, 'He definitely wasn't. But I agree with the first half of the quote.'

Howard's troubles with the police did not end when they dropped the case against him for pretending to be an Military Cross holder. In many people's estimation, the crimes for which they nailed him were more serious than masquerading as a war hero. Nobody can be physically hurt or killed by a bogus claim. But getting drunk and driving a car can wreck innocent lives. Howard was convicted of drunken driving on three occasions, and it was more by luck than any judgement on his part that nobody was injured through his irresponsible actions. Had a pedestrian or cyclist been in front of his wheels they could easily have been killed.

On 14 August 1953 he crashed his car while driving out of London along Cricklewood Broadway at three in the afternoon. The explanation given at the time was 'over-work, plus drinking on an empty stomach'. Howard was found guilty, fined £50 with £7 15s. costs and lost his licence for twelve months, but halfway through the penalty period it was restored to him. The lesson appears to have been promptly forgotten. On 14 May 1956 Howard's soft-top Alvis car rammed the back of a Bentley driven by Alec Morris, a company director. Morris had slowed down prior to leaving the North Circular Road. Howard helped him on his way. 'It's his fault,' he told the policeman at the scene, 'He didn't put out his damned flipper!' Morris called him a liar and declared that his indicator had been visible for 'a considerable distance'. According to the prosecuting counsel, Mr Noakes, when Howard stepped out of his car 'he was staggering about, and the officer came to the conclusion that he was under the influence of alcohol'.

Interviewed by Dr Denys Howells at Edgware police station, Howard barked his replies in a manner which the police doctor described as 'loud, ending in a deafening note'. Howard admitted to having drunk 'three Guinnesses and a couple of double whiskies'. Despite being able to walk sufficiently steadily along a straight line chalked on the interview-room floor, Howard lost the case and received a fine of £100. His licence was taken away for nine months.

In Hollywood, during the filming of some extra scenes for *Mutiny on the Bounty*, Howard met the writer John Mortimer in a restaurant called the Retake Room. Mortimer asked him if he would be interested in appearing in one of his plays when they both got back to England. Not wishing to get stuck in a long run, but ever the polite gentleman, Howard replied that he would be delighted. Shortly after returning to Arkley he was off on another plane, to Kenya to begin filming with William Holden in *The Lion* (1962). For Howard it was a routine assignment, enjoyable because of the location, but returning to his and Helen's hotel one evening, along the dusty road to Nanyuki, his car collided with a Kenyan Army lorry. Howard sustained several cuts and bruises to his face, but expert make-up got him in front of the cameras again in a couple of days. The lorry hit the passenger side of the car where Helen was sitting. She considered herself lucky to have escaped with a broken arm. It came within inches of being a much more serious accident. There is no suggestion that Howard was drunk on that occasion.

Immediately following his return from Kenya the play for which Mortimer wanted him was ready to go into rehearsal. It was called *Two Stars for Comfort*, and the cast included Isabel Dean, Esmond Knight and Patricia Healey. Rehearsals began on 20 February, six weeks after his car accident in Kenya. The 'two stars' in the title referred to the Ronay-style rating of a small riverside hotel of which Howard was the slapdash proprietor. Isabel Dean played his wife, the real manager of the place and the reason why the establishment had any rating at all.

Although Howard badly needed a rest, he told Helen not to arrange anything until the play reached the end of its run. It opened in Blackpool and during April 1962 it transferred to the Garrick Theatre in London, where it settled in for six months. Soon into the London run, Howard realized that he had created his own nightmare. The play was a very good one, he said, but trapped in London for the summer he became impatient and, following the pattern of earlier frustrations, he began drinking more heavily. But even that had its limitations. He told friends, 'I need something else to break the monotony.'

When the offer arrived of a new Anglo-American television production, to be filmed in London, of Ibsen's *Hedda Gabler*, with him playing Lovborg to Ingrid Bergman's Hedda, and with Ralph Richardson and Michael Redgrave also in the cast, it seemed exactly what he was looking for: a prestige production with a trio of great names. He could film *Hedda Gabler* on the days they required him and continue with the play each night.

But it was relaxation that Howard needed, not more work. By the time they began filming *Hedda Gabler* Howard was exhausted; more than he would admit, even to himself. Months of overlapping demands on his time and concentration had drained his energies. He was running on empty, but, always the instinctive performer, he threw everything into his acting and left the personal side of his life to fend, more or less, for itself. By a unanimous verdict, his performance in *Hedda Gabler* was outstanding, partly through technical mastery but equally through the way he looked. Dilys Powell once wrote that Howard had a 'face for tragedy'. In *Hedda Gabler* that face, sombre, worldly-wise, tight-lipped to cauterize the strong emotions, possessed a poetry all of its own.

Filming the final scenes took longer than planned, and on 4 June, after three days of solid work on the television production before racing to the theatre for his evening performances, he arrived at the Garrick with only minutes to spare before the curtain went up. Everyone was in a state of panic. After working almost fifty hours in three days Howard was at the end of his rope. He was ill-tempered and fidgety, and his movements on stage were described as those of a man in a sleep-walk. Afterwards, to calm his nerves and to celebrate the completion of *Hedda Gabler*, he had a couple of drinks backstage. Then, as he often did, he drove to the Park Lane apartment of Al Parker and his actress wife Margaret Johnson and drank three more whiskies. It was after midnight when he set off to drive to Arkley.

Motoring along the Ridgeway in Mill Hill he failed to notice some roadworks, hit a temporary barrier and ran over a hurricane lamp. Even though nobody else was involved, and the damage to his vehicle was minimal, PC Michael Walker, the policeman who drove up to investigate, smelt whisky on his breath. Howard was promptly arrested, driven to Edgware police station where he was seen by Dr Abraham Matthews and charged with driving while under the influence of drink or drugs. On 6 June, two days later, he was remanded on bail at Hendon Magistrates Court. His solicitor David Jacobs told the magistrates that his client pleaded not guilty and elected to go for trial. Jacobs added, 'Mr Howard strongly refutes the charge and will be bringing medical evidence.'

At the Middlesex Sessions on 24 September his defence relied heavily on the testimony of another doctor, called Norton, who had examined him in the police station immediately after Dr Matthews and declared that Howard had been fit to drive when he saw him. Howard's lawyer, Christmas Humphries, laid his defence on with a trowel. He described Howard as a 'man at the end of his tether' who drank too much occasionally to 'give him energy to carry on a task which was almost more than he could bear'. During the previous ten months, he went on, Howard had scarcely had a day off work. During the month before the alleged offence he had consistently worked a seventeen-hour day. Exhaustion, not drink, was the reason why he had collided with the roadworks barrier. Humphries called the accusation 'borderline' and formally requested an immediate acquittal.

The prosecution argued that Howard did not have to work such long hours. Nobody forced him. He was a wealthy man and a free one. He chose the hours he worked. Besides, tiredness was no defence for law-breaking. Howard had a job that millions envied. He was a privileged human being enjoying a lifestyle beyond the reach of most people. There was no justification for treating him more leniently than anybody else on a drink-drive charge.

The police doctor, Matthews, testified that Howard had failed the ubiquitous finger-to-nose test, had staggered when asked to turn around and had shouted in response to being questioned. (Margaret Johnson, a witness for the defence, pointed out that the loudness of Howard's voice, which had been trained to reach the back of a large auditorium, did not prove that he had been boozing. 'He can roar like a lion, even without drink. I've heard him!' she declared.) Matthews also revealed that Howard had taken longer than five minutes to write out a four-and-a-half-line paragraph. PC Walker raised a laugh when he told the court that on asking the actor if he knew he had collided with some roadworks Howard had growled at him, 'Yes, but it's a bloody awful lane to drive along.'

However, Matthews's evidence was no laughing matter. He concluded that Howard 'was under the influence of drink to such an extent that he was incapable of having proper control of a car', a view supported by the clinical examination which indicated 'an intoxication level equivalent to having consumed between six and eight double whiskies on the day of the collision'. The verdict was guilty. Taking into account Howard's previous convictions for drink-driving, they had no option but to impose a lengthy ban. A gasp went around the room when the period was announced – eight years. The judge, Mr Ewen Montague, told Howard, 'On the clearest possible evidence you were well under the influence of drink on that night. You have had a warning, but we cannot think that it will be in the public good to send you to prison.' He went on, 'The public needs protection from you, because, even after that warning, you are a man who drinks vast quantities every night – according to your own evidence.'

Howard left the Sessions in a state of shock and bewilderment.

Others felt that he had been extremely lucky to have escaped a prison sentence. He couldn't blame anyone but himself. Nobody had been hurt, but Howard could take no credit for that. He was lucky that the extent of the damage was some broken roadworks and a flattened hurricane lamp. However, three arrests and convictions in less than ten years suggest that there were many other occasions when he was above the limit at the wheel of his car but was fortunate enough to not collide with anything or come to the attention of the police.

Personally, I think Howard never understood the seriousness of drinking and driving. His conduct when the police had arrived on the scene at Mill Hill in 1956 clearly indicates that he thought of himself as the victim, not the criminal! When I was at his house, he was aware that I had driven to Arkley because we always went to the Gate in my car, yet he expected me to drink booze from the moment that I arrived in the morning, at lunchtime and right through the afternoon. There would be a hint of annoyance, a twitch of the face, an exasperated sigh when I insisted on keeping a clear head for the journey home. His catalogue of arrests and disqualifications should have taught him something, but it never seemed to.

12
WHEN IN DOUBT

I'm on the screen for about two minutes. What am I supposed to do in two minutes? Turn a heap of shit into gold dust?
– Trevor Howard discussing his supporting role in *Persecution* (1974)

TREVOR Howard hated discussing his films, but since they would not go away, and in any case were central to the biography, he had no option but talk about them. The occasions had to be chosen carefully. He had to be warmed up beforehand. It was no use barging in when the mood wasn't right. You had to make the right sort of noises and let him see that you were batting on his team. And then, only when the spirit moved him – or spirits more often than not – would he open up and let you tiptoe inside his thought processes.

I once asked him which he thought was his best film. 'None of them!' he roared, adding slyly, 'but I was proud to be in *The Third Man*.' It was the nearest I ever heard him get to congratulating himself. And even then he was thinking not of himself but of Welles and Cotten. As to what he thought was his worst film, he could offer no guidance other than the terse invitation, 'Take your fucking pick!'

I said, 'I think, actually, it was *Persecution*, the one you made with LanaTurner.'

Howard agreed that it was a 'stinker' but said it wasn't his fault: 'I spent a couple of hours on that film. One at London Zoo. The other in someone's fucking hallway. I'm on the screen for about two minutes. What am I supposed to do in two minutes? Turn a heap of shit into gold dust? They're always doing that to us. Their motto is, when in doubt, wheel the old fuckers out! Larry [Olivier] didn't mind. Brought him some tidy pay-days. I'm talking too much. Have another drink.'

The truth was that Howard hated being idle. He became cantankerous and out of sorts after weeks of doing nothing. Michael Hordern once said to me, 'The problem with being out of work is that you have nothing to take your mind off being out of work.' This is true, of course, for everyone. Unemployment black-spots become trouble zones because people lose hope. They need the discipline and optimism and goal-setting that work provides. So, too, do actors. Roles of any kind are better than sitting at home watching daytime television.

When I wrote my book on character actors some years ago I asked Michael Hordern about a film that he had been in. 'Was I?' he inquired, 'Well, goodness me.' He had no idea when it was made or what it was about and, quite clearly, he didn't care. It had been a job of work. Simply that. 'I would love to help you, but my acting life is a total blank,' added the man who had turned absent-mindedness on the screen into an art form. There is always the slender hope among actors that a terrible role will lead directly to a better one, and occasionally it does. Hordern understood – and Howard too – the importance of regular appearances, of being seen. Producers are fickle and memories are short. If you aren't part of the parade it quickly moves along without you. Actors who start out being choosy about their roles often abandon that policy just to keep busy. Peter Cushing had a neat reply when I asked him why he never seemed to turn down a part. 'I'll start refusing work,' he told me, 'when my local supermarket stops asking for my money.'

After *The Heart of the Matter* Howard's film career took a downturn. *The Stranger's Hand* (1953) had him working again with *Third Man* writer Graham Greene and co-star Alida Valli in what proved to be a failed attempt to recreate in Venice the atmosphere and tension of their earlier collaboration in Vienna. Howard had gone into it with high hopes, and its failure to catch fire took him by surprise. Director Mario Soldati missed a golden opportunity to wring visual drama out of the submerged city. It would be two decades before Nicholas Roeg demonstrated how it should be done in *Don't Look Now*.

Howard next appeared in a French film, *The Lovers of Lisbon* (1953), supporting Daniel Gélin and Françoise Arnoul. Directed by Henri Verneuil, it was a fairly complex murder mystery which Howard, as a British police inspector, eventually solves. The plot was neatly crafted around Gélin and Arnoul, leaving Howard to plug the gaps. He played it straight and made a credible policeman, and the film's modest success on the Continent owed more to its French stars than anything Howard had contributed.

It was his friend Euan Lloyd who came to his rescue in 1955 with the offer of a role in *Cockleshell Heroes*, a filmed tribute to the Royal Marines in wartime. Lloyd was then production assistant with Warwick

Films, an independent US company whose films were financed and distributed by Columbia Pictures.

Warwick had been set up by Irving Allen and Albert 'Cubby' Broccoli. Their plan had been to make high-quality films for the international market using American stars in European locations. It could have been a winning formula had the quality of the scripts matched their ambitions. Alan Ladd agreed to come to Britain in 1952 to make two films under the Warwick banner, after tax complications in the United States made it advantageous for him to spend some time outside the country. *The Red Beret*, his first movie for Warwick and the company's first in Britain, was a half-decent effort, spoilt in the main by the unsuitable, last-minute casting of Susan Stephen as Ladd's romantic interest to replace the Canadian actress Diane Foster who had pulled out at short notice.

The original script of *Cockleshell Heroes* was unsatisfactory. A young London screenwriter who had previously rewritten some scenes for one of the British-made Alan Ladd movies was therefore hired to give it more edge and make it sound more British. Lloyd remembered driving to his home in East Sheen in Surrey to collect the first ten or so pages that he'd written. 'I was to make that trip at least a dozen times to pick up the script as it became ready.' The writer, then at the beginning of a distinguished career in films, was Bryan Forbes.

The storyline, showing men in training for combat during the first half of the film and with the mission for which they have been trained occupying the second half, has almost become a blueprint for war films, but Warwick were among the first to use it successfully in *The Red Beret* and, three years later, in *Cockleshell Heroes*. Irving Allen hoped to press Howard into service and used Lloyd's friendship with the actor as a means to get to him.

'You're his buddy,' said Allen. 'Get to work on him.'

Lloyd replied, 'I can show him the scripts, but he makes up his own mind.' When Howard read the outline of *Cockleshell Heroes* he was immediately interested. Lloyd had an easy time getting his signature. Securing an American star proved more challenging. Several of them turned it down. The eventual choice was José Ferrer, a versatile, cultured actor who was seen as something of an intellectual. Allen wanted to avoid repeating what some critics felt had been a mistake in *The Red Beret*, – casting an all-purpose American hero to lead British troops into battle – although Ladd had played a private who initially turns down the offer of a commission. Ferrer, with his precise mannerisms and cosmopolitan track record (he had recently played the artist Henri Toulouse-Lautrec and the composer Sigmund Romberg) seemed an acceptable compromise. Ferrer, who at the time was keen to try his hand at directing, liked the plot but did not want to film in Britain. Allen offered him a compromise. If Ferrer would agree to co-star he could direct the picture as well. Ferrer agreed.

In *Cockleshell Heroes* Howard played Captain Thompson, an officer in the Royal Marines who is seconded to a special volunteer unit commanded by Major Stringer, played by Ferrer. The men's task is to infiltrate Bordeaux harbour in a fleet of five two-man canoes and, using limpet-mines, blow up the enemy merchant ships moored there. The Navy would require massive air cover to get near enough to attack them. The only way it can be done is by a highly trained force of marine frogmen who can strike silently under cover of darkness and attach the mines beneath the water-level.

At first Thompson, an experienced, 'rule-book' officer, despises Stringer's lack of formality with the men. He watches contemptuously as Stringer's training methods fail. But the senior officer is willing to learn from his mistakes and Thompson's ideas prevail, which results in a tighter, more disciplined fighting unit. The attack takes place in virtual silence and at night. Thompson is captured by the Germans along with two other Marines, and their refusal to collaborate with the enemy seals their fate. As the firing squad does its work, the ships in the harbour explode, the men's sacrifice neatly coinciding with the destruction of the enemy ships. But success proves costly in terms of lives. Of the ten men who set out only two survive.

The film was a fairly uneven action drama which borrowed good and bad elements from other war movies – we have the tarty wife from *The Cruel Sea* (1953) and the good-guy serviceman going missing so that he can confront his wife's low-life lover from *Waterloo Road* (1944). A scene showing the men undergoing an initiation test, returning to base camp under their own steam using a variety of disguises, provides some welcome light relief to a film which is predominantly sombre and violent.

Ferrer gave Howard his first experience of working with an outsize Hollywood ego. The English actor was not impressed. Interestingly, their screen selves paralleled their off-screen relationship. Even the dialogue had a prophetic ring about it. Ferrer/Stringer, the officer in charge, tells Howard/Thompson, 'I'm the one who's responsible for the success or failure of this project. We'll do it my way. Is that clear?' Later Howard/Thompson tells him that the men have been laughing at him behind his back from Day One. Howard delivered the line with evident relish.

Lloyd conceded there had been a degree of needle between the two actors, but it was imperceptible to anyone else. 'I only knew about it because Trevor said a couple of things to me over drinks late in the evening,' Lloyd told me. 'Nothing was ever said to Joe. Trevor was too experienced a pro to reveal his feelings in that way. But Joe never made any effort to be popular.'

One thing that riled Howard was Ferrer's belief that he was a ladies' man. He used to boast of his successful conquests with women, although married at the time to his third wife, Rosemary Clooney, and the father of five children. Howard's view was that men who talked about it were not usually much good at it. He made fun of the false nose that Ferrer had worn in his recent film *Cyrano de Bergerac*, suggesting to one of the British actors that the nose was 'probably longer than Joe's prick'. He told Euan Lloyd that Ferrer's looks would be improved if he had the false nose grafted permanently on to his face. Lloyd told me, 'Having Joe star in the film was a mistake. It would have been much better had a British actor played that part. Sadly, that wasn't Warwick's policy.'

The scenes supposedly set in Bordeaux harbour were filmed on the River Tagus, near Lisbon. Howard, who was never safe in a small boat, almost drowned himself and fellow-actor David Lodge when he overturned their canoe. Lodge managed to struggle out of the craft, but Howard finished upside-down in the water, unable to swim clear. Some real marines, dressed as extras in Nazi uniforms, leaped into the water and rescued them.

The production of the film had its share of difficulties. Keeping Howard away from drinking dens proved a headache for Lloyd. Under express instructions from Allen, he kept a tight rein on Howard, whose thirst was well known. Once, after filming all day in Lisbon, Howard said to Lloyd, 'Let's go out and have a few jars tonight.' He had more than a few. Two o'clock the following morning saw them in a beer joint – 'not a bordello but near enough', recalled Lloyd – with Howard out cold in his chair, his body slumped forward on a table-top. Lloyd asked if a room could be found for them, and he spent a sleepless night on a settee thinking about the career that he was about to lose, while Howard dozed in the only available bed.

Lloyd told me, 'I got him up at six forty-five, poured down his gullet several cups of the strongest coffee available outside Turkey, then stuck him under a cold shower. He screamed like a stuck pig and I imagine he wanted to kill me, but I got him on the set in time for the first shot, at eight thirty in the morning, and guess what? He was word perfect. You'd think he'd been up half the night learning his lines. Amazing.'

Lloyd's biggest headache by far was arriving at Estoril in Portugal for the start of filming to be told that permission to shoot the movie had been rescinded by the Portuguese government. He could not understand why. All the relevant permits had been authorized by senior officials. When he drove up to the Palace hotel, after the long journey by road from Britain, Allen and Broccoli were waiting for him on the hotel steps. They were in a state of panic.

Broccoli said, 'Euan, we can make our film only if we make one for them, too. That's the deal. I don't like blackmail of any kind, but there it is. Our hands are tied.'

Lloyd asked, 'What do you mean, a film for them? What sort of film?'

Allen replied, 'They want a short documentary about Portugal to expand the tourist trade.' He glanced at his wrist-watch and added, 'As of this moment, Euan, you are the writer, director and producer of this documentary. Keep the costs down, but do a good job.'

The following morning, refreshed after his journey from England, Lloyd got a cab into the centre of Lisbon and spent the day touring all the popular sights. That evening he went to a night club, where the star of the cabaret was the locally well-known *fado* singer Amelia Rodrigues. *Fado* is an exhilarating folk style and Rodrigues accompanied herself on the guitar.

Lloyd told me, 'She sang this song, "Coimbra", in Portuguese. By the time I left the club I virtually had the documentary structured in my head and knew that "Coimbra" was the perfect theme for it.' The next morning, Monday, Lloyd phoned a friend of his, Teddy Holmes, who worked for Chappell, the music publishers. Holmes told him, 'I know the song you're talking about. As a matter of fact we published it, with English lyrics.'

Lloyd asked him, 'What's it called in English?'

Holmes replied, 'April in Portugal.'

Lloyd now had the title of his documentary as well. He thanked

Holmes and went immediately to tell Allen the good news. Less than a day after arriving from England he had his movie outline completed. The Portuguese authorities were sufficiently impressed by Lloyd's phone call describing the planned documentary that they immediately restored permission to make *Cockleshell Heroes*. Howard provided the narration for *April in Portugal*. His resonant voice, the colourful scenes and the haunting theme tune made it a documentary of considerable style.

Lloyd and Howard visited several countries to promote *Cockleshell Heroes*. Columbia Pictures paid for Howard to travel first class, but Lloyd, through shortage of cash, had tourist-class tickets. Howard, however, usually managed to charm one of the stewardesses into allowing Lloyd to join him in the first-class section. In Paris they stayed at a small hotel, the Splendide, near the Place de l'Etoile. One cold, blustery night they were having drinks in a small bistro in a back street off the Champs-Elysées when a stocky man in a trenchcoat and slouch hat, accompanied by a second man, walked in. Howard grabbed Lloyd by the arm. 'It's him!' he hissed.

'Who?'

'Him!' Howard repeated and fell silent.

It was like a scene from a movie. The man in the hat studied in turn every face in the bistro. He looked more intently at Howard than at anyone else and then slowly, deliberately, made his way across the floor towards Howard's table. He stood there unsmiling. Lloyd wondered for an anxious moment if the man might be some woman's aggrieved husband intent on revenge.

Still unsmiling, the stranger thrust his hand. 'Gabin,' he said. Just the one word. Gabin.

Howard stood up, grasped the man's hand firmly in his own and responded, in mock French, ''Oward!' They embraced, left the bistro together, and that was the last that Lloyd saw of Howard for forty-eight hours. It was, as Lloyd told me, 'a breathtaking moment, this chance encounter between two cinema giants'. Howard has been compared many times with Jean Gabin and also with Spencer Tracy in terms of their acting technique. All three were capable of rock-solid performances. They could reveal great depths of character and emotion without showing anything on the surface. But it was there, unmistakable and rivetingly beautiful, in their weathered faces and all-knowing eyes. All three had their admirers, but many critics had begun by the mid-1950s to put Howard out in front. One was Richard Whitehall, who wrote, 'A seeming extra dimension to the actor's imagination has enabled him over the past decade to rescue films of small merit by the perceptive quality of his playing. Howard assumes a true mantle of greatness, a talent well able to cast a giant shadow over most of his contemporaries, much wider in range than the two players – Gabin and Tracy – whom in method he most resembles. Gabin is, by now, firmly in the grip of his own myth. Tracy has an equal grasp of the intimate revelation of character but lacks Howard's flow of subterranean passion. No one can watch his performances without being aware that he has the passion and humility of the true artist.'

From second lead in *Cockleshell Heroes* Howard slipped a further notch in his next movie, *Run for the Sun* (1956), as a Nazi hiding from justice in the Amazonian jungle. When his hiding-place and identity are discovered by a novelist, played by Richard Widmark, who crash-lands near by, Howard must prevent him reaching civilization so that he cannot tell his story. The only way that the intruders can escape is to kill their way to freedom.

Run for the Sun was a familiar tale, another reworking of Richard Connell's short story, 'The Most Dangerous Game', where a mad scientist, Zaroff, bored with killing animals, turned the pursuit of an unwanted visitor to his private island into a blood sport. The problem with *Run for the Sun* was that we had seen it all before and would see it again. Widmark was passably good as the crusading novelist, and Jane Greer, as a journalist, provided the love interest (for Widmark, not Howard), but the film offered few surprises, and the ending was as certain as night following day. Turning the villain into a Nazi gave it a topicality of sorts, but Howard made him far too contemplative, far too normal for the audience to hate him. He once told me that he had been offered the role of Adolf Eichmann in a television film about the trial in 1961 of the infamous Nazi. He said to me, 'I would have done it, but Helen said, "No, you can't. Surely not. You'll have everyone liking him."' Howard's villains were difficult to hate because they were never shallow or over the top. They had a gritty integrity that came from within, which made it difficult to believe that he could ever be part of anything irredeemably evil, twisted or shoddy.

Careerwise, the years between 1955 and 1960 contained little to enthuse Howard. No offers of any significance came his way. Once the sought-after prop forward, after nineteen films he seemed to be heading for the substitute's bench. The year 1956 saw an explosion of raw new talent in the theatre, with John Osborne's *Look Back in Anger* at the Royal Court, and this was quickly followed – although the cinema took a couple of years to catch up – by other dramas by new writers from provincial towns describing working-class life as they knew it. Cosy, complacent middle-class attitudes and preoccupations suddenly became unfashionable. Howard was forty-three when *Look Back in Anger* opened, and he looked every year of it. For him, and for other actors of his generation, there could be no going back to the thoughtful romantics or trapped lovers of a few years before.

His performances were 'robust' and 'reliable' rather than outstanding. The parts were supporting rather than central, in US-funded movies where an American star was as essential as wings on a plane. Apart from the cheapness of making films in Britain – and there were tax incentives for Americans to do so – with the lifting of post-war restrictions on travel, food rationing finally ending in 1954 and jet airliners available for faster, more comfortable long-distance travel, the American tourist invasion got under way. Among the thousands who arrived were many former GIs taking the opportunity to show their families where they had been stationed during the war. Quite a number of them were accompanied by their English-born wives – 'GI brides' – revisiting parents and letting them meet their grandchildren.

Hollywood seized on the opportunity to show these sights to American audiences in glorious Cinemascope – never more blatantly than in Mike Todd's *Around the World in Eighty Days* (1956), made in Todd's self-developed widescreen process, AO, and starring David Niven as Phileas Fogg and the Mexican comedy actor Cantinflas as his faithful valet Passepartout.

The film opens with a solemn introduction by Edward R. Murrow, the one-time UK-based war correspondent, which seems curiously out of tune with the rest of the film. We see Hyde Park's Rotten Row and a mock-up of Horseguards' Parade before moving through the doors of the Reform Club, where crusty old men insult each other and the waiters. Asked in he would like ice in his drink, an old buffoon retorts, 'Ice? What do I look like – a polar bear?' Fogg enters to the chiming of Big Ben, establishing that he is a stickler for punctuality. He rejects his copy of the *Daily Telegraph*, offered to him on a tray, because someone has read it before him. 'Send out for a fresh one,' he commands a dismayed flunkey.

Wearing bushy sideburns, built-up eyebrows and a moustache,

Howard plays Fallentin, a club member who bets against Fogg completing the journey in eighty days. He hasn't much to do except react to the updates on how the travellers are faring. When they do badly, he wears his 'I-told-you-so' smirk. When they catch up again, he affects to disbelieve the news. It is a small role but no smaller than most of the guest appearances, which included Noel Coward as an employment agent, Charles Boyer as a travel clerk, Ronald Colman as a railway official, Peter Lorre as a ship's steward, Marlene Dietrich as a bordello madam, Red Skelton as a town drunk and Buster Keaton as a train guard.

Around the World in Eighty Days set many records. It had more star guests, more extras, more overseas locations than any film before it. Four million air passenger miles were clocked up making it. Two thousand camera set-ups were used. Seventy-five thousand costumes were designed or supplied. Todd spared nothing to make this the biggest and greatest movie of its day, and, while nobody could argue about its ambition and scope, opinions differed sharply as to whether or not it was all that great. To some, it was inspired film-making; to others, it seemed tiresome and overlong. For me, the truth lay somewhere in between.

When Howard arrived in Hollywood he was met at the airport by Robert Newton, who had gone there in 1951 to make *Treasure Island* and stayed on. Newton, who also appeared in Todd's *Around the World in Eighty Days*, had taken the trouble to find out when Howard would arrive so that he could meet him. Howard never forgot his generosity. He told me, 'I hadn't known Bobby terribly well in England. I thought it was a wonderful thing for him to do. Before long he was throwing double brandies at me while he had to settle for ginger beer, poor devil.'

Newton wasn't aware of it, but Howard had good reason to feel grateful to him. Newton's failure to turn up for *They Made Me a Fugitive* in 1947 had led to Howard taking over his role, one in which he set a new standard in screen toughness. When Howard told him about it, Newton arched that famous eyebrow and said, 'Glad to have been of service, dear boy.'

Howard told me that Newton's alcoholism and early death at fifty-one had saddened but not surprised him: 'Bobby was a sad figure around Hollywood. He hated the place, but there was nothing for him in England. He married a wardrobe mistress out there called Vera, who worshipped him, bless her, so that was fine. But he was lost in

America. He couldn't fit in like Niven or Colman. He wasn't part of the colony. They didn't want him. But he had a heart of gold.'

Back in Britain Howard was invited to play a merchant ship's captain in *Manuela* (1957), directed by Guy Hamilton, whom he knew well. Hamilton was a close associate of Carol Reed's and worked with him on *An Outcast of the Islands*. Later he married Howard's co-star in *Outcast*, the Algerian actress Kerima. Again the reviews praised him for his 'sensitive' playing, but it was all rather wasted on a film that would never amount to anything. However, it was to Howard's credit that he got the character noticed. The critic Dilys Powell called his performance 'superb' and added, 'I can think of no actor like Trevor Howard for suggesting the heartbreak behind the bleak, the unwavering look.' A cynic might say that he wasn't acting at all. He was merely contemplating his future, or lack of it, in the film industry.

And if that was true, his next job of work would have deepened his gloom. He played a nasty villain opposite Victor Mature in *Interpol* (1957). Euan Lloyd produced it, and since the word Interpol is virtually unknown in the United States it was renamed *Pickup Alley* for the American market. Lloyd told me, 'Trevor didn't want to do it after reading the script. I was pressured by Warwick Films to get him on board.'

The deciding factor was the locations. They frequently were, in Howard's case. Filming something less than perfect in a nice climate and getting paid for it was better than sitting around at home watching the grass grow. Lloyd knew that sooner or later the question of travel would arise. When it did, Lloyd told him they would be shooting in 'Rome, Genoa, the Italian Riviera and probably the south of France.' Howard pulled a wry face and said, 'Tell you what, Euan. I'll just take a second peep at that script.'

Although the film wasn't up to much, Howard never regretted making it. He and Victor Mature had enormous fun both off and on the set. Mature's attitude to movie-making was refreshingly obtuse. He prided himself on never having had an acting lesson in his life, and in one of his movies, *The Sharkfighters* (1953), he claimed that the giant rubber sharks used in the long shots were better actors that he was. Once, refused membership of an exclusive gentlemen's club in Los Angeles where actors were not allowed to join, Mature denied that he had ever been an actor. 'And I have over fifty films to prove it,' he said.

One day Mature said to Howard, 'Look, Trevor, I have a bit of a problem. I need to work on a couple of scenes with you. I have some time tomorrow afternoon, around three thirty. Can you come along to my room? It won't take long. You'd be doing me a big favour.'

Howard said, 'Yes, of course.' They were staying at the same hotel in Genoa, and Mature liked a drink. It promised to be an interesting afternoon. When Howard arrived with Lloyd at Mature's suite they found the door open. Hesitating for a moment in the corridor, they were overheard by Mature who called out, 'It's OK, guys. Come on in.' They walked in and found Mature, undressed, on the bed with three sexy-looking girls. 'Oh, yeah, the script,' he said, without looking round. 'You don't mind if I finish this first?' Howard saw the joke immediately and roared with laughter. But the joke was on Mature a few seconds later when, unexpectedly, his Italian girlfriend arrived and stumbled into the phoney orgy staged for Howard's benefit. Of course she didn't know it was a set-up and, cursing loudly in Italian, she immediately attacked the occupants of the bed. The girls scurried for cover, leaving the naked Mature to defend himself as best he could.

The harder she punched, the more Mature seemed to enjoy it. Incensed further by the realization that she could not physically hurt him, she threw open his wardrobe, grabbed an armful of his suits and hurled them as far as she could through the open window. It was a blustery day and the strong breeze carried the flashy garments to the four corners of the crowded piazza below. The townspeople on whom the clothes landed paid little attention. Italians are used to outbursts of emotion.

Howard watched all this mayhem with classic English reserve, and when the girl paused momentarily to consider her next move and to recover her breath, he said to Mature, in his best Cliftonian accent, 'You went to all this trouble for me? How *very* thoughtful!' Lloyd recalled, 'Victor's performance that afternoon was better than anything he ever did on the screen.'

The Key (1958) reunited Howard with director Carol Reed, which delighted him. He felt safer in Reed's hands than in almost any other director's. He was third-billed below William Holden and Sophia Loren, who were, at the time, very hot. Holden's movie *The Bridge on the River Kwai* (1957), directed by David Lean, was still sweeping all before it. Sophia Loren had recently been Cary Grant's love interest both on and off the screen in *The Pride and the Passion* (1957), and although she was never the critics' pin-up girl audiences loved her.

The Key held the best promise for Howard since *The Heart of the Matter* in 1953, and he grasped it with both hands.

The Key was written and produced by Carl Foreman, a blacklisted American film-maker whose credits had included *Champion* (1948) and the classic western *High Noon* (1951). He had made a home for himself in Britain and earned his living by writing film scripts anonymously. In 1957 he convinced Columbia Pictures to finance productions that would again carry his name. The first of these ventures was *The Key*, adapted from *Stella*, a Second World War novel by Jan de Hartog about the private lives and public heroism of tug-boat captains. The story struck a familiar chord with Foreman, who had seen service in the war. It contained both lively action sequences and strong personal conflicts, two recurring ingredients of his work. Foreman believed that its subject matter, and the mandatory conversion of the Dutch hero to an American, would make the film popular in the United States, while its salute to the heroism of British and Dutch crew members, executed in a plain, documentary style, would go down well in European countries.

Howard played a tug-boat captain in wartime who inherits the key to an apartment from a previous occupant shortly before his death. The hazards faced by tug-boats helping merchant ships in war are enormous, and the life expectancy of the crews is only slightly longer than that of a house-fly. Consequently, each occupant of the apartment hands a spare key to another captain who can then move in, as the next on the list, should they not return. This sensible arrangement is made more desirable by the fact that whoever gets the key also gets to share the apartment with the mysterious Stella, played by Sophia Loren, who can be a love-goddess or a whore or just someone decorative to have around. It is up to them how they see or use her.

Howard's tenancy doesn't last very long. His successor, William Holden, is considerably luckier. Having been killed off at the end of his last film, *The Bridge on the River Kwai*, Holden's fans expected him to survive in *The Key*. And survive he does, despite the best efforts of the treacherous seas and a Nazi submarine to kill him. But his survival unnerves the girl, who, it seems, can only love men who are on their way to their deaths. When they live long enough to love her in return she goes to pieces. The love element of the story is flimsy, almost surreal, but the realistic sea chases and the scenes of brave men making the most of their time, whether celebrating, loving, fighting or dying, are impressive. Reed engenders in the apartment and in the men's eyes an ever-present, tantalizing veil of doom, and by use of imaginative camerawork – always a strong point with Reed – Stella assumes at times a stark, banshee-like presence which combines in a single image the men's greatest hopes and worst fears: love and death.

According to Robert F. Moss, in his biography of Carol Reed, the European ending, where Holden sprints after but fails to get on the train carrying the girl out of his life for good, was abandoned in the United States for a happier one in which the couple are reunited. In the acting stakes, by Moss's reckoning, Howard was the clear winner. He called his performance 'sturdy and reliable as always, every inch the tough old salt which the script asks him to be. Unhappily, the script doesn't require him to be a particular salt, with individual pains, predilections, tics and obsessions.' Holden, he added, 'like most Hollywood leading men, gives no sign of an inner life . . . he is as reliable as his tug and even less interesting'. Moss describes Sophia Loren as 'usually mediocre in English-language films, and *The Key* is no exception'. Critic Robert Murphy noted, 'The dictates of the international box office – lots of naval manoeuvres and a turgidly American hero – result in a fascinatingly enigmatic melodrama being buried within a stolidly conventional war film.'

The Roots of Heaven (1958) was a film Howard keenly wanted to make. Based on a best-selling book by Romain Gary, it was about a man named Morel who is obsessed with preventing the slaughter of African elephants. Howard's love for elephants, nurtured during his years as a child in Ceylon, fitted him well for this role, but his problem, as with all Hollywood-financed projects, was that he still hadn't broken the ice with American audiences. A direct approach by his agent, Al Parker, to Darryl F. Zanuck, the cigar-chomping head of production at Twentieth Century Fox – who owned the film rights – failed to impress. Zanuck wanted William Holden.

Howard's fortunes began to look up when Zanuck named John Huston as the film's director. Huston, whom he knew, was an old hand at making films about men driven crazy by their obsessions, like Dobbs in *The Treasure of the Sierra Madre* and Ahab in *Moby Dick*. Huston always insisted on total control of his films and would accept no interference from the front office. Howard felt that if he laid his cards on the table with Huston, there remained a slim chance that he might still land the role. And he did, but only after Holden declined. The film included

Eddie Albert and Errol Flynn, with Orson Welles in the kind of small, juicy part at which he excelled. Huston had given Welles a one-scene role in *Moby Dick*, and he had practically stolen the picture.

With the remainder of the cast and crew mainly European, the unit gathered in Paris prior to heading off, *en masse*, for its African location. Flynn's role was that of a ravaged former Army major who joins Morel's band of angels because he has nothing better to do. Flynn had nothing better to do either. He was at a very low ebb in his life. His finances has been drained by profligacy and expensive court battles. He was a pale imitation of his former self. Huston knew the role would not place too many demands on him. Despite having gone to seed, he could still flash that winning smile and had lots of loyal, adoring fans.

Making the film meant living rough in tropical conditions where the midday temperatures soared to between 130 and 140°F. Even at night the temperature rarely dropped below a stifling 100°F. Filming was impossible after the sun reached its height. People could not sleep at night because of the heat, and the danger of malaria was always present. Oddly enough, Flynn and Howard, the two heartiest drinkers on location, were among the least affected by the heat and the mosquitoes. Flynn put it down to his constant intake of vodka and fruit juice, plus the fact that he had spent time in the jungles of New Guinea. 'If you can survive there, you can survive anywhere,' he declared.

The only female in the cast was Juliette Greco, a stunning half-Corsican, half-French actress with long dark hair and a sultry voice. She would sit in the shade strumming a guitar and singing Left Bank songs. Howard thought she was very pretty, but nobody explained to him what she was doing there. One day he said to Flynn, 'Who's that girl with the guitar?'

Flynn replied, 'That's Juliette. But don't do a make on her, old sport. She's Darryl's discovery.'

'Discovery? Does that mean he's fucking her?'

Flynn laughed. 'I've heard on the grapevine, cherub, that you have made a few small discoveries of your own.'

Another story, probably just as apocryphal, had Helen in Paris badgering her husband to introduce her to Flynn. She would not go home until she had met him. They went to Flynn's hotel room, tried the door and, finding it unlocked, ventured inside. There was no sign of its occupant. Howard called out Flynn's name and from behind another door a voice responded, 'In here, sport.' Helen, nearest the door, opened it. There, spread out in his bath, submerged in soap suds, was the great swashbuckler himself. He clearly had not expected a female visitor, but the old charm had not deserted him. 'You will forgive me, dear lady,' he teased, 'if I don't stand up.'

The Roots of Heaven was, according to the director's biographer, Stuart Kaminsky, 'another example of Huston's exploration of an apparently doomed quest by a group of vastly different people, led by a man obsessed . . . Morel's crusade is clearly seen as a religious obsession. His followers are disciples, elevated by the righteousness of his cause and ready to follow him to their death.' The film struck different chords with different reviewers, ranging from "excellent" and "artistically fine and spiritually exuberant" to "disappointing" and "curiously unconvincing".' Howard was considerably buoyed by the whole experience, especially getting close again to his beloved elephants, but would probably have agreed with Huston when the director confessed to the *Los Angeles Times*, 'There were depths to the story that were never, never touched.'

Howard's next film was *Moment of Danger* (1959) with Edmund Purdom and Dorothy Dandridge. Purdom had enjoyed a brief spell of fame in Hollywood when he was brought in to replace an overweight Mario Lanza in *The Student Prince* (1955). But despite clean-cut good looks Purdom rapidly lost his grip on stardom. Bad publicity over his affair with Tyrone Power's wife, the actress Linda Christian, did not help his cause. In *Moment of Danger* he and Howard play thieves who double-cross one another. Again Howard gave a co-star a serious acting lesson and, without blinking an eye, made Purdom look callow and empty.

Sons and Lovers (1960) was in a different category. Howard had always admired D.H. Lawrence's writings for their candour and earthiness. The books were a landscape of painful dilemmas, paradoxes and tormented relationships. Of all Lawrence's books, *Sons and Lovers* is judged to be the most autobiographical. Formerly a young coal-face worker, Lawrence based his novels on his first-hand knowledge of mining communities. His fictional self leaps from the pages of many of his books.

Howard played Walter Morel, a rough and ready Nottinghamshire miner whose wife, played by Wendy Hiller, and their three sons have grown apart from him. The eldest, William, has gone to London. The second son, Paul, played by Dean Stockwell, dreams of becoming a successful artist, which pleases his mother who wants none of her sons to become a miner. When Arthur, the youngest of them – who against her wishes has followed his father down the pits – is killed in a coal-face accident, the tragedy sets his parents at each other's throats. Walter accuses his wife of treating him like a dog and storms out yelling, 'I'll see you again when I see you', to which she replies, 'And it'll be before I want to!' She is also jealous of Paul's girlfriend, Miriam, played by Heather Sears, whom she accuses of trying to shut her out of her son's life.

Paul enjoys a brief fling with Clara Dawes, played by Mary Ure, a married woman separated from her priggish husband. But the end of that affair, and the death of his mother from a heart attack, does not restore him to the arms of Miriam. 'I want to be free,' he tells her. 'I don't ever want to belong to anyone again.' As the credits roll, Paul catches a train to London where he will study at art school, thereby fulfilling his dead mother's last and dearest wish.

Dean Stockwell was the choice of American producer Jerry Wald to play Paul. Nothing in the track record of the former child star suggested him as the man for the role. He made a poor stab at an English accent and none at all at a Nottinghamshire dialect. The result was a miner's son who seems to have spent half of his growing years in stockbroker Surrey and the other half in Massachusetts.

Howard told me that Stockwell took time before a scene to psych himself up for it. Everyone waited patiently while he paced to and fro, coaxing himself into the right mood. Wendy Hiller thought it most odd. One day he went to great lengths to explain to her the rationale behind his technique. Wendy listened politely until he had finished and then inquired, innocently, 'Yes, but does it do any good?'

Howard was the film's greatest asset. He looked as rough-hewn as the coal stacked at the pit-head. His dirt-streaked face, proud, gruff manner and every movement of his body rang true to life. His son's artistic ambitions cut no ice with him. He wants an honest day's labour out of him instead of 'scholarships and holidays and spouting algebra'. Howard's performance struck many chords – blustery when demanding respect, subdued when struggling for words to express tender feelings – and all of them immensely moving to watch.

Richard Whitebait, in *Films & Filming*, wrote, 'Trevor Howard's performance is no mere virtuoso display. That craggy, gargoyle face, never entirely in repose, is capable of sustaining the most searching close-up because strange things are going on behind the eyes – the curl of the lip or the jib of the jaw is always expressive; the minutiae of expression dividing the great from the merely competent actor . . . By an almost monastic simplicity of method, Howard can draw a spectator deep into the heart of a character without making one aware, until much later, that one has been fed an essential psychological detail – the look he gives his waiting wife when he brings the dead son to the surface after the pit explosion in *Sons and Lovers* tells more about the relationship of this couple than half a page of dialogue.'

Wendy Hiller, too, was utterly believable as the clinging mother who, after losing one son to the pit, fights like a tiger to prevent the other one being sacrificed. Perhaps one should not be too critical of Stockwell's performance. With English co-stars of the calibre of Howard and Wendy Hiller, in as English a book adaptation as *Sons and Lovers*, it was never going to be easy terrain for an American to infiltrate. It was ironic that Twentieth Century Fox wanted Stockwell from the beginning but couldn't make up their mind about Howard until the last minute. British director Jack Cardiff recalled, 'They wanted someone who was more of a star than a first-class actor to play the father.' Howard's performance earned him his first nomination for an Academy Award, and many believed that he had a good chance of winning.

Howard believed so himself when, accompanied by Helen, he arrived in Los Angeles for the presentation ceremony and found a note in his hotel room from Hedda Hopper, the influential Hollywood columnist, inviting him to be her escort at the glittering occasion. However, a couple of hours before they were due to meet the phone rang. It was Hopper's secretary announcing a change of plan. She couldn't accompany Howard after all. Burt Lancaster would escort her. That phone call told him where the vote had gone. Later that night Lancaster picked up the Best Actor Oscar for *Elmer Gantry*.

13
CAPACITY TO TRANSFORM

People would go up to him and he would react not as a movie star but as a bloke who never saw himself as anything special. That's an unusual, and endearing, way for an actor to be. – Jack Gold, Director of *Catholics* and *Aces High*

Man in the Middle (1964), directed by Guy Hamilton, co-starred Robert Mitchum. Howard's face brightened at the mention of Mitchum. 'I had met Bob in Mexico in the mid-fifties. Yes, as long ago as that,' he said. 'I was making *Run for the Sun*, and he was down there making a western. I think he said it was called *Bandido*. My co-star was Jane Greer, who had worked with Bob a couple of times. He came to England to make *Man in the Middle*, and we had a fine old time making it. Only reason I did it was Bob, really.'

Mitchum had his own reasons for escaping to England at the time. Hollywood gossips had blackened him for an alleged affair with Shirley Maclaine during the making of *Two for the Seesaw* (1962). Moving his family to England took them out of the spotlight long enough for he and his wife Dorothy to sort themselves out. Mitchum played an American GI stationed in India at the end of the Second World War who shoots a British sergeant and is placed on trial for murder. His defence is that at the time of the killing he was suffering from temporary insanity. Howard played the British Army psychiatrist whose job it was to prove or disprove Mitchum's claim.

The film was nothing special, but Howard registered well during his brief appearance. 'Mitchum is the star, but Howard takes command,' declared the London *Evening Standard*. Mitchum wouldn't disagree with that verdict. 'The great thing about Trevor is that you'll never catch him acting,' he told a television interviewer many years later.

In *Father Goose* (1964) Howard co-starred with Cary Grant. The unit spent several weeks on an island in the South Seas. As the producer as well as the star, Grant had chosen Howard to be his straight man in what turned out to be an uneven comedy about a war-dodging beachcomber, played by Grant, who is compelled by an authoritarian Australian naval commander, played by Howard, into manning a strategic South Seas observation post during the Second World War. The transformation of Grant, from a scruffy layabout to a heroic patriot, was the whole point of the film, but it proved more than a one-joke outing for both of them. With Universal Studios' resources behind them, it was visually stylish and satisfying in all departments. Howard's initial reservations that Grant the producer might over-indulge Grant the actor were swiftly swept away.

'Cary was a team player,' Howard recalled. 'The comedy worked because we all had good dialogue. He made sure of that. It was a happy experience. Sure, I was essentially his straight man, but you could do a lot worse than be a straight man to Cary Grant in a beautiful location in a multi-million-dollar production.'

Father Goose was a commercial success, partly because of the excellent chemistry between the two actors. The film's screenwriters, Peter Stone and Frank Tarloff, won an Academy Award for their efforts. Neither had expected to be in the running and were bowled over when the announcement was made. Clutching their Oscar, Stone looked across to where the star was sitting and said, 'My thanks to Cary Grant, who keeps winning these things for other people.'

By 1964 the James Bond wagon was in top gear, and spy movies were crowding the circuits. Every major studio had at least one Bond-style caper in the making. Director Jack Cardiff came up with what he thought was a fresh viewpoint – the super-cool spy hero who hates his job and pays others to dirty their hands for him. This was the basic idea for *The Liquidator* (1964), with Rod Taylor, Jill St John and Trevor Howard.

Taylor, an established Hollywood tough guy, played a timid café owner in London who gets sucked into spying against his will. He cannot bring himself to kill, so he hires a dodgy-looking assassin, played hilariously by Eric Sykes, to do the job for him. David Tomlinson also appeared in the film as a super-smooth double agent. Taylor and St John were in the film to satisfy its American backers. Taylor was badly miscast; it needed a lighter touch than he could deliver.

Howard played the equivalent of M in the Bond movies, the no-nonsense spymaster who issues the orders and counts the bodies. Jack Cardiff, who had directed Howard in *Sons And Lovers* and *The Lion* (1962), immediately thought of him when casting Colonel Mostyn. It was a stroke of luck that he did. Along with Sykes, Howard provided the film's occasional good moments.

A spy movie with a difference was set in motion when the United Nations decided to sponsor *The Poppy Is Also a Flower* (1965), one of a planned series of television feature films financed by Xerox – who put up $3.65 million – to show various aspects of UN work around the world. The plan was to screen the films on television in the United States and show them in cinemas around the world. Top directors, including Otto Preminger, Alfred Hitchcock and Joseph Mankiewicz, were invited by the US Ambassador to the United Nations, Adlai Stevenson – an unsuccessful presidential candidate – to become involved.

Terence Young, the director of the first two James Bond movies – *Doctor No* (1962) and *From Russia with Love* (1963) – was invited to make a film of his choice as one of the series. Young accepted and asked Euan Lloyd to be his producer. Lloyd recalled, 'Terence and I went to Washington, to a reception at the White House where the idea was launched. Terence decided to do a film about the UN's efforts to combat the international traffic in drugs. Joe Eisenger, a writer friend of his, did the script.' The budget of $600,000 provided by Xerox was insufficient, but the company could not increase Young's budget without increasing everybody else's, and his request for more cash was rejected.

Nevertheless he decided to upgrade the production, and if that meant they had to beg, borrow or persuade stars to work for nothing then so be it. Lloyd, a tireless fixer when he needed to be, flew to Hollywood to rope in some famous names, carrying with him a letter from Adlai Stevenson which underlined the US government's support. Lloyd did not return empty-handed, although enthusiasm for the film in Hollywood was generally muted. Some he propositioned promised to think about it. Only Harry Belafonte, he recalled, turned him down flat. Yul Brynner, Rita Hayworth, Steven Boyd and Gilbert Roland were among those who said yes. From Italy he got Marcello Mastroianni, from Egypt Omar Sharif and from Austria Senta Berger.

One of American television's most popular actors of the 1960s was E.G. Marshall, who looked like Bob Hope's stockier elder brother and whose series *The Defenders*, about a father-and-son attorney team (Robert Reed played Marshall's son), has been described as one of the best courtroom drama series ever made. It was therefore something of a coup when Marshall agreed to come to Europe for the fourteen-week shooting schedule for a dollar a week plus expenses, at a time when highly paid offers for his services were flooding in. Marshall's admiration for the work of the UN was a factor in the decision.

He was cast as the FBI chief who, with his British counterpart from Scotland Yard, traces the dope trail from its origins in Iran and Afghanistan to the pushers in various back streets of Europe. Lloyd thought that Trevor Howard would be excellent for the Scotland Yard inspector, but the question of wages, or lack of, had to be overcome. There had to be a limit on how far friendship would stretch. Lloyd waited until the last second to mention the money. His sales pitch emphasized the sunny locations, the star names and the UN involvement.

'Yes, but how much will you pay me,' asked Howard.

'A dollar a week.'

Howard looked relieved. 'Thank God for that. I thought you were going to ask me to do it for nothing.'

Despite having got Howard for less than the price of a decent cigar, Young did not treat him, or any of the cast, with kid gloves. Howard had a scene to do on a luxury yacht moored in Monte Carlo harbour. He was provided with an elegant white made-to-measure tuxedo to wear in the scene, which was to take place in the middle of an on-board party. Gilbert Roland, as a Mafia boss, has discovered that Howard is an undercover cop and plans to kill him and push him into the harbour. Howard was to be given the jacket at the end of the shooting, and he didn't want it scuffed or dirtied in any way. It was worth many times more the salary he was getting for the film.

It was therefore a disappointment when Young told him that instead on the stand-in going overboard Howard would have to do the shot to facilitate a close-up. The actor glanced at the oily, smelly water below the pier, smiled tolerantly and shook his head.

Lloyd told me, 'Terence was a typical director. He insisted on actors doing what they were told. He said to Trevor, "Get on with it, man. You're being paid enough to make this picture!" to which Trevor shrieked, "*What* did you say!" Gilbert Roland, who was on already on his marks, said, "If you do it, Trevor, I'll do it. I'll follow you in. We're in this thing together, amigo." Of course, Roland had no intention of getting wet. But it wouldn't matter, because by then the jump would have happened.' Once again, Howard, the eternal innocent, was fooled by a glib promise.

A net had been placed just under surface of the water to enable Howard to be scooped out the moment the cameras stopped turning. His reappearance after the jump was greeted by loud cheers. The immaculate tuxedo was, of course, ruined, but Lloyd had a nice surprise in store for him after he had dried off. A second, identical jacket had been made for him by the wardrobe department. As Howard marched off with the new tux across his arm, Young called out to him jokingly, 'Put it on then, Trevor. I need another take.' Howard's reply was a stream of invective.

The film brought together on the screen for the first time Howard and Jack Hawkins, the two actors most frequently identified with military or naval commander roles in British post-war films. They were old friends, of course, and often ribbed one another about being stereotyped. At the end of a thumping war scene Hawkins was once asked by a reporter what he would like to do in his next film. 'Make love to a woman instead of a bloody battleship,' he replied tartly.

When the day's filming was over, Howard and Hawkins would disappear to a little bar near by, sip gin fizzes and swap stories. One day on the set Hawkins practically lost his voice, and the experience seemed to unnerve him unduly. Later that night at their favourite café Hawkins explained why. Five years previously he had been diagnosed as having throat cancer. Radiation therapy had been successful, but it was a once-only treatment. If the cancer recurred, Hawkins was told he would have to rely on surgery, which would mean the loss of his voice. Sadly, as most people know, the cancer returned, and he died in 1972.

Of all the cameos in *The Poppy Is Also a Flower*, the largest and most flamboyant was that of Yul Brynner, who played the colourful Colonel Salem. Brynner agreed to appear in the film as long as he was allowed to wear black, his lucky colour since *The Magnificent Seven* (1960). Against the bleached sands of the desert he cut an imposing figure. Howard's verdict on the film was 'interesting, though by no means great'. He could not remember how he had spent the few dollars he had earned for making it.

Triple Cross (1965) straddled true life and boys'-own fantasy. Based on the true exploits of a wartime double-agent, it emulated the style of the Bond films unnecessarily – the truth would have been more than sufficient to sustain a lively adventure movie. Eddie Chapman, a professional safe-cracker, spies for Britain until caught in the act by the Germans. To save his skin he agrees to work for the enemy. Both sides watch him like a hawk. Any false move could get him killed by either side. Terence Young kept the thrills coming, but it was kids'-stuff heroics rather than a serious attempt – like *Odette* or *Carve Her Name with Pride* – to show the realities of behind-the-lines espionage. Christopher Plummer played Chapman, and his opposing 'bosses' were played by Howard and Brynner respectively.

Brynner and Howard were on the opposite sides of a different argument in *The Long Duel* (1967), a story set during the last gasp of British rule in India in the 1920s. Brynner was a rebel chieftain with a history of guerrilla raids on the British. Howard was the policeman ordered to arrest him. As the chase develops, both men begin to respect each other. They see one another as human beings with identical values, not simply the mouthpieces of the opposing ideologies.

Surrounded and trapped in his hideout, with the British troops closing in, the bandit chief wrings a promise from Howard that he will take care of his son, and when Howard is halfway down the mountain with the boy at his side Brynner turns his rifle on himself.

Spain had been chosen to replicate the Indian bandit country, and interiors were completed at Pinewood after location shooting ended in the spring of 1967. Produced and directed by Ken Annakin – who had directed *The Longest Day* (1962), *The Battle of the Bulge* (1965) and *Those Magnificent Men in Their Flying Machines* (1965) – compared to his earlier work this film was rather disappointing. The script seemed muddled, and a silly, intrusive love affair between the policeman and another officer's daughter about half his age served no clear purpose. The best scenes were between Howard and Brynner. You could believe in these men but not in much else *The Long Duel* had to offer.

Singapore was the setting for *Pretty Polly* (1967), a Noel Coward story of little interest. A young girl, Polly, played by Hayley Mills, and her aunt, played by Brenda de Banzie, interrupt their world cruise at Singapore for an interlude with the girl's uncle, an old reprobate who grows rubber trees, played by Howard. During their stopover Polly falls in love with a local Malaysian boy, and the aunt drowns. Her uncle is unperturbed by these dramatic happenings. Singapore could sink into the sea and he would not notice. He is sloshed most of the time, after what the hotel boy admiringly calls 'evenings of unforgettable merriment'.

Pretty Polly had practically no substance. Coward deemed it 'awful' and everyone in it 'horrid', and he wasn't talking about the fictional characters. But it gave Howard an opportunity to be an amusing rascal and, for once, was able to use his hell-raising image as an excuse for some passable jokes. At his sister's funeral, when the grieving hotel boy at his side says, 'These are morose circumstances', Howard mumbles, 'You're right. I've run out of scotch.'

There were no comic lines in *The Battle of Britain* (1967). The lines filling the screen were rows of Spitfires and Hurricanes intercepting enemy bombers over the Home Counties in 1940. It was a familiar story – an unprepared Britain giving the Luftwaffe a bloody nose. The dog-fights over British south coast were filmed with style by director Guy Hamilton and his aerial cameramen. Air battles can cause confusion among audiences who mostly can't tell a Messerschmitt from a minced pie, but these are thrilling air sequences viewed both from the ground and inside the aircraft, arguably the most watchable ever photographed.

On the ground the action divides between the strategists and the pilots, the former seemingly a bunch of anxious-looking men who stare at maps and gripe about the shortages. Throughout the film Laurence Olivier as Air Chief Marshal Dowding behaves as if his mind is somewhere else. In a neutral country perhaps. The pilots just want to enjoy themselves between sorties. One even finds time to get married.

Howard played the officer in charge of Britain's defences. He buzzes around in a dazzling white boiler-suit (has nobody told him about camouflage?) barking orders at moving objects and keeping that upper lip as stiff as a propeller blade. With a number of expensive stars playing cameo roles, it was not always possible to get them together. In one scene Howard and Patrick Wymark – as another piece of top brass – squabble about resources in front of Dowding. Crafty editing allowed Olivier to be somewhere else that morning. We are not supposed to spot it, but Howard and Wymark are bickering in front of an empty chair.

Produced by Harry Saltzman and Benjamin Fisz, the film was three years in preparation, considerably longer than the Germans took to plan the real thing. Costing $5 million, *The Battle of Britain* proved in the end too rich a mixture, and, rather like a bird that overeats, it struggled to get off the ground. But only the critics carped. Audiences still celebrating England's victory over the German football team in the World Cup of 1966 gave it a great reception.

Howard could not remember a single thing about *Twinky* (1969). No amount of persuasion would unzip his memory on that one. I said to him, 'You played Susan George's grandfather, and the director was Richard Donner.' He went into 'if-you-say-so' mode and locked the door behind him. I said, 'The star was Charles Bronson. You remember him, surely.' Diplomatic lockjaw set in at the mention of Bronson. He stared into space for a couple of seconds and then shook his head.

Night Visitor (1967) was a psychological melodrama directed by Laslo Benedek, the Budapest-born director whose biker movie, *The Wild One* (1953), starring Marlon Brando, had kicked off the teen rebel genre and sparked off a storm of protest sufficient to delay its general release in Britain until 1968. The violence in *Night Visitor*, a pedestrian melodrama by comparison, was criminal insanity, which does not photograph too well. The film starred Max von Sydow and Liv Ullmann and was made in Sweden and Denmark. Von Sydow played an asylum escapee seeking revenge on those who had him locked away for a crime they had committed. Howard and Rupert Davies provided robust British support. Howard couldn't make sense of the storyline and had 'nothing worth hearing' to say about the film, but it was enjoyable, he recalled, working again with Benedek, who had directed him in *Moment of Danger* a decade before. They were able to continue their reminiscences about Vienna, a city they both knew well – Howard from his time on *The Third Man* and Benedek from his days as a psychiatry student at Vienna University during the 1930s. Not surprisingly, mental aberration of one kind or another featured in many of Benedek's films.

By 1970 the free world had become so lethargic towards the Cold War that the only people giving it a second thought were film-makers hoping to make money out of it, urging the broken-winded old spy genre to complete another circuit of the track.

One of the more inventive of the movies that poked fun at the espionage business was *Catch Me a Spy* (1971), co-produced in Britain by Kirk Douglas's company, Bryna Productions, and starring the boss himself. The film, mostly about rival spies being captured and exchanged, had a lightness of touch to it, a satisfying pace and sufficient changes of location – ending up in the wilds of Scotland – to keep it entertaining. Douglas was the superspy who rescues an amateurish Briton, played by Patrick Mower, from the clutches of his communist captors.

Howard was second-billed as a crusty Foreign Office official, a role that allowed him to play comedy within the context of a straight role. Some of his lines would be considered, in these enlightened times, politically incorrect. A good deal of the humour is directed at the dissimilar cultures of East and West, and it works reasonably well. Example: during an exchange of spies a Russian agent falls through the ice and drowns because his luggage is too heavy, weighted down with 'souvenirs of Western decadence'. He won't leave the West without his LP of *The Sound of Music*. When he drowns, everything sinks with him except a soggy copy of *Playboy*.

Several jokes are made about the awfulness of Russian culture. When Mower's captors boast that they haven't tortured him, Mower replies glumly, 'Have you seen Russian television?' Most critics agreed that the idea, a good one, had not been developed correctly. Richard Coombs wrote that the director, Dick Clement, had 'assembled all the ingredients of a good lightweight thriller – neat and ingenious plot, attractive cast, inventive comic touches – but [he] has failed to blend them into an effective whole. What emerges is a succession of disjointed scenes with no controlling style or momentum.' Coombs added, and few would disagree, that Howard had been 'sadly wasted'.

Filming of *Ludwig* (1971), a four-hour epic directed by Luchino Visconti, was undertaken in the director's native Italy, and although Howard was on the screen for only ten minutes, he felt that his trip there was justified. Visconti is a respected name in European cinema and a favourite of British actors seeking challenges and recognition abroad. Dirk Bogarde is a case in point. One of their collaborations, *Death in Venice* (1971), extracted from Bogarde a performance of startling sensitivity, one that the actor believed was his best ever.

Ludwig was not in that category, but it was a handsomely mounted if overlong saga of the life and times of the nineteenth-century King of Bavaria, who, if you believe Visconti's account, went mad. Audiences risked a similar fate if they attempted to watch it from start to finish. Helmut Berger played Ludwig, and he was supported by Romy Schneider and Silvana Mangano.

Working with Visconti was an eye-opener for Howard, who thought by then that he had seen everything. He told me, 'Visconti works like no other director I know. He had four cameras, but you never knew where they were. You couldn't see any of them. You had no idea which one was on you. And I was told they all had different lenses. All you were told was "You walk from here to there" or "Stand still." You never knew what kind of shot he wanted. And if you asked him, he wouldn't bloody tell you. All he'd say was: "Don't worry about it." So I didn't!'

Howard's performance as the composer Richard Wagner, who enjoyed the patronage of the king, was brief but noteworthy. Vincent Canby, in the *New York Times*, described him as 'a rather British Wagner' (what on earth did he expect?), adding that the composer appeared to be a 'profoundly interesting combination of self-absorption, craftiness, genius and vision . . . the comparative understatement of Howard's performance rivets the attention'.

Elizabeth I and Mary Queen of Scots were feisty cousins who both knew what they wanted. Unfortunately, they both wanted to be Queen of the same country, which locked them into a bitter feud. It should have been the stuff of high drama. Veteran American producer Hal Wallis and director Charles Jarrott certainly thought so and fused their talents for a second crack at Tudor history. The reception given to their earlier collaboration, *Anne of the Thousand Days* (1969), with Richard Burton as Henry VIII, encouraged them to think that its success could be repeated.

Playing Elizabeth I in *Mary Queen of Scots* (1971), Glenda Jackson scarcely had time to swap costumes. Only six weeks separated the completion of the television recording of *Elizabeth R*, in which she had starred, and the first day of filming for Wallis on the Scottish Borders. Vanessa Redgrave played the doomed Mary. These two fine actresses complemented one another splendidly – Jackson with her strong, rather masculine face and strident voice and Redgrave with her milk-white skin and large, tragic eyes.

The historical facts of Mary's doomed attempts to hold on to the throne of Scotland and to topple Elizabeth are well known. The film opens with Mary's arrival in Scotland from France, where she had been exiled. Before reaching Edinburgh she is denounced as a papal lackey by the reformer John Knox, who shuffles though the bleak Borders landscape denouncing anyone of a different faith to his own. But Knox's fiery accusations are merely the opening salvo of a continuous broadside which for Mary ends on with her head on the block at Fotheringay Castle in 1587. Everybody she trusts either fails or abandons her. Her half-brother plots against her. Her husband is a drunken, jealous fool. The Scottish lords resent her Catholicism, as well as the fact that she is a woman. To spare the life of her second husband she is forced to flee to England, straight into Elizabeth's frosty embrace.

The discovery by Elizabeth's flinty chancellor, played by Howard, of letters implicating her in a plot to overthrow Elizabeth – inexplicably stored under the floorboards of her cell – spells disaster. Elizabeth promises to pardon her if only she will beg forgiveness in writing, but the headstrong, misguided, ill-advised and tragic queen-in-name-only has already made up her mind. 'I must die. It is my destiny,' she tells Elizabeth. 'It will torment you till the end of your days.' Her prediction is accurate on both counts.

Howard is on screen for only a couple of scenes, looking stately and wise behind a neatly trimmed beard, yet his brooding presence permeates the story. You sense that Elizabeth will not make a move without consulting him, that he is the one with the real power, using it to taunt the Spaniards, to keep the lesser lords from fomenting trouble, to keep the wheels of government turning smoothly. Elizabeth's only scenes are the ones where she is in a state about Mary. Didn't she have anything else on her mind? Sadly, there are no real sparks in the battle between Elizabeth and Mary. Their conflict has no more firepower than two netball captains from genteel private schools disputing a penalty decision. The other members of the cast, however, work hard to create an atmosphere of menace and intrigue, and some overdo it – Timothy Dalton as the foppish Lord Darnley sweats so much you wonder if Holyrood Palace is having problems with the heating.

Jackson was told that the role required her hairline to be receded by three inches. A skin-coloured adhesive strip worked fine in long shot but was visible in the close-ups, of which there were many. She had no alternative but to have the front of her head shaved every day. She asked her hairdresser, Harold Leighton, 'There won't be any lasting effects, will there?' Leighton replied, 'Well, after so many shavings your hair might not grow back again.' Jackson said nothing. She just settled back in the chair and waited for Leighton to start cutting. But to minimize the number of times that her forehead would need to be shaved, the schedule was revised to allow her scenes to be filmed back to back. Her performance, from start to finish, was compressed into three and a half weeks. Howard, who had a number of key scenes with her, was out of breath at the pace of filming. He told the director, Charles Jarrott, 'I've just spent over a year on *Ryan's Daughter*. Now I have to do this picture in three and a half weeks. Isn't there a middle way?' But there wasn't. The queenly Jackson's needs came first.

The film has more than its share of solid doors being thrown open and of cunning plots being intercepted. However, I thought the mixture of ambition, desperation and madness which make up life inside the royal palaces had been brewed competently enough by Charles Jarrott. Not everyone agreed. Richard Coombs criticized the film's 'complete failure to present the conflicts visually. People simply congregate against various settings for these encapsulated readings from history.' Ian Woodward's biography of Jackson suggests that she shared this gloomy view of the finished movie. He quotes her as looking back at it 'with horror, and [she] referred to it as the first film of which she was ashamed to be a part'. If he had the opportunity, I can just imagine Howard telling her, 'What can you expect, if all you were prepared to give it was three and a half fucking weeks!' Personally, I would have preferred fewer dark interiors, claustrophobic passageways, tiny cell-like rooms and perspiring Scotsmen. The most watchable scenes for me take place out of doors.

Although Howard shared star billing with Sean Connery in *The Offence* (1972), he had only one scene of any importance. Admittedly it was a key scene, but that hardly justified calling him the co-star. Once again Howard's repeated complaint that companies offered him small roles and matching fees only to then plaster his name in large letters on cinema hoardings seemed justified. In 1972 Connery's box-office appeal did not extend beyond James Bond. His other movies went down poorly in America. Howard, by then, was better known in the United States because of *Mutiny on the Bounty*, *Ryan's Daughter* and *Von Ryan's Express*. Directed by an American, Sidney Lumet, *The Offence* was clearly intended for transatlantic travel, and Howard's name above the title made good marketing sense. He might bitch about it in the bar afterwards, but small roles were Howard's bread and butter, and he would have been the first to concede that they were a damn sight better than doing nothing.

The Offence, written by John Hopkins – who had made his name during the early 1960s as a scriptwriter on the British television police series *Z Cars* – took a gloomy, grainy look at the damaging effects on a policeman's mind who sees too much violence in the course of doing his duty. Detective Sergeant Johnson, played by Connery, is an otherwise conscientious copper tormented by images of past murder victims, suicides and dead children. When a child molester on his patch strikes for the fourth time – Johnson finds the victim alive, sobbing in a dark wood – the experience pushes him over the edge. He takes his fury out on the first suspect brought in for questioning – a wonderfully creepy performance by Ian Bannen – who dies in hospital from the thumping Johnson dishes out.

Howard played Lieutenant Cartwright, a police chief sent to stir things up and restore the service's good name. To find out why Johnson flipped, he must force the officer's paranoia to the surface, which he does in a brutal, terse battle of words. From the minute he sweeps into the interrogation room Howard's dour, abrasive superintendent is out for blood. 'You think you're a hard case? I was bloody shouting and swearing when you still wet your bed!' Cartwright sees Johnson as a cancer within the force. Johnson hates Cartwright because he sees him as an bureaucrat from headquarters.

The acting of the four leading players – Connery, Howard, Ian Bannen and Vivien Merchant as Johnson's downtrodden wife – is tight and efficient, in keeping with the no-frills, documentary-style of storytelling. Clyde Jeavons commented, 'Connery's hard, reticent style suits the acerbic copper, while both Vivien Merchant and Trevor Howard seem curiously subdued in their set-pieces. Ian Bannen brings off a minor *tour de force* with his depiction of bewildered, tormented hysteria.' Jeavons thought that Sidney Lumet's 'portentous, leaden direction' failed to exploit the 'underlying substance of John Hopkins's script'.

Pope Joan (1972) is the story of the peasant girl in Italy who fools everyone into thinking she's a devout monk and lands the top job. Unfortunately nobody warns her that getting pregnant while being a Pope is a bad career move. One minute she is riding triumphantly around the city of Rome; the next she is being torn limb from limb by a hysterical mob. What, I wondered, were important international actors like Liv Ullmann, Maximilian Schell, Keir Dullea and Franco Nero doing in this tripe? But you don't have to take my word for it – or Howard's huffy silence – that *Pope Joan* was a rotten waste of time and talent. Peter Buckley wrote in *Films & Filming*, '*Pope Joan* is without a doubt the most sententious, trite, pompous and intellectually offensive movie of the year . . . in total, the most inept, amateurish piece of film-making I've been forced to sit through.' Sylvia Miller called it 'a hagiography of gloomy and ludicrous mawkishness; often it is only the limp solemnity of Liv Ullmann which quells one's laughter.' Dilys Powell said, 'I thought *Pope Joan* was rather terrible, but suddenly it was transformed by the appearance of Trevor Howard in a minor part, Pope Leo. I thought at the time, "Please, don't take him away. Don't show me any more of this dreadful film." But I wanted to go on watching Trevor Howard. He had an extraordinary capacity for transforming an uninteresting film into something exciting.'

It was, therefore, with a sigh of relief that Howard received the script of Ibsen's *A Doll's House* from Joseph Losey. The play, in its time, had been a controversial tract on radical feminism, but social progress had caught up with it. Nevertheless Ibsen had written from the heart, and the emotions and attitudes he described have their parallels in contemporary society. Losey, an Anglicized American since the blacklist of the early 1950s, certainly thought so. His was a maverick talent, strongly influenced by Brecht and Pinter, and he had no serious rivals in Britain at the time when it came to exploring complex, quirky themes of both classical and modern origin. In his autobiography *Snakes and Ladders*, Dirk Bogarde wrote, 'Like all the greatest directors, Losey never tells one what to do or how to do it. Ever. Only what not to do. Which is very different . . . There is no waste of chatter, no great in-depth discussions about motivation, no mumbo-jumbo about identification, soul or truth. You get on with it.'

Howard arrived in Norway, eager to 'get on with it' in November 1972 with some of the other cast members, including David Warner and Edward Fox. Jane Fonda, the star of the film, was already there. A strong advocate of feminism, she was the kind of woman Howard had difficulty understanding, let alone liking. Trouble flared almost immediately when it became apparent that Fonda wanted to accentuate the play's feminist content. According to Losey, 'she wanted to stand on the rooftop and holler at the top of her voice.' No serious interpreter of Ibsen would dream of behaving in such a way. Losey was polite but adamant. Fonda responded by fetching from America her own scriptwriter, Nancy Dowd, who wove her ideas into the text and presented them, in written form, to Losey every morning.

An edgy stalemate developed, with winter drawing in, the nights growing longer and everyone getting miserable. Michael Meyer, a leading authority on Ibsen and a close friend of Howard's, told me, 'They were filming in a little town in the wilds of Norway. I had planned to visit them after everyone had settled in. Then I got a card from Trevor and Edward and David saying, "For Christ's sake, don't come, because when you see what's being done to Ibsen you'll jump in the nearest fjord." I took their advice and stayed away. It was a dreadful film, and Jane Fonda was awful in it. Absolutely awful.'

Howard told me, 'I just wanted to finish the thing and get home before everywhere froze over. I could see the film not being one thing or the other.' Losey stuck to his guns throughout his arguments with Fonda and saved a film which, had she got her way and been allowed to extinguish the subtlety, would undoubtedly been panned by the critics and deservedly so. Losey's delicate touches, such as the fluid camera movements, and his respect for Ibsen's text ensured that the film is watchable although less than engrossing. Leslie Halliwell said it had 'too much solemnity and the central part [Fonda's] is miscast'. Clyde Jeavons, however, praised Howard for performing 'at his superlative best'.

In 1973 Howard joined the cast of *Craze*, a shocker notable only for the fact that Hollywood bad guy Jack Palance was its star. His blinkless stare and fly-trap mouth – remember *Shane* (1953)? – suited his role as a nutter who sells his soul to an African demon god and then has to become a serial killer to keep his part of the diabolical bargain. Palance made a passable attempt at showing a spirit in torment, but it was the presence of Howard, Hugh Griffith and Diana Dors in cameo roles that made the film tolerable. Howard had never taken part in a horror movie and found the experience execrable. 'Mad, all of it,' he said. 'Palance was supposed to be mad, so you could excuse him. But the rest of us, no excuse at all. We must've been off our fucking heads.' Chris Petit was critical of its 'poor and perfunctory script'. He added, 'We are left depending on the numerous cameo roles [which] ensure that the film is in safe hands, but ultimately their brief appearances can't compensate for the yawning gaps elsewhere.'

Rescue, of a sort, was at hand, when Jack Gold asked Howard to be in *Catholics* (1973), a television film made for American CBS television by Sidney Glazier. Written by Brian Moore, it was about a refusal by an

Irish Catholic abbot to modernize the Mass when ordered to do so by his superiors. This lands him in deep trouble. Filmed mostly in the ruins of a monastery in Sherkin Island in County Cork, with some interiors completed at Cahir Castle, *Catholics* was a serious, intelligent film, and Howard's run-in with the modernizers, represented by a younger priest, Martin Sheen, is fascinating to watch. The clash of consciences leaves both of them shaken and seriously questioning whose is the right direction. John J. O'Connor described it in the *New York Times* as 'nothing short of magnificent', full of 'craggy gruffness and sophisticated humanity'.

Asked by a journalist if he had undertaken any special preparation for the role, Howard replied crisply, 'Of course not.' It wasn't intended as a put-down. He was simply being truthful. His preparation followed established lines. He learned the script and then slipped himself into the mind-set of the character. Everything we saw on the screen flowed from that. His performance was delightfully natural and precise. Graham Greene was so impressed by it that afterwards he wrote, 'I can't describe how moved I was by your performance; there were tears in my eyes at the end and I had to take a pill to sleep. For me, it was one of the two finest performances I have ever seen on the screen or the stage – and I say "one of the two" only because otherwise you mightn't believe me.' The pragmatic author had written the note, he said, 'with the cold wisdom of the next morning, not in the flush of first enthusiasm'.

Jack Gold recalled for me his experience of working with Trevor Howard on that film and on two others, the sci-fithriller *Who?* (1974) and *Aces High* (1976). 'I had always been a fan of his,' said Gold. 'He helped us out at the last minute in *Who?* as a Russian intelligence officer opposite Elliott Gould. It was CBS who suggested him for *Catholics*. I was delighted that they saw him as an "OK" name.'

The shoot was fast and furious; eighteen days spread across several Irish locations. Exteriors of the Sherkin Island location required the fitting of a canvas roof because there were no roofs on any of the derelict abbeys in Ireland. Gold said, 'I think Trevor felt stretched in a way that he hadn't been for ages. This was a major challenge for him, especially at the end, where the emotional input from him had to be enormous. I thought that he was terrific in it.' He went on, 'He drank a bit, as he always did, but he was no problem at all. It never affected him. He was one of those guys who plays hard, but he's also very professional. He hadn't time to be cranky. It was an intensive period. We were either working or travelling.'

I asked Jack Gold how he rated Howard as an actor. He replied, 'He was absolutely marvellous in character parts. His range was enormous. And he was dependable, like the rock of Gibraltar. As a director, you could relax, because you knew that his part of the film was going to be OK. You only had to suggest something to him and he responded. We had a collaboration rather than an actor–director situation. One might just say, "Look, I think you can show more" or "Bring it down a little" or "That looks like a bit of mannerism creeping in", and he'd be fine with that. Most actors welcome sensible direction, otherwise they're in a vacuum.

'He was never prickly with me or with anybody else that I was aware of. I found myself more than once comparing him with Humphrey Bogart. There was a terrific reality about the two of them. Both were men's men, but underneath you'd find layer after layer of sweetness and charm. People would go up to him, and he would react not as a movie star but as a bloke who never saw himself as anything special. That's an unusual, and endearing, way for an actor to be.'

It was back to more routine matters with *Eleven Harrowhouse* (1974), an entertaining yarn about a diamond heist masterminded by Howard and carried out by an American professional thief, played by Charles Grodin. John Gielgud and James Mason had smallish roles in the film, their first together since *Julius Caesar* (1953).

In the first half of the film the comedy is mainly observational – Grodin's bewilderment at the English upper-class lifestyle. Howard is a landed gentleman whose criminal activities are more to do with escaping boredom than making a profit. Behind this sparky comedy of manners is an equally engaging spoof on a genre which by the mid-1970s sat up begging to be satirized. The director's competent control of the narrative slips awkwardly during the final quarter of the film, allowing it to stray dangerously close to slapstick, but despite this change of pace it remains an enjoyable film to watch, and Howard is in excellent form as the mad joker behind the robbery.

Howard was dismissive of *Persecution* (1974), which brought Lana Turner to Britain and on which he did next to nothing, got paid in shirt buttons and finished up having to carry the film, because Lana Turner, married seven times and looking every day of her fifty-three years, had nothing more to offer – at least nothing that anyone wanted to watch. In the movie Howard played her ex-lover. She is crazy and evil in equal proportions. She dominates her weak son, then murders her daughter-in-law and their child. Suggestions of witchcraft and demonology turn what was already a sorry mess into unrelenting farce. Verina Glaessner wrote, 'Lana Turner . . . labours to hold her head high and bear up despite the Grande Guignol all around her tipping into embarrassing silliness.'

14
MELANCOHOLIC

He still had, at that time, the reputation of being a hell-raiser. My recollection of him is at variance with that. I saw him as someone immensely patient and rather melancholy.

– Corin Redgrave

An episode of the Crimean War provided Howard with his most colourful role in years, Lord Cardigan, who led the Light Brigade charge commemorated in Tennyson's poem. *The Charge of the Light Brigade* (1968), directed by Tony Richardson, had a difficult, protracted history before reaching the screen. Richardson and John Osborne, former colleagues at the Royal Court Theatre in the 1950s and collaborators – as director and screenwriter respectively – on *Tom Jones* (1962), felt that the fatal charge was a perfect cinema vehicle for their film company, Woodfall Films. It had everything except love interest, but they felt that need not stand in their way. Richardson's original favourite to play Lord Cardigan had been Rex Harrison, but friction between them over a misleading press report, which wrongly suggested that the American actor George C. Scott was in the running, gave Richardson time to think again, and the part went to Howard. With hindsight, Harrison seems a trifle lightweight for Cardigan.

Cecil Woodham-Smith's book *The Reason Why*, which Richardson described as 'brilliant historical writing', provided a definitive account of what really happened, what went wrong and the tragic aftermath. The battle had attracted film-makers before Richardson, but in Britain these had come to nothing. Warner Brothers had made a version of *The Charge of the Light Brigade* in 1935 with Errol Flynn, which was 80 per cent fiction. The film rights to *The Reason Why* were owned by the actor Laurence Harvey who, after co-starring in *The Alamo* with John Wayne (who also directed), had spent several years looking for a similar sort of story in which to direct himself, as Wayne had done. He bought the rights to the book because he was struck by the parallels between the two incidents; that is, they both had small groups of brave men being overwhelmed and decimated by a stronger, better-equipped enemy.

Richardson hoped to make his film without reference to the Woodham-Smith book. As a piece of history as much in the public domain as any other famous battle, other accounts of it existed, notably Alexander Kingslake's *Invasion of the Crimea*. Richardson had agreed with Osborne that the writing should steer well clear of Woodham-Smith's approach so that nobody could accuse them of plundering Harvey's property.

That may have been the intention, but Osborne's script sailed dangerously close to the wind, and Harvey responded with a lawsuit accusing them of contravening copyright. Oscar Beuselinck, the lawyer for Woodfall Films, compared the two versions and concluded that Osborne had, in Richardson's words, 'helped himself liberally to stylistic phrases and descriptions in *The Reason Why*'. Harvey, to his credit, sought only to recoup his financial losses. He acknowledged that it had been an enthusiasm for the subject comparable to his own which had landed Richardson in hot water and that Woodfall had no intention of stealing from him. With a measure of goodwill on both sides, the matter was quickly settled out of court – for a sum reputed to be £12,000 – and Woodham Smith's book got a mention in the credits.

The Crimean War began as a dispute between Russia and several European countries over the guardianship of the Holy Places in Palestine, then under the control of the Turks. When a pact signed in Vienna proved ineffectual, two of the European allies – Austria and Prussia – withdrew, leaving France and Britain to prevent Russia's expansion to the south, where the region could be destabilized and, worse still, Britain's vital overland trade routes to India intercepted.

When Russian troops began to move south, Turkey responded with a declaration of war and called on Britain and France to honour their promises. Thus the scene was set for military confrontation. The gloves finally came off in March 1854. It was a war in which, tactically speaking, Britain should never have become embroiled. Her army was hopelessly unready and poorly managed and had not seen action since Waterloo, nearly forty years previously. Its commander-in-chief, Lord Raglan, had spent the intervening years desk-bound in Whitehall and was sixty-six years of age.

Lord Cardigan, who commanded the light brigade, and Lord Lucan, who was in charge of the cavalry, were equally spent old warhorses. To complicate matters, they were arch-rivals, distantly related, and they loathed one another. Their gung-ho days on the battlefield were a distant memory. Richardson's film was essentially in three parts, showing the cavalry preparing for war, travelling to Crimea and settling in and, finally, the famous charge of the 'six hundred' – historians now put the number at closer to seven hundred – out of which less than two hundred men and only a similar number of horses survived.

A series of cartoons by Richard Williams during and after the credits explain in simple graphics how the crisis emerged. We first see Cardigan, astride his horse, reviewing his columns of cavalry. Riding between their ranks, he mutters to himself, 'If they can't fornicate, they can't fight and if they can't fight, I'll flog their backs raw for all their fine looks.' Cardigan represents the old-style army officer, rich, high-minded, pedantic, who gets his way through floggings and cash payments. An alternative, more enlightened view is offered by Captain Nolan, played by David Hemmings, who hates cruelty and stupidity. He sums up his attitude 'in a word, kindliness'. When an unschooled horse throws its rider to the ground, Nolan tells another officer, 'Horses are taught not by harshness but by gentleness.' Cardigan and Nolan are on a collision course from the very beginning.

The film remains true to the documented descriptions of the charge. The cavalry under Lucan lines up in the hot sun. The light brigade under Cardigan stands forward, while the heavy brigade, under another commander, waits in reserve. The Russians have captured some British gun positions on nearby heights, and Raglan debates whether to send in the light brigade to recover them. At this point commands are misinterpreted, panic sets in and the general disorganization plus over-eagerness by some troops to engage the enemy leads to the disastrous charge. By an ironic twist, Turkey was the only country where the film could be made. The terrain was ideal, and Turkey still had sufficient horsemen doing military service – standing off the Russians cavalry across the border as they had done more than a century before, but this time as part of the NATO balancing act – to play both armies. A deal was struck with the Turkish government whereby Richardson could borrow the troops when he wanted them for the price of their upkeep. If a real war broke out, he was told, they would have to be withdrawn immediately.

Filming began in May 1967. The site where they filmed the charge was a huge valley – some twenty miles from the unit's headquarters in Ankara – which closely matched the drawings and lithographs of the terrain of the actual charge. Finding so perfect a spot was a tremendous bonus, but each step forward was matched by a fresh crisis that set everything back once more. For the chaotic battle of Alma, for example, the numbers of infantry needed ran to several thousands. It was impossible to provide them with quarters comparable to the cavalrymen, who were much smaller in number. The peeved infantrymen mutinied, and it took Richardson's formidable negotiating skills, and patience, to convince them that they had not the resources to satisfy everybody.

When the troops disembark *en masse* at the port of Sebastapol, the scene was filmed at Istanbul, using land troops instead of sailors to fill the barges. Richardson had to employ the men that he was given; he could not pick and choose whom he wanted. The smallish boats were loaded at a nearby jetty then sailed into camera range with the men and horses and guns crammed tightly on board. Unused to being in barges in choppy waters, the men became seasick and threw up over each other. Richardson found to his horror that instead of the troops lined shoulder to shoulder, looking landwards with the light of battle in their eyes, they were 'out of sight, writhing on the decks, awash with vomit'. It was a struggle to clean their faces and tunics and stand enough of them upright to get the shots he needed.

Filming the charge did not go according to plan either. The army personnel were suddenly withdrawn to take part in a major defence exercise. Their withdrawal left the unit with a serious man-power shortage. Richardson could not incorporate any sweeping long shots to show the full panorama of the battle, which had been his original intention. The audience is shown, instead, mainly close-ups of the action, the thundering hooves, cannon being fired, men falling from their horses, hand-to-hand fighting, followed by interminable close-ups of blood-soaked bodies crumpled on the ground and dazed survivors in gloomy disarray.

The Charge of the Light Brigade was a triumph for Howard. Given the chance to show what he could do, he performed magnificently. The real Lord Cardigan was a piece of vintage theatre, a classy dresser, a man of huge vanity, a great hit with both well-bred, respectable ladies and low-bred vamps. Howard played him as a feisty, colourful authoritarian. He knew that anyone accusing him over going over the top could simply be told to check the facts. And, to be fair, he didn't go over the top. It was a controlled performance from start to finish, and his scenes contain an energy that is missing when he is out of the picture.

Some scenes and female characters were added to help make it a woman's picture as well, but these were pale counterpoints to the main action. Nolan has an amorous fling with another officer's wife, played by Vanessa Redgrave, while inside a tent near the battle zone Cardigan practises his seduction skills on a warrant officer's wife, played by Jill Bennett.

Screen appearances during the 1960s were rare for John Gielgud, who as the bemused Raglan provides moments of unexpected black humour. Woken by a commotion outside his window in Crimea, he balks at the sight of French troops, having forgotten they are his allies. But, despite Gielgud milking every line for all that it was worth, and some solid competition from the ever-reliable Harry Andrews, it was Howard's show and nobody could steal his thunder.

But there were times when his actor's dislike of learning lines nearly got him into trouble with Richardson. Corin Redgrave, who played Captain Featherstonehaugh, told me a story he heard from Alan Dobie. 'When Trevor had a good deal of dialogue on a particular day and hadn't learned it the night before, he would say to Tony, "Could you explain it to me?" and they would walk off into the desert together. And by the time they returned, Tony explaining, Trevor nodding, repeating the lines as he walked, he would have managed to learn them.'

The reviews at the time were mixed. Dilys Powell wrote that the film was 'uneven but often brilliant'. Alexander Walker called it 'two hours of brilliant period reconstruction . . . as such, it is Richardson's surest, most incisive film to date and one that will bite deep into my memory.' Ian Christie joined the many critics who found it all rather confusing. He wrote, 'It is a beautiful production, but if its aim had been clearer it could have been a great one.' John Simon put it more strongly, describing it 'almost as inexcusably muddled as the British commanders at Balaclava'.

It would, I feel sure, be wrong to judge the film entirely on contemporary reviews which may have reflected, in some small way, the hostility of a predominantly right-wing press for the left-wing views of Richardson and Osborne, who were accused of anti-officer bias. The officers at the top are seen as out-of-sorts racist incompetents and those lower down as class-conscious dummies who couldn't be trusted to water the flowers. While no doubt the system in place at the time created a number of officers who were, in Nolan's words, 'stupid, inconsiderate and lazy', the criticism of the officer classes contained in the film was too sweeping to be believable. Where were the good guys, apart from Nolan and Lewis? When the chips were down – or, rather, when the charge was ordered – the gallantry and patriotism of these men, irrespective of rank or background, deserved greater recognition than this film grudgingly provides.

Howard had been allocated a horse which, really, had no place in the line-up. Redgrave told me, 'The stunt arranger and riding master knew very little about horses. He had blarneyed his way to the top of his trade with the help of good looks, a convincing line of chat and a considerable flair for self-promotion. He talked the film company into sending him out to the location six weeks ahead of shooting in order to select the principal horses. The Turks recognized him for the bull-shitter that he was and sold him some absolute duds, charging a high price into the bargain. The horse chosen for Trevor looked reasonably impressive but was completely broken-winded. Worse still, it had a serious kidney ailment. The vet's treatment made it piss frequently, making an absolutely revolting smell. Poor Trevor was partnered with this medically unsound horse for three months in Ankara. But he bore it very stoically and professionally.'

American critics, in particular, disliked the film for the way it seemed to glory in military stupidity. The Americans, fighting their own war in Vietnam, drew an obvious parallel between the British failure in Crimea and their own unwinnable engagement in South East Asia. Rex Reed called it 'a colossal waste of everyone's time, including mine'. It was the wrong time to release a film of that kind in the United States.

Were it to be made today one suspects that its reception would be quite different. The cartoon sequences with all their Hogarthian robustness were concise and innovative and compressed a complicated history lesson into a few, easy-to-follow sketches. Skilful editing, rapid cross-cuts and imaginative camera settings ensure that the pace of story-telling never falters, even during the wistful romantic interludes.

This is a story that never ceases to fascinate and about which the 'what-if' questions continue to be raised more than a century and a half later. Richardson's film is worthy and watchable. Its outstanding moments belong to Howard and justifiably so, according to Redgrave, who told me, 'I had immense respect for his acting. I remember his performance in the film vividly, especially his seduction of Mrs Duberly. On broader lines, I thought then, and I think it now, that Trevor was the perfect embodiment of a Graham Greene hero. Greene has always been one of my favourite novelists. But Trevor was a private man, and also of a generation older than I, so I saw little of him on location in Ankara. He still had at that time the reputation of being a "hell-raiser", the term used by the tabloid press for actors who drank a great deal, danced on top of tables and got into arguments in nightclubs. My impression of him was somewhat at variance with that. I saw him as someone immensely patient and rather melancholy. But that was merely an impression, based on instinct rather than evidence.'

The screenplay for *Conduct Unbecoming* (1975) was by Barry England, from his original play which had been a success on the London stage. As a theatre piece, the conflicts between a group of Army officers in India in the 1890s seemed to work reasonably well. The plot was quite a simple one. An officer's widow, played by Susannah York, is molested on the way back to her quarters late one night after a party. A young officer is put through a hush-hush trial, and his guilt seems certain until the officer who defends him, played by Michael York, exposes the tensions and the phoney respectability of his peers.

To avoid a scandal, the guilty man, when eventually unmasked, is made a tempting offer. If he shoots himself, the offence will be quietly forgotten and his records will show that he died with honour. The film ends as he blows his brains out. Little was done to expand this claustrophobic snail's-pace tale beyond the original set-piece courtroom drama from which it was adapted. Howard played the regiment's commander-in-chief who drifts in and out of the proceedings in a marvellous tunic and bushy Cardiganesque whiskers but who fails to make any impact, and Stacy Keach was the officer conducting the trial. Critic Tom Milne called it 'an alarmingly creaky adaptation of Barry England's play'.

Opinions differed on the quality, and suitability as a film subject, of *Hennessy* (1975), which told of a maverick Irish terrorist's attempt to kill the British Royal Family during the opening of Parliament. Rod Steiger played a Belfast demolition worker, half crazed by the killing of his family, who becomes a willing terrorist, and Howard played a police officer. The use of newsreel footage showing the Royal Family, which reduced them to bit players in a movie that cynically exploited the politics of Northern Ireland, was roundly condemned at the time, and its distribution was blocked as a result. Four years later the Earl Mountbatten of Burma was murdered by IRA bombers while holidaying in Ireland. This obviously had no connection with any film, but it justified the distributors' decision to drop *Hennessy* like a hot potato. It has never been screened on British television.

The difficult subject matter took nothing away from Steiger's performance, as twitchy and intense as we had ever seen him. David Pirie described him as 'better than he has been for ages' and the casting, locations and use of newsreels (although criticized by others) were, he added, 'spectacularly good'.

If British cinemas could do without *Hennessy*, they could have equally done without *The Bawdy Adventures of Tom Jones* (1975), a remake of the Henry Fielding novel filmed successfully by Tony Richardson in 1961. This adaptation was a musical based on a stage version which had done reasonable business in the United States. Nicky Henson played Tom, and Howard took on the role of Squire Western, which had been played with zest by Hugh Griffith in the earlier film. Griffith was a difficult act to follow, but Howard made a wonderfully seedy, eye-rolling, randy Squire, stealing nothing from Griffith's performance because he didn't need to. Chris Petit thought it was a pity that several 'distinguished names who should have known better' had lent themselves to this 'smutty version' of *Tom Jones*, but other reviews were more tolerant. Howard thought that critics who tried to write serious reviews of *The Bawdy Adventures of Tom Jones* were 'pretentious bastards, completely off their heads'.

The Bawdy Adventures of Tom Jones was the first of half-a-dozen costume dramas of variable quality in which Howard played smallish parts. *In The Count of Monte Cristo* (1975), another remake, he played a prisoner in the notorious Chateau d'If, in which Edmond Dantes, played by Richard Chamberlain. is unjustly imprisoned. As an old prisoner in the adjoining cell who knows where some treasure is hidden and who shares his secret with the luckless – up to that point – Dantes, Howard has a couple of key scenes with Chamberlain. Most of his dialogue is spoken through a thick grey beard and a thick grey wall. Made originally for television in the United States and shot in Rome (one of Howard's favourite locations), the film was given a cinema release in Britain, where it was judged to be inferior to the 1934 version made in Hollywood with Robert Donat. This did not stop Howard being nominated for an Emmy for his performance.

Another much-filmed story is *Kidnapped*, written in 1866 by Robert Louis Stevenson. Peter Finch played its swashbuckling Jacobite hero

Alan Breck in an unsuccessful 1960 version. Remade eleven years later, Michael Caine donned a kilt and sporran as the supporter of the Bonnie Prince's doomed cause. But, unlike Finch, Caine brought a weary, post-1960s cynicism to the role. Howard had a smallish part to play, but once again, with minimal gestures and a brooding, resonant voice, he registered well as the Lord Advocate in Edinburgh who must ultimately decide the fate of the captured rebels cooling their heels in a shabby Scottish dungeon. The brevity of his role was fortunate on this occasion. Shortly after his few days' work, and with his cheque banked, the film ran into financial difficulties. For a while it was doubtful whether it would ever be finished. However, a complete shutdown was averted by the securing of alternative funds, but morale among the cast and crew remained at rock bottom. Some salaries, apparently, were never paid in full.

A statement always worth repeating is the pointlessness of war. Films have taken their place alongside novels, poetry and works of art decrying man's inhumanity to man. *Aces High* (1976), directed by Jack Gold, was not a great anti-war movie in the category of *All Quiet on the Western Front* (1930) or *Paths of Glory* (1957). But the message was similar, that young men are sacrificed or driven crazy or brutalized by the experience of war, often for shamefully meagre gains. Set during the First World War, *Aces High* focuses on a squadron of young pilots and portrays the effects on them of constantly flying dangerous missions. Malcolm McDowell played a gung-ho squadron leader, Simon Ward was a shell-shocked pilot and Peter Firth was the decent, new guy forced to learn the brutal game of war the hard way. Howard and Ray Milland played senior officers who sit around a table wearing anxious expressions and drinking tea.

Howard was originally offered a central role in *Eliza Frazer* (1976), Timothy Burstall's retelling of an Australian folk-tale, but when he realized that his trip to Australia to make the film coincided with a test series over there, he told Burstall he preferred a role that would take up less of his time. The prison camp commander Foster Fyans, perhaps? Burstall said, 'You could do it easily, Trevor, but we'd only need you for two weeks out of the fourteen. It's hardly worth your time coming to Australia for that.' Howard replied, 'Oh yes it is.' He would have polished the camera lenses as long as they paid his fare and gave him time off to watch England versus the Aussies.

Susannah York played Eliza, the title role, a spirited widow of the master of a clipper ship which sank off an island – later named after him – *en route* from Sydney to Singapore with a cargo of tea in the 1830s. Eliza survived the ordeal and remarried. The film did not get a cinema release in Britain, although it has been screened on television.

Marty Feldman was best known as a television comedian in the UK, instantly recognizable by his wild eyes and straggly hair. He was inventive and zany and anarchic, a diarist of life's absurdities. Originally a talented writer of radio comedy – his early collaborators formed the core of the Monty Python team – it was thought that his humour was essentially British-based and would not transplant easily in the United States, where his real ambitions lay. However, in 1974 he went to Hollywood and became part of Mel Brooks's creative entourage. At the time Brooks had embarked on a series of spoofs of classic Hollywood genres, starting with *Blazing Saddles* (1974), and Feldman arrived in time to appear in *Young Frankenstein* (1974) as the cheerful hunchback Eye-Gore. Brooks's next film, *The Adventures of Sherlock Holmes's Smarter Brother* (1975), in which Feldman also had a part, as Sergeant Sacker, gave him the idea for a spoof of his own. If Sherlock Holmes could have a smarter brother whom nobody had heard of, Beau Geste, the handsome, dashing French Foreign Legion hero, could have an ugly twin hidden away whom the family were too ashamed to mention.

In Feldman's film, *The Last Remake of Beau Geste* (1977), the joke is that the ugly, idiot twin brother, played by Feldman himself, is the hero, not Beau, a conceited oaf who would prefer to study his looks in a mirror than face marauding tribesmen. Feldman thought it would be funnier to make it in monochrome, using the same sort of cheap backgrounds and amateurish back-projection that makes the 1939 original movie such a howl these days. Brooks had made *Young Frankenstein* that way, to emphasize that the mad scientist was still the same old black-and-white monster-maker, only this time with his pants around his ankles. But Universal studios, which financed Feldman's comedy, wanted him to make something more lavish and in colour. It did not want to be associated with a low-budget film, and to get his hands on the money Feldman had to compromise much of his original vision. The result was a mish-mash of old sight gags and crisp one-liners welded on to the framework of a big screen epic, and the whole thing teetered unsteadily between satire and banality. Howard played Sir

Hector Geste, father of the clan, a bluff old bounder still boasting lots of lead in his pencil, married to Ann-Margret, the twins' glamorous stepmother. His scenes were filmed in Dublin, denying him a trip to the Spanish location. He welcomed the opportunity to work with Feldman, whose wacky, off-the-wall comedy he admired, and also with Spike Milligan, who played his doddering man-servant.

Howard told me, 'Marty said to me one day, "I've got more money than I need and I'm going to spend it all." If he'd turned it down, they might have closed the picture. What he made had some good bits, but it wasn't consistent.'

Howard's next film, *Slavers* (1977), might have benefited from some lighter moments, but, alas, the German director, Jürgen Goslar, seemed determined to make audiences suffer as acutely as the African slaves in the story. Howard played a cynical, grizzled slave trader living in Africa during the 1880s. Captured slaves were forced to make long treks to the coast to be shipped off, in chains, to plantations and other places of work. The film exploited this brutal trade as a backdrop to an absurd love triangle.

Jennifer Selway called it 'black exploitation at its worst', adding, 'It's nasty to watch, unless you relish brandings, rape, cruelty to animals, spurting arteries, vultures working over dead natives, baby trampling, assorted deaths and repeated shots of ankles chafed to the bone by iron anklets . . . Had these images been used to make a coherent condemnation of slave trafficking in the nineteenth century, then the film might have been able to claim some validity. Goslar, however, makes them incidental to the actions of a few despicable whites, with whom you wouldn't share a shelter in an nuclear bomb attack.' And that is where the film lets itself down and why it was so widely ridiculed.

From Africa Howard went to Hollywood to deliver a cameo in *Meteor* (1979), a big-budget disaster movie directed by Ronald Neame, who had co-produced *Brief Encounter* and directed *The Golden Salamander.* Neame had kicked off the disaster movie cycle in the United States with *The Poseidon Adventure* (1972) and virtually ended it with *Meteor*. But the genre had already run out of steam by 1977. *Meteor* showed how badly the engine was misfiring. The industry need not have worried, however. Its next mammoth crowd-pleaser, *Star Wars* (1977), was in preparation.

In *Meteor* the story was that a collision between two giant asteroids in outer space had knocked one of them off course, and large chunks of it were spiralling towards earth. Unless the planet could take evasive action, we would soon be just a memory. The solution? Simple. Coordinate the detonation of nuclear explosions at strategic points on the earth's surface which will divert our endangered planet on to a new, safe trajectory.

With such a barmy storyline the film – unlike the asteroid – had an uphill battle to stay on course. The hammy 'let's scrap the Cold War' politics and a risible love story, between an American scientist and a female Russian interpreter, made the whole thing so awful that the only print of it should have been dispatched to another galaxy.

Henry Fonda played a furrowed-brow American President (a good choice: he had begun playing presidents – Abe Lincoln – in 1939). Howard played Britain's representative in the high-level squabble to save the world. He chipped in his pennyworth over a satellite link. Riveting it was not. Tom Milne called the film 'shabby, unspeakable, and inept' and warned people to 'see it on peril of death by boredom'.

During 1978 Howard made three films, two of them with extravagant budgets and the other with scarcely a budget at all. The latter, *Stevie* (1978), was based on Hugh Whitemore's successful play about the British poet Stevie Smith, who in the film was played by Glenda Jackson. Although Stevie was a real person, the supporting character whom Howard played was not. He was supposed to be an amalgam of many of Smith's admirers, friends and critics, a cash-saving device, some called it, to provide a narrative to a film better suited to being a radio play. Howard was the link between the plot and the audience. In Shakespeare's time he would have been called the Chorus.

Howard remembered that everything was a bit rushed. It always seems to be with Jackson. He told me, 'She was in a play or something at the same time, so it was all a bit fraught. But it was a good little film, although a bit abstract for some people's taste, I'm sure.' I contacted Jackson to ask her about *Stevie*, but she was too rushed off her feet, trying to become the Mayor of London, to comment.

After a quick rest Howard took off for Bora Bora to appear in *Hurricane* (1978), a new version of the 1937 Goldwyn movie which had included a spectacular studio-tank hurricane and the world's first glimpse of Dorothy Lamour's legs. The remake, like *Meteor*, tried to cash in on the popularity of disaster movies, but it was too late. The parade had passed by, and people were not interested. Italian moviemaker Dino de Laurentiis, a throwback to the profligate Hollywood directors of the 1930s, spent an amazing $22 million bringing the story (such as it was) to the big screen. A five-star hotel was specially built on the island of Bora Bora to accommodate the actors and the crew. The cast included Jason Robards, Mia Farrow, Max von Sydow and Timothy Bottoms and, of course, Howard. Director Jan Troell was given instructions that nothing must be spared on the hurricane at the climax of the film. De Laurentiis told him, 'Anything you want, get it and send me the bill.' Troell could hardly say to him, 'Anything? Well, how about a script?' The images of destruction were as good as contemporary technology and superior art direction could achieve. The problem for the film was that, unlike the flood waters, the characters were one-dimensional, and when, during the storm, some of the them were swept away like bits of cardboard audiences could not have cared less.

The film relied on special effects, and coming at the last gasp of the disaster genre they simply were not enough. What was needed was a new idea. *Star Wars*, the movie phenomenon of 1977, provided it. A year later, *Superman – The Movie* appeared. Cinemas began filling up again. Interest had been reactivated, which gave the British technical side of the industry a much-needed boost because *Star Wars* was made at Elstree and *Superman – The Movie* at Pinewood.

Howard had a small part in *Superman – The Movie* (1978) as one of the Krypton elders. So did his close friend Harry Andrews. Maria Schell, his lover in *Heart of the Matter*, was also in it. Christopher Reeve played Superman, but the biggest ripples on the set were caused by Marlon Brando, lured to Britain by a salary of £2.25 million (around $3.37 million) for just over a week's work. When news of Brando's pay-cheque reached Howard he almost had a fit, and although they were on the same set for two days Howard avoided him. Watching Brando read his lines from boards held up behind the cameras – his customary practice – Howard said to Harry Andrews, 'Look at him! He'd want two million to read the nine o'clock news!' Asked by a reporter if they had buried their differences over a pie and a pint, Howard replied, 'No. I can get on with most people but not with Marlon Brando.'

The Wild Geese (1979), directed by Andrew McLaglen, brought ageing boozers Richard Burton and Richard Harris together as mercenaries fighting to restore a deposed African leader to power. The film was a commercial hit, probably because audiences wanted to say goodbye to the two Richards before one of them finally slid below the froth. The first to go was Burton, five years later.

MacLaglen and his *Wild Geese* producer Euan Lloyd felt that the theme of war-mad old men taking on bad guys who were young enough for them to babysit instead of fight had sufficient box-office appeal to give it another go, so they made *The Sea Wolves* (1980). In place of the Great Tipplers, they put the two most abstemious, sure-footed stars ever to climb into uniforms – Gregory Peck and David Niven. Reginald Rose, who had written *The Wild Geese*, also wrote *The Sea Wolves*, based on James Leasor's novel *The Boarding Party*. One critic noted that when Roger Moore joined Peck, Niven and Howard as the fourth star, at fifty-one he was, compared with them, a mere babe-in-arms.

The Sea Wolves was the story of a territorial unit known as the Calcutta Light Horse Infantry which, in 1943, successfully sabotaged a German attempt to broadcast propaganda from the neutral harbour of Goa in India. Based on a real-life incident, it was a good idea, but, with the exception of Moore, the actors had too many miles on the clock to have the stamina for these antics. Chris Peachment called the film 'a risible affair with the geriatric schoolboys wheezing about, getting hernias . . . Peck and Niven shamble aimiably through the dross as if it were a Navaronian old boys' reunion (class of '44), and Roger Moore finds new ways of smirking in a dinner jacket.'

Occasionally, when the quartet – who got along famously – sat up drinking at the end of the day, it did not pass unnoticed that Niven had difficulty pronouncing certain words. He had to try several times before he could get some words to sound correct on the soundtrack. Howard wondered if he might being having a few snorts in his trailer before work began. But the reason, when it emerged shortly afterwards, shocked them profoundly. It was the beginnings of the motor neurone condition that led to his death in 1982.

15
STONE THE CROWS

I wanted the best actor I could think of, and Trevor was the best actor I could think of. – Kieth Merrill, director of *Windwalker* (1980)

FROM the heat of India Howard travelled to the snow-capped mountains and wide vistas of Utah. But if the view from the air as he and his wife flew into Salt Lake City suggested to them that he was in for a quiet, peaceful few weeks, it was a cruel deception. The job he had in front of him was completely different from anything he had attempted before. Here was a challenge, physical and intellectual, that would both exhilarate and exhaust him. If anyone had told him when he was in India that within a few weeks he would be 12,000 feet up in the Uinta mountain range playing a full-blooded Cheyenne Indian chief in a film where the dialogue was spoken in Cheyenne, and that he would be the only non-American among the cast and crew, he would have brayed like a donkey.

Yet there he was, with a sprig of feathers in his long white wig, wearing natty buckskins, looking every inch an ancient redskin chief. True, he did have ancient red skin, but that wasn't why he was chosen. Indeed, the director, Kieth Merrill, had some explaining to do to the American movie press, who thought the casting of Howard as a Red Indian bizarre to say the least. The young director faced his critics squarely. 'I wanted the best actor I could think of, and Trevor was the best actor I could think of,' he told them bluntly.

To my knowledge, Merrill's film *Windwalker* (1980) has not been seen in Britain, either in the cinema or on television. I am indebted to Helen Howard for loaning me her personal copy of the film on videotape; and angry, too, that cinema-goers in Britain have been denied the chance to enjoy a film of such haunting beauty and truth. For this reason I shall describe it in some detail.

Windwalker opens with an old Cheyenne warrior, the eponymous Windwalker, played by Howard, lying on some skins in a tepee, clearly nearing death. He tells his family, 'I am a burden. It is time I nourished the earth.' A series of flashbacks recall the high and low points of his life. These include his pursuit and marriage to Tashina, the girl with whom he grew up. One flashback shows them as children playing with bows and arrows in the forest. Another shows the birth of their twin sons and her death a couple of years later when an attempted abduction of her by a jealous rival is tragically bungled. The raiding party abducts, instead, one of his twin sons, who is brought up to adulthood by some Crow Indians, deadly enemies of the Cheyenne.

The old man has spent much of his life grieving for and trying to trace his lost son. All his efforts have failed, and finally, sadly, he yields himself up to the Great Spirit in the sky. The voice-over in English puts it succinctly. 'I never saw my son again. It is a good day to die.' But the Great Spirit is not ready for him and, although he is laid out on his funeral platform, with the farewell ceremony complete and his grieving family trudging back to their tiny encampment, the old man reawakens. This proves fortunate, because with his remaining adult son, Smiling Wolf, unable to defend the women and children from ambush by the Crows because of injury, the Old Man's wisdom and battle plans are essential for the family's survival.

But for the old man it isn't a simple case of regaining his strength and eyesight to deal with the Crows. He has first to fend off a pack of killer wolves and then to kill a large brown bear whose hibernation he accidentally disturbs. The bear is furious at being awoken midway through his long winter sleep.

The final showdown appears, at first, badly weighted against the Cheyenne. Here are five fierce war-painted Crow warriors against an old man, who everyone thought had already died, plus a handful of freezing, frightened women and children. But the Great Spirits have not restored the old man to his family so that he can fail them. One by one, the attackers are disposed of or taken prisoner until only their leader, Crow Eyes, the one who had abducted the old man's son many years before, remains. He is taught the error of his ways, but not killed, in a furious hand-to-hand fight with a new and unlikely champion of the depleted Cheyenne. And, yes, the old man does see his abducted son again before continuing his 'walk on the wind' to an emotional reunion with the spirit of his long-dead wife Tashina.

Windwalker is a simple story of a life-or-death struggle in the wilderness in sub-zero temperatures against a cunning, ruthless, stalking enemy. But the simplicity of the story is expanded to epic visual dimensions by Reed Moot's enchanting camerawork, which puts the snow-clad mountains, deep ravines and gloomy, leaden skies right at the centre of the action. Here is a landscape to be enjoyed and admired but, equally, respected and feared because it can kill as silently and efficiently as any raiding party, and Moot's photography hints at the treachery behind its awesome beauty.

Scene after scene enchants the eye. The moody vista shots behind the opening credits quickly give way to lush green woodlands where the young Windwalker and Tashina's childhood games become tender declarations of adult love. Dialogue takes second place to sensuous glances and handclasps and imaginative camera angles. The scene where the Windwalker learns of his wife's pregnancy is filmed in mid-shot silhouette against warm autumnal colours. He discards the deer he has hunted to crouch down and put his ear to her stomach.

Hands are an important feature in the narrative. The affectionate handclasp between the lovers when her father consents to their marriage is followed by the Windwalker's clenched-fist shout of triumph. Having picked Tashina up in his arms after hearing that she is carrying his child, he also punches the air ecstatically. Returning to find her dead after the failed abduction attempt, he tenderly holds her hand, a repeat of their betrothal handclasp. And in the final scene, when the lovers are reunited, their joining of hands marks the moment of his rejuvenation. The close-up shows the old man becoming young again – the age he and Tashina had been on the day she was taken from him.

The montage that follows the fifteen-minute ambush sequence is visually very striking. We see dark rivers scything through snowscapes, shadows moving across snowy peaks, a weak sun boxed out by veiled clouds, close-ups of icicles and rocks, to the accompaniment of Merrill Jenson's music, which switches seamlessly from lush strings to fiery percussion as the old man's funeral cover is blown back by the icy winds and his eyelids tremble then pop open. Later in the film there is a wonderful shot of Howard's face upturned in silent prayer for Smiling Wolf, his injured son – a face that could have been hewn from the land itself, the solemn totem-pole profile, that patrician beak of a nose rising from the grooved, dented face like some weathered mountain peak.

Another scene, one of many that linger in the mind, is between the captured Crow and a little Cheyenne girl too young to go outside and help kill his friends. She isn't afraid of his intimidating looks and warpaint. With marvellous, unquestioning innocence, she just wants to help him. She offers to share her supper, and he takes a bite of food. She then bites off another morsel and puts it into his mouth. A warm smile lights up her face. She has no fear of this savage, who before they met had been trying to kill her family. All she knows is the curiosity of a child, and she wants to please him; her spontaneous show of warmth melts his heart, possibly for the first time in his adult life. He watches her as intently as before, but the hatred for her tribe, for her family, is gone. The scene is played in silence but for the noise of a crackling fire and the two of them eating. The child's eager, trusting smile melting the heart of a cruel warrior is a moment of pure joy, natural and charming.

The only English spoken is the periodic narrative of the Windwalker, spoken on the soundtrack by Nick Ramus, who plays both his adult sons. Every line of dialogue is in either Cheyenne or Crow, and Howard underwent a crash course in Cheyenne to prepare himself for the role. His first day's filming required him to lie on the elevated funeral platform in bright sunshine. He wore tinted contact lenses to cover his blue eyes, but, unaccustomed to such lenses, he found them extremely uncomfortable. After putting up with the pain for several hours, he asked Merrill to let him perform without them, pointing out that it wasn't unknown for Indians to have blue eyes. Merrill agreed, but there were other ordeals in store for him. He had to wade through frozen rivers, ride a white stallion up treacherous slopes covered in snow and wrestle a giant grizzly bear. Such activities would have been mundane for a young Cheyenne brave of two centuries earlier, but for a 65-year-old British actor whose physical condition left a lot to be desired they proved exhausting and dangerous.

His run-in with the scavenging wolf pack was filmed without him having to be in the same frame as them, so the stunt could be arranged using a double. This was not the case with the grizzly bear. Filmed in a studio-built cave, the two of them had to be seen in action together. Armed with only a lance, Howard lay down on the floor of the cave and awaited the arrival of his hairy adversary. He admitted to me that he had felt nervous, because, however well trained a large brown bear may be, such animals have minds of their own. They can be unpredictable. Bright lights or sudden noises can make them forget their script. One swipe of a bear's giant paw, even with its claws trimmed, can leave a hideous scar or knock a man senseless, depending on whether or not it closes its fist. And if a grizzly takes a dislike to you he is likely to lie on top of you, because that is how bears dispose of their enemies.

Howard said to Merrill, 'Let's see if we can wrap this up before he gets bored with his new profession. I'd hate to be the one who gives the expression "Cut" a whole new meaning!' The scene was completed without incident, to everyone's relief. When he returned home, Howard was full of praise for his new friend. He told me, 'The bear was wonderful. He knew his lines and didn't complain once. That's more than can be said for some actors I know.'

For both director and star, *Windwalker* was an experiment that paid remarkable dividends. Decades of seeing Hollywood Red Indians as po-faced, alien, monosyllabic stereotypes with folded arms had persuaded audiences that this was how native American tribes had been in real life. Unlike those earlier portrayals which had, literally, nothing going on behind the impassive stares, Howard gives us an insight into the family ties and tribal loyalties that motivate such people. The emotions of the old man are extreme; despair on his death-bed as he mourns the son he has not been able to embrace since he was a small boy and joy when he unexpectedly rediscovers him. These are powerful emotions which a lesser actor than Howard would have to 'act' for us so that we, too, could experience them. He doesn't need to do this. He conveys them, powerfully, vividly, by simply thinking them. The others actors are uniformly excellent, especially Nick Ramus, as the Windwalker's grown-up twin sons. The film is an ensemble piece, each element necessary for the success of the others. As if taking their cue from Howard, nobody in *Windwalker* overacts. What we see are the simple courage and unbreakable loyalties that help a small defenceless family survive unbelievable hardships and dangers, and this is achieved with a complete absence of stage effects or cliché. You have to keep reminding yourself that you are watching a film with actors, that this isn't a documentary.

The American reviews below indicate what a loss to British cinemagoers the decision not to release the film in the United Kingdom has been. Judy Stone, of the *San Francisco Chronicle*, wrote, '*Windwalker* is a rare and riveting adventure, a spectacularly beautiful movie on all counts . . . Howard brings strong dignity to the part and a certain humorous style to the perplexing situation in which he finds himself . . . it is one of those few movies that the whole family can not only enjoy but feel enriched by.' Marty Meltz of the *Maine Sunday Telegraph*:

'In its total effort, stunning results, and wonderful ethereal ending, *Windwalker* is a singularly outstanding film and a conspicuously separate experience from anything we've ever seen. It is a film to make American cinema proud for what *Windwalker* is, and ashamed for what other Indian films have not been. A milestone in US motion picture history, *Windwalker* is in a class of films numbering one.'

Malcolm Johnson wrote in the *Hartford Courant*, 'The film is dominated by Howard's presence, with its self-knowledge, assurance and humour, as the old man who cannot simply lie down and die.' Bruce Kirkland of the *Toronto Sun* agreed. He wrote, 'Trevor Howard is marvellous as Windwalker, despite playing an Indian for the first time in his illustrious career. He seems to merge with his character in body and spirit.'

Bill Cosford in the *Miami Herald* called the film 'well made and satisfying, a happy surprise' and added, 'Trevor Howard plays the old grandfather, which seems to be *Windwalker*'s concession to the box office. But even this ploy works. Howard has been made up to look quite ancient, but he suffers it well . . . There is even a hint of humor in Howard's performance, which is enough to set *Windwalker* apart from other films about American Indians. *Windwalker* allows for humor and for a surprising range of other human emotions as well.' Charles Neil of the *Vancouver Magazine* praised 'a strong performance by Trevor Howard (obviously chosen to give the movie box office appeal but inspired casting, nevertheless) who brings warmth and humanity to the role'.

The film contains a dedication to the memory of Michael Hurst, who had worked as a researcher for *Windwalker*'s co-producer Tom Ballard's Santa Fe International production company and was a friend of *Windwalker* author Blaine Yorgason. It had been Hurst who originally spotted the cinematic potential of the book and who persuaded Ballard to take an interest in it. While working on the first draft of the screenplay with Yorgason, Hurst developed cancer, from which he later died. The final screenplay was credited to Ray Goldrup, with Yorgason as the author and provider of additional material.

Helen made her customary visit to the site of the film, but she and her husband almost didn't meet. She told me, 'I went to see Trevor in Utah, but owing to a misunderstanding I arrived not knowing where he was or where I was staying. At Salt Lake City airport I said that my husband was making a film and described it, and one of the crew happened to be there and took me to where the were filming. It was a real stroke of luck. But I couldn't find him. Nobody seemed to know where he was.'

Helen asked various members of the crew, but nobody had seen him. She went into the make-up trailer, but still there was no trace of him. All she could see was an actor in Indian clothes and a white straggly wig being worked on by a make-up artist. She recalled, 'It was Trevor, but he was wonderfully made up. I didn't recognize him at all. He looked at me, but he wasn't expecting me to arrive until the following day, so he didn't recognize me either. We both looked at each other and thought: Who's that? Afterwards, we had a laugh about it.'

Sir Henry at Rawlinson End (1980) was a slice of surreal madness which took everyone, including Howard, by surprise. Why anyone would want to finance, or, indeed, watch, a fleshed-out version of this repugnant radio character is hard to imagine. But Charisma Films came forward with the cash, and audiences loved the cranky, demented Sir Henry.

Filmed versions of off-the-wall radio characters, such the Goons, have usually failed. It is a very thin line between inspired zaniness and toe-curling embarrassment. Even the Monty Python films have been accused of over-stretching the material. *Sir Henry at Rawlinson End* runs for just under an hour and a quarter, and you never get the feeling that his creators are struggling to fill the time. The madness keeps coming at you, like a blizzard.

Sir Henry Rawlinson lives in a decaying country mansion surrounded by senile servants, peculiar relatives and a wife from whom, at bedtime, he retreats behind a coil of barbed wire. He is half monster, half wayward child – 'I don't know what I want but I want it *now*!' He insults everyone and hates everything except drink, of which he can't get enough – the family motto is 'Omnes Blotto'. 'If I had all the money I ever spent on drink, I would spend it all on drink,' he roars across a dinner-table strewn with rotting food, empty bottles and guests whose faces are on the point of falling into their food. 'When I eat something, that's the last I want to see of it!' Then he staggers outside to a barbed-wire compound where he keeps two German prisoners of war as pets and abuses them by mimicking Lord Haw-Haw over a tinny loudspeaker, '*Jarmany calling . . . Jarmany calling . . .*'

Filmed in grainy monochrome, *Sir Henry at Rawlinson End* is an excursion into lunacy filled with quirky one-liners, but really it defies description. There has never been a film like it. Nobody connected with it seems to know what it was or why it came to be made. It gives the appearance of just happening, like a rotten harvest or a hole in the road. It took three weeks to film, mostly in and around Knebworth House in Hertfordshire, at a cost of half a million dollars, chicken-feed by contemporary standards. At first, Vivian Stanshall, founding member of the Bonzo Dog Doo-Dah Band, who produced it, disagreed with the selection of Howard as Sir Henry by his director and script collaborator Steve Roberts, on the grounds that he was too old and that people saw him as a dramatic actor. Roberts argued that the pulling power of Howard's name was more significant. 'This isn't a role anyone can do,' said Roberts. 'We need someone audiences will love despite his hateful behaviour, who won't ask for the earth because, frankly, we haven't got it to give them and who will put bums on seats. That's Trevor Howard.'

Stanshall was eventually persuaded, and the rest, as Sir Henry might say, is geography. The supporting cast, including Patrick Magee, Denise Coffey, Sheila Reid and the delightful J.G. Devlin as a fawning manservant named Scrotum, play their parts dead straight, giving the madness engulfing them an occasional chink of respectability – normality, even.

Roberts revealed afterwards that Howard, who avoids chit-chat where possible, developed an effective defence against the chattering of J.G. Devlin, an Irish actor who could make monologues an Olympic event. Devlin was not aware that all the time he was yakking away not a word was penetrating Howard's cleverly concealed ear-plugs.

'Directing Trevor Howard is absurd, really, because what can you teach the man?' said Roberts. 'It's lunatic. You stand there, trembling a bit, because here is a man who knows everything. But the magic about him is this. If you say "I'm not quite happy about this", what he spots is that you really mean "I don't know what the hell I'm doing." And he immediately says, "Well, the way I'd tackle it is very simple, sport. I think we'll have a go at it that way." And what he's doing is teaching you what you ought to have known in the first place without letting you know that.'

A deer-keeper at Knebworth House, who appeared briefly in the film as a zany violinist, told me that he watched Howard filming the scene in which the German prisoners break out of their barbed-wire compound. Sir Henry reacts to their escape by shouting 'Bum!' Just that one word. Without a trace of a smile the man from Knebworth recalled, 'Each time Trevor said the word, it was different. He gave the director thirty different-sounding bums to choose from. I had no idea there were that many ways you could say it.'

One day I arranged with Howard to have a few beers at the Gate, and when I arrived to collect him – I had a Jaguar in which he enjoyed being ferried around – he was in unusually high spirits.

'What's up, Trevor?' I asked. 'Won the pools?'

He patted me on the elbow. 'Better than that, sport,' he chortled. 'I've just been on the phone to Celia Johnson. We're doing a film together.'

It was almost enough to make the journalist in me stop the car and rush to a public phone box (there were no mobile phones in 1980). Trevor Howard and Celia Johnson, the lovers in *Brief Encounter,* were making a new film together! 'As what?' I asked. 'Husband and wife,' he roared triumphantly. 'I knew I'd get her in the end.'

They had both signed to appear in a television film, *Staying On*, (1980), a touching story about bygone days in India, based on a Booker Prize-winning novel by Paul Scott. India was, in fact, a continent much in the minds of British film-makers during the early 1980s. Scott's novels, notably the Raj Quartet, of which *The Jewel in the Crown*, his first volume of the four books, was made into a memorable fourteen-part television series, and Richard Attenborough's *Gandhi* (1982) were just two prime examples.

Staying On came at the tail-end of Scott's novels about life among the British expatriates. It was set in 1972, a long time after the mass exodus of the former British ruling classes from India had been completed. Colonel Tusker Smalley, played by Howard, and his wife Lucy, played by Celia Johnson, are a middle-aged couple who have stayed on in their little house in Pankot after Independence. Scott called them 'the last survivors of Pankot's permanent retired British residents'. Tusker and his wife are failures. They stayed on, but now they are hanging on. To their dignity, which has all but evaporated. To the remnants of a lifestyle they can no longer afford. They have neither money nor assets. Even their lodgings, in a guest quarter of a once luxurious hotel, are in jeopardy. The hotel owner, Mrs Bhoolabhoy, played by Pearl Padamsee, who has little sympathy for the English, wants them out.

Tusker is a belligerent old fraud. He keeps up appearances by damning and blasting away at everything he doesn't like or understand. And the list keeps growing. Scott describes his anger as 'the main thing that kept him on the boil, and so, alive. Tusker was a man who needed irritants. Often, he invented them.'

In the novel Lucy is small and slight, with blue-rinsed hair, who cares only about being a 'good woman' for Tusker. Played by Celia Johnson, she could never be anything but a model of reason and old-world decency. The couple live as they have always done, fussily, tidily, everything in its place, but in the India of 1972 they are anachronistic and, worse, irrelevant. Their day has been and gone. They exist merely to exist, and nothing in front of them can ever again be as good as what they have had.

In 1979 Howard flew to Canada to make a thirty-minute television film called *Night Flight*, figuring that a leading role in a half-hour 'quality' drama was better for him than a small part in a worthless big film. That was the reason he did it, he said. The story was about opening up mail transport flights across South America during the 1930s, when frail monoplanes struggled across barren wastes, often through fierce tropical storms. The human story could be equally dramatic. These risky patrols put tremendous strain on the pilots and on their families, too, who waited in poor light or no light at all, listening anxiously for the first purr of their engines coming in to land

The film focused on one particular hazardous flight through a raging storm. The pilot, Fabien, played by Bo Svenson, runs into horrific weather and loses his way. Fabien's wife, played by Celine Lomez, frets and waits while his boss, Rivière, played by Howard, tries to guide him home using the radio. Rivière used to fly the mail routes himself, so he knows everything that is going through Fabien's mind. Now grounded by age, his job is to run the operation smoothly and to get the pilots back safely. But it is more than a job to Rivière. When his pilots are in trouble he agonizes over every mile until their wheels touch down. The radio link between the two men becomes the pilot's lifeline, but in *Night Flight* it fails, and Fabien is killed.

The original story was written during the 1930s by Antoine de Saint-Exupéry, a French air-mail pilot who flew the same skies in the tiny open-cockpit plane he described in his book. He reminds us that it was through these courageous, pioneering flights that air-mail services to remote regions eventually became established.

The autobiographical sources gave everybody on the film enormous respect for the material, and they did it justice through the strength and sensitivity of the central performances, Howard's in particular. The *New York Post* stated, 'Trevor Howard . . . manages with a few inflections and a few expressions to deliver both a man and a theme.' Several weeks afterwards Howard met me at the door of his house, brandishing a newspaper clipping. It was a review of *Night Flight* from a Canadian newspaper which read, 'Howard was never better as the hard-bitten veteran who would much rather be in the plane than on the ground waiting.' Receipt of that clipping had made his day.

After attending the film's press show in Canada, Howard and Helen flew back to Arkley, where he immediately began preparing for *The Missionary* (1979), which had been written by former Monty Python star Michael Palin. It was a comedy, set in 1906, in which the Reverend Charles Fortescue, played by Palin, returns from an African mission, and is promptly persuaded by his fitness-mad Bishop, played by Denholm Elliott, to establish a Christian refuge for prostitutes. 'Find out what they do – and stop them doing it,' commands the Bishop.

To raise funds, he trawls around a few stately homes and encounters the predatory Lady Ames, played by Maggie Smith, who seemingly has two objectives – to get him into bed with her and to murder her filthy-rich fruitcake of a husband, Lord Henry Ames, played by Howard, who served under General Gordon. So far so good. But what started out as a half-decent comedy then plunges into farce. A succession of weak Python jokes follow, some of which are done to death, such as the cadaverous butler who cannot find his way round the stately home and who marches visitors around the lake and into linen cupboards in his search for the drawing-room.

Howard has some amusing lines; when asked if he will help people less well off than himself, he gasps in horror, 'That means *everyone*!' He has a better idea. 'Leave the ungrateful buggers alone,' he roars, sounding just like that fellow at the head of the filthy table at Rawlinson End. For Palin to write, co-produce and star in this film was, in my opinion, a triumph of self-belief over good sense. It was too big a job for him, and the cracks show. Fortescue is too lightweight a character to carry the storyline. His innocence, like that of his soppy fiancée, played by Phoebe Nichols, rapidly palls, and we are left with not just one but two characters who, especially when they are together, are intensely annoying. The supporting roles are mainly sketches on paper, and the ending, in which Lady Ames hires a hitman to shoot her husband on a remote Scottish hillside only to fall victim herself to the inept assassin, is muddled and unfunny.

After *The Missionary* Palin moved on to what he does best – factual television, sharing with us the world as he sees it – and each journey that he makes is filled with fascinating, intimate, amusing detail which shows the artistry of a true diarist.

'My husband was a terrible man. The drinking and the wenching. Oh, if only you could know how much I have suffered all these years.' No, that quote wasn't from any of my interviews with Helen Cherry. It was dialogue spoken by the newly bereaved Wife of Lyonesse in *Sword of the Valiant* (1982), an Arthurian romp which for outright silliness took the biscuit. At any moment you expected Graham Chapman to appear over a hill to the clip-clop of coconuts.

The plot is similar to Python's *Holy Grail* caper, but this was serious stuff. You were not supposed to laugh. Sir Gawain, played by Miles O'Keeffe, achieves instant knighthood when he accepts a challenge from the wily, all-powerful Green Knight, played by Sean Connery. He is given twelve months to solve a riddle set by the Green Knight or he will forfeit his head. The film chronicles his highs and lows along the way – the high point being his infatuation with a comely maid named Linet, played by Cyrielle Claire, and the lowest point, possibly, his spell in the torture chamber of the evil Baron Fontinbras.

If you are prepared to enjoy the daft premise, the film isn't bad. It chunters along at a reasonable pace, and the usual mish-mash of brainy dwarfs, ladies being transformed into birds or red frogs and severed heads reattaching themselves to their carcasses are all there. Howard plays King Arthur as a cross between Santa Claus and a pensioner on a day trip who can't wait to get home – sometimes pleasant, at other times tearing out his hair. He frets that his knights have grown too fat and cowardly since they stopped warring with their neighbours. 'I'm bored with you all,' he shouts as he cancels their Yuletide banquet. Their unanimous refusal to take up the Green Knight's challenge proves him correct.

Sean Connery as the Green Knight struts around in a ridiculous glittery wig and a cape of what appears to be sieved vegetables. One can only assume that he was in it purely for the money. Miles O'Keeffe, who plays Sir Gawain and who made his name romping with Bo Derek and a playful chimp in *Tarzan the Ape Man* (1981), looks dishy enough in an all-white Puss-in-Boots outfit occasionally bared to the waist, but there is no suggestion of a personality – critic Mike Bygrave said he had 'Bjorn Borg's head bolted on to Arnold Schwartzenegger's body' – and one tires quickly of the great physique and the near-perfect cheekbones.

The performance I enjoyed most was Ronald Lacey's obnoxious, leering, cowardly Oswald. Lacey gets as close to pantomime villainy as anyone can, and not for the first time. He, at least, enters the spirit of the thing and refuses to yield to the attempted seriousness of the director and co-writer Stephen Weeks, for whom it was all familiar territory. Weeks had directed *Gawain and the Green Knight* (1973) on a tighter budget and consequently with a less starry cast, but this second attempt fared no better than his first. The dialogue, at times, is throw-away, more of which would have elevated the film into a completely different category. As he is about to be strapped on to the rack in the sadistic baron's dungeon, which is littered with the corpses of earlier guests, Gawain coolly inquires of his burly torturer, 'Does your mother know you do this for a living?'

When Howard first looked at Alain Tanner's shooting script of *Light Years Away* (1981), based on a French novel, *La Voie Sauvage*, by Daniel Odier, the only words that made sense to him were the directions. Everything else seemed insane. But, on the plus side, the director was greatly respected in Europe, a man who admired Brecht and Beckett. And wasn't real life was a bit crazy, anyway? You didn't need to live in Beckett's mad world to encounter absurdities. They stare at you from everywhere: income tax forms; people on cruise liners; the English cricket team. Howard figured that he might as well be in a crazy film as sit at home and go crazy by himself.

Jonas, the main character, played by Mick Ford, had already figured in Tanner's film *Jonas qui aura 25 ans en l'an 2000* (*Jonah Who Will Be 25 in the Year 2000*). In *Light Years Away* it is the year 2000, and Jonas, having reached the age predicted in the earlier film, drifts through a barren landscape, stopping beside a deserted garage. There he meets Yoshka Poliakoff, played by Howard, a creaky, creepy old Russian immigrant who claims to have remarkable powers which, he promises Jonas, if certain conditions are observed he will share with him. Jonas thinks he is insane but harmless enough, so he plays along with the old man.

After that, nothing much happens. We're in Beckett country. Jonas has to prove himself worthy of Yoshka's trust (by acting out odd fantasies, such as filling up imaginary cars with non-existent petrol from a dry pump) to earn the right to share his amazing secret. The film is a mystery, a comedy and a tragedy all rolled into one, and these elements overlay and interact with each other almost seamlessly. To separate them, or to try to explain them by means of conscious imagery, would, somehow, be pointless. Consequently, the film went over most people's heads, but then much of Tanner's work does. One suspects that he would be tempted to plunge off in a wildly different direction if he ever suspected that the audience could understand what he was up to.

Critic Jennifer Selway called it 'mysterious without being mystifying or unduly solemn. Clear as mud, in fact, with the compelling logic of a dream.' Other critics felt that Howard was well on the way to becoming a national treasure. In *The Times* David Robinson wrote, 'The old man, lurching between senile crabbiness and beautiful serenity, is Trevor Howard, whose vast gifts British films consistently squander.' Dilys Powell, again, thought that he was excellent. She called his performance 'perfectly graded'.

Howard won the 1982 Best Actor Award from the London *Evening Standard*, and the film earned the Special Jury Prize at the Cannes Film Festival, despite its ambiguity of plot and the fact that its Swiss-born director was working for the first time in English. It is amazing, really, the reluctance of juries to rubbish anything they don't understand. They seem at times too ready to equate incomprehensibility with quality. Sometimes you can, but much of the time you can't, and with *Light Years Away* you have to make up your own mind. For me, it had far too much premeditated dullness.

Howard spent three months working on the film, paying close attention to everything Tanner said, pondering and puzzling it all out, but he remained completely baffled. 'If it had an inner meaning, I couldn't see it,' he told me, 'but other people's lunacy can be good for us. I always like Ireland. It's a very civilized country.' I told him that my mother came from County Waterford. 'There, what did I tell you!' he roared delightedly.

As a director, Richard Attenborough (now Lord Attenborough) liked to work on big canvasses, perhaps because so much of his acting career had been in small-scale dramas. He appears at his best handling broad historical themes, such as in *Oh What a Lovely War*, *Young Winston*, *A Bridge Too Far*, *Cry Freedom* and so on. One of the biggest films of its time was *Gandhi* (1982), which handed an Oscar on a plate to a previously little-known actor, Ben Kingsley. I'm not suggesting that Kingsley did not earn it. But the film showcased his performance in a way that made audiences take notice.

It opens with Gandhi's assassination and state funeral in 1949 and goes back to 1893 when, travelling to Pretoria by train as a young attorney and new to the ways of South Africa, he experiences apartheid for the first time – a guard throws him off the train because, as a coloured person, his first-class ticket is worthless.

This experience fuels his opposition to unjust laws, both in South Africa, where he is imprisoned, and back home in India. Howard has a small but significant role, as Judge Bloomfield, who presides over a court trying Gandhi for civil disobedience. Gandhi admits his guilt, declaring simply, 'I believe non-cooperation with evil is a duty and that British rule in India is evil.' Bloomfield has no choice but to imprison him, for six years. After passing sentence, the judge adds, 'If, however, His Majesty's Government should, at some later date, see fit to reduce the term, no one will be better pleased than I.'

Attenborough postponed shooting the scene, which took two days, until Howard was free to do it. Several years afterwards, when I was involved in a project with Lord Attenborough, he discussed Gandhi with me and his 'desperation' (his word) to get Howard to play the judge: 'I said to him, "I'll need you for two days, Trevor. You tell me when you can do it." God, yes, I wanted him. He was more than just that judge. He was the face of compassion, of the fair play that many senior British administrators in India were capable of. The film is honest about many of the faults associated with colonialism, but the judge was the other side of that coin: a man of stature, a fair and humane man. Through him, I made the point that some bloody good men were out there, too. Those forty or so words of the judge had to be pitched absolutely right. Trevor was marvellous. Truly. There is no actor whom I can think of capable of doing what he did with that scene.

'Why was he so marvellous? I'll tell you. It all goes back a long way. Trevor's generation of actors came from the theatre, and we were, as English actors, obsessed by the text. The legacy of Shakespeare and Wilde and Shaw and others had put the emphasis on words, often to the detriment of the performance.

'Then, at the end of the war, Trevor came along, relatively unfettered by stage technique, although he had done some. Suddenly, in a small part in *The Way to the Stars* – and it had to be sudden because he only had half-a-dozen lines – he created a character of quite devastating reality. What he did in that film was introduce a standard of documentary reality in performance – not quite as earth-shattering as Brando did a few years later in America – but which over here created, and deserved to create, a huge impact.'

I asked Lord Attenborough if Howard had been difficult to act with.

'Not in the sense that he was ungenerous or stole from you. God knows, he didn't need to. The difficulty, if that's the correct word, was for others to match that reality which he had. It made you question your own performance in a way you hadn't done before, because you had never been put under the microscope quite like that before.

'If I had to summarize what Trevor did that we shouldn't forget, it wouldn't be an individual performance, good though so many of them were. I would say it was the way he opened the door to realism in film acting. He set a standard of reality and truth in the cinema that was wholly unknown before he came along. If you want to know where the recognition and prestige that British films have enjoyed internationally since the 1940s originally came from, it began with Trevor, initially. He was the turning-point.'

Howard's final performance of any length (or depth) was in *Dust* (1984), a Belgian production directed by Marion Hansel, which was filmed in Spain. The script was based on a book by the South African writer J.M. Coetzee. Howard played the father, a farmer living in a remote part of South Africa with his dowdy unmarried daughter Magda, played by Jane Birkin. The daily routine is hard and boring and, although the young woman is sad and frustrated, she tolerates the situation because that is how life is and nothing is likely to improve. In her eyes, however, they get dramatically worse when her father takes advantage of his position and has sex with Anna, the young wife of his black foreman. In a fit of jealous rage Magda kills the old fellow and buries him out in the bush.

Howard's performance was sluggish to say the least. Maybe that was how it was written or maybe he had, by then, begun the slow wind-down. Where his character found the energy to have sexual intercourse with Anna is anyone's guess. Jane Birkin is believable as the daughter who wants her father's love so badly that she chooses to have nothing rather than share it. After the film was finished Jane wrote a sweet thank-you letter to Howard, describing him as a 'sweet companion, wonderful fun, moving and truly inspiring'. Unfortunately nobody could find nice words to say about the film. It failed to get a cinema release but was shown on British television in the early hours of the morning when only drunks, insomniacs and security guards are watching.

16
FULL CIRCLE

He roused up a bit and recognized me, but he was terribly weak. He didn't say anything. I sat there holding his hand. It was the end of forty-three incredible years.

– Helen Howard

As the 1980s wore on, television provided Howard with more opportunities to work than the film industry. As someone whose mood dipped and whose drinking soared when he was idle for any length of time, these offers were, literally, life-savers. Howard's liver had taken a non-stop pounding throughout his adult years and, while his system's capacity for regeneration could not be faulted, from the beginning of the final decade of his life the punishing routine to which he subjected himself began to show on his face.

His nose seemed to inflate and become more reddish in colour. The pores on his skin widened, rather like fork-holes in pastry during cooking. The gargoyle effect became more extreme. His concentration would wander off at tangents, and his memory, which had frequently been annoyingly selective, became less reliable than at any time previously. It was for him a constant source of irritation that most of his best performances on American television were not shown during his lifetime on British screens. The position changed little after his death. One would think that, somewhere within the endless diet of trashy American made-for-TV films and repeats shown in Britain, room could be found for his and other British stars' higher-quality US television work, but that appears not to be the case.

It would be interesting, for example, to compare the Trevor Howard of *Brief Encounter* with the US television production of *Tonight at Eight* (1954), an American adaptation of the Noel Coward play *Still Life* from which they were both derived, in which Howard repeated his role as the charming doctor, this time opposite Ginger Rogers. The production was directed by Otto Preminger, a controversial film director with whom few actors formed a cordial relationship. Howard was no exception. The American market was not the same as that which David Lean had in mind when making his 1945 classic with the actor. Nevertheless, the lack of subtlety of Preminger's direction went beyond anything Howard could have expected on this, his first working trip to the United States and on which he had placed high hopes. Howard told me that Preminger had said, shortly after they met, 'Forget that other damn movie. In mine, you buy her a coffee, pick her up and pinch her ass!' Howard told me, 'There was a song around at the time called the "Crazy Otto Rag". That was him all right.'

The coolness between them at the start of the production never improved. Howard found him crass and overbearing, and when it was time for the British actor to catch a flight home they were barely on speaking terms. Many years later the two of them met, by accident, at a nightclub named Toots Shor's in New York City. Preminger, who watered his grudges in a greenhouse, said to Howard, 'You don't like me, do you?' It was a statement of fact, but since Preminger had phrased it as a question Howard felt he deserved a reply. 'You know damn well that I don't!' he said. That was the end of the conversation.

In 1963, a distinguished American television director and winner of eight Emmy Awards, George Schaefer, offered Howard the title role in his television production of *The Invincible Mr Disraeli* (1963). The lean-faced British statesman of Victoria's reign, best known for acquiring the Suez Canal and for proclaiming Victoria the Empress of India in 1877, had been played many times, most memorably by George Arliss in 1931 and by Alec Guinness twenty years later. Howard had Greer Garson to co-star as his wife, and the English actress Kate Reid played Queen Victoria. Also in the cast were Denholm Elliott, who had worked with Howard in *The Heart of the Matter*, and Geoffrey Keen, Howard's old colleague from the Stratford 1939 season.

The company's New York rehearsals coincided with the annual St Patrick's Day festivities, of which Howard took full advantage. But for most of the time, and particularly on the nights before he had an early-morning camera call, Howard kept a tight lid on his drinking. At the end of one of Disraeli's highly charged speeches to a packed House of Commons, the crew broke into spontaneous applause, a rare occurrence in television filming.

In the *Los Angeles Times* Cecil Smith wrote, 'Trevor Howard's performance as the immortal "Dizzy" was as lustrous as these tired eyes have seen have seen in many a year . . . The cast was without blemish and

George Schaefer's colour production, as usual, was superb. But, ah, *that* Mr Howard.'

During 1978–9 Howard made two television films in Britain. One was called *Easterman* (1978), a routine cops-and-killers thriller with Howard as a tough, hard-drinking CID chief inspector trying to catch a criminal who attacks police officers. It was a self-contained episode in a six-part series made under the title *Scorpion Tales*. Patrick Allen played a senior police officer. The second film, *The Shillingbury Blowers* (1979), was a sub-Ealing comedy about the disruption caused to a village brass band when a new, youthful conductor arrives and imposes fresh ideas on it. Soon everybody is taking sides, for and against the newcomer.

Produced by Greg Smith as the pilot for a television series, and filmed only a few miles from Elstree, *The Shillingbury Blowers* was a gentle comedy that seemed curiously out of step with the flinty, more abrasive television offerings of the early 1980s. Howard played Old Saltie, a veteran cornet-player and influential band member who vehemently opposes any changes. He is a cunning old buffer who sees off the challenge of a newcomer who tries to drag the band into modern times. In acting terms, Howard did a similar job on comparative newcomer Robin Nedwell, who played the pop musician-conductor.

Most people know the name Jonathan Swift as the eighteenth-century author of *Gulliver's Travels*. But he was also widely read for his other satires and poetry and was the Dean of St Patrick's in Dublin. Howard got a chance to play him, as a grumpy seventy-years-old, in *No Country for Old Men* (1981), filmed by Tristram Powell for BBC television. Set in the Dublin deanery in 1737, when Swift was an old man, the film used flashbacks to take us through important milestones in his life, including his romantic involvements and the work he put into writing *Gulliver's Travels*. Filming was done in an old house near Ross-on-Wye which Tristram Powell recalled having visited as a schoolboy. Howard told me that he thought the house might have belonged to one of Powell's relatives.

Jonathan Swift was a complex and paradoxical character for any actor to attempt. He was strong-willed, short-tempered and impossible to get to know. Swift was described by his fellow-churchman and contemporary Tom Sheridan – played in the film by Cyril Cusack – as 'a patriot who hates the land of his birth, a misanthrope who leaves his money to the public benefit, a Protestant who speaks for the whole people of Ireland, a man of true religion who shuns all show of piety'.

Howard always made a careful study of the historical figures he played before deciding how to assemble the character inside his head. After studying a collection of Swift's writings and his biography, Howard conceded to me the difficulty he had trying to mould the conflicting strands of Swift's life into a coherent and convincing whole. He said much the same thing to critic Michael Billington: 'It was a smashing role to play . . . one had to try to knit together all these contradictions.' He quoted an example: 'He [Swift] is full of sexual disgust, yet he could also write tender love poems.' Howard added, 'There's one marvellous scene where a group of ragged-arsed paupers come begging for alms. First he attacks them, then he gives them money. When his sub-dean praises him for doing the Lord's work, he says, "No, sir, I have extenuated a public vice at the expense of my pocket and their pride." It's marvellous when an actor is given a variety of moods to express in a single scene.'

Howard also applauded the speed with which the film was made. He told me, 'Four weeks was all it took. Tristram Powell is a good director. Didn't keep us pissing around for months like some do.' Once again, he had been severely challenged, in a production where – in his opinion – time wasn't wasted. Consequently he loved every minute of it. So, too, did many leading critics. In a discussion of Howard's recent television work, *The Times* commented, '*Catholics* . . . *Staying On* . . . and now *No Country for Old Men* have brought Howard to our small screens with gratifying regularity and consistent distinction.'

Howard's performance as the composer George Fredric Handel in John Osborne's *God Rot Tunbridge Wells* (1984) lacked more than it contained. It was not very watchable, which was rarely the case when Osborne was the writer. Casting Howard as the composer in old age seemed the correct thing to do, according to director Tony Palmer. Osborne had reservations, but they both wanted Howard quite badly despite the clearest possible signs that his health was deteriorating. No amount of bravura could conceal his decline.

With a tight shooting schedule and low funds, progress had to be maintained. Palmer had no alternative but to suggest 'prompt' boards to help the actor with his words. He was surprised when Howard agreed to it without an argument. He had expected a tetchy response from an actor whose scorn for 'idiot cards' (as Howard called them) was widely known and who had mocked Brando for using them. But by

1984 Howard had drunk the bottom out of his memory and he knew it, and he accepted Palmer's suggestion without equivocation.

Although he was yet not fully aware of it, the end was accelerating to meet him. He was seventy-two but looked ten years older. Alcohol had affected his liver, but it had not stopped him drinking. Howard had no traditional hobbies, such as gardening or collecting things, and the cricket season in England seemed to finish almost as soon as it had begun.

By 1984 it was rare for him to reach midday in a sober condition. The strain placed upon Helen increased, along with his helplessness, as time went on. Her love had endured many severe tests during their long years of marriage, but as he sank deeper and deeper into a near-permanent alcoholic haze, enlivened occasionally by his desire for a heated argument, the mother-figure she had always been to him emerged more defiantly pure and defensive of him than she had ever been. Whatever her private fears for the future, she continued to love him and care for him devotedly, and she was determined that, for as long as she could, she would keep his gradual and irreversible decline a secret from the rest of the world.

It was, of course, easier to manage the situation while he stayed at home. A problem arose when she accepted work that took her away from Arkley for any length of time. She wanted to continue acting – and did, when an interesting role was offered – but making arrangements for someone to come to the house and look after Howard was not easy. He adamantly refused to have anyone stay overnight. Matters came to a head when she was offered a good part in a television film, *Time After Time* (1985), based on a novel by Mollie Keane, to be made in Ireland under the direction of Bill Hayes. John Gielgud and Googie Withers were to co-star with her. It was exactly right for her, but she could not leave Howard at home to fend for himself. He wouldn't remember where anything was. He might fall downstairs or electrocute himself. If she accepted the film, he would have to go with her.

It marked a significant reversal of their traditional roles. For years Helen had accompanied him to locations all over the world, ordering taxis and room service, making sure that he ate regularly, that his socks were washed and keeping him company – and he appreciated everything she did for him and the spirit in which it was done. In Ireland in 1984 they were together on a film set because she was in demand and he was too helpless to be anywhere except beside her.

Hayes thought it would fun to give Howard a couple of lines in the film, the tiniest of tiny cameo roles. It was a mistake, as John McCallum, who had accompanied his wife Googie Withers, told me, 'He couldn't say the words. He struggled, bless him, but he had lost it by then. Completely. It was sad to watch. But poor old Helen had no choice but to bring him along. If she'd left him at home he'd have starved!'

Why, I asked McCallum, in his opinion, had Howard lost it? 'Drink did it, without a doubt,' he replied. 'He couldn't stop. Didn't want to stop. This is how bad it was. I knew exactly when he was arriving from England, so I met him off the plane at Dublin Airport. He'd had a few already. We went into the bar, downed a few more, then went to our hotel where we had a meal and chatted for an hour or so, about old times mostly. I suppose we had half-a-dozen whiskies each. Helen and Googie had been out together somewhere. Afterwards, when we got to our room in the hotel, Googie burst out laughing. She'd heard Trevor ask Helen if they had any whisky in the bedroom. When Helen said no, he was shocked. He said to her, "How the hell am I going to get to sleep?"'

The conversation amused McCallum for many years afterwards. He told me, 'He'd had a real skinful that day and was going to carry on for the rest of the night. Bloody amazing. But Helen was marvellous with him.'

During 1985, Howard made three television films, one for British audiences and the other two for American viewers only. The British production, *Foreign Body* (1986), was directed by Ronald Neame, at whose request he was given the role. It could loosely be described as a sex comedy, with Victor Banerjee as a young Indian con-man whose pretence at being a doctor gives him an opportunity to bed lots of attractive young women. Howard played an elderly doctor. Lacking both the appealing innocence of the *Doctor* film series of the 1950s and 1960s and a charismatic leading man, *Foreign Body* was a dead weight from beginning to end. Nobody seems to have heard of it.

The only fact worth mentioning about *Christmas Eve* (1986), the first of two American productions in which he made brief appearances, was that it marked the return to active service of former Hollywood star Loretta Young. She played an old woman, stinking rich and close to death, whose final wish, to be reunited with the younger members of her family, is granted through the intercession of a mysterious old man, played by Howard, who seems to have the answer for everything. For audiences who enjoy having their heart-strings pulled it probably worked. I found it tedious beyond endurance.

Peter the Great (1986), Howard's other US television movie of that year, was a mini-series with blockbuster ambitions. The cast list was impressive, including Maximilian Schell, Vanessa Redgrave, Omar Sharif, Laurence Olivier, Mel Ferrer, Lili Palmer, Ursula Andress and many more. Schell played Peter the Great, the Russian tsar, who during the latter part of the 1800s wanted to transform Russia from a giant, insular going-nowhere nation into one ready to take advantage of the scientific, industrial and cultural breakthroughs of the more progressive countries, bearing in mind that during this period the strides forward in these areas were massive. Peter did not want Russia to drop behind, but his ambitions were seen by many as radical and dangerous. Howard played Sir Isaac Newton. Leo Tolstoy and General Gordon were among the historic figures who flit in and out of this lavish production, which, despite its War-and-Peace pretensions, was basically a simple story that deserved to be told more expertly.

Back in Kenya in 1941 a small group of wealthy, bored socialites became known as the 'Happy Valley set'. They had parties every night at which they drank until they fell over. Infidelity was a way of life. Their antics went unnoticed in Britain, because at the time German bombing raids were grabbing the headlines. It took a high-profile murder trial to expose the whole sordid set-up. The murder victim was the Earl of Errol, hereditary High Constable of Scotland. Chief suspect was Sir Jock Broughton, a millionaire landowner whose young wife Diana was having an affair with Errol. There had been rumours that the two lovers were about to embark on a new life together. Broughton had apparently been insanely jealous of Errol. Everything pointed to him being the killer.

In the subsequent trial Broughton was acquitted, partly from lack of evidence and partly because Errol was a notorious womanizer who many thought had received his just desserts. But the notoriety that engulfed Broughton after the trial left his life in ruins. He returned to Britain and, soon afterwards, committed suicide. Several accounts of the Happy Valley lifestyle, the murder and acquittal have been published. The film *White Mischief* (1987) was based on a 6,000-word article by Cyril Connolly and James Fox that appeared in the *Sunday Times Magazine* in December 1969. The feature aroused a fresh wave of interest in the case. When

Connolly died in 1974 Fox continued with his researches and published in 1982 his definitive analysis of the Errol murder.

In the film Charles Dance played the Earl of Errol, Joss Ackland was Broughton and Greta Scacchi was Diana. The director, Michael Radford, wanted Trevor Howard in the smallish role of Jack Soames, Broughton's friend and fellow Old Etonian, a notable marksman and big-game hunter in Kenya. Initially, and with good reason, questions were raised about Howard's fitness, particularly whether or not he would be able to withstand the rigours of filming on location in Kenya. Sarah Miles, who had already been cast as Alice de Janzé, a bizarre member of the clique and a former lover of Errol's, seemed the obvious person to ask. She repeated for me the advice she had given to the producer. 'He asked me if I thought that Trevor could still do a good job. I thought he could and said so. But with one important proviso. He must have Helen with him. I said that if Helen wasn't around to look after him I would have serious doubts.'

Howard arrived in Kenya, not with Helen but with David Williams, his driver and long-established friend from his home village. Williams, now retired and living in Devon, told me over lunch at his local pub, 'Trevor wasn't terribly well, and Helen couldn't cope with him any more. She asked me to look after him. I had been their driver for several years, knew them well and had some medical experience. I accompanied him to Kenya and, after that, to Ireland.'

Their flight to Nairobi began uneventfully, but, Howard being Howard, he needed careful supervision. Fading health had not dulled his artfulness. The naughty schoolboy in him awaited his chance, and while Williams took a nap Howard downed several double brandies in rapid succession. By the time the plane landed at Nairobi the actor needed a wheelchair to get him to his car.

That by itself would not have been serious had there been sufficient time for him to sober up and to acclimatize to the altitude and humidity of Nairobi. The leading members of the cast and the crew had been given several days to get over their flights and adjust to the conditions, but Howard had been scheduled for an early call on the morning after his arrival. He was due to begin filming with virtually no rest. It would have drained the reserves of a man half his age, extremely fit and sober on arrival. For Howard the demand was simply too great.

Sarah told me, 'I couldn't believe that Trevor was being rushed in front of the cameras so soon after arriving. I was upset for him and even more so when he arrived without Helen. And he wasn't steady on his feet. I immediately thought: I must cover myself here, for I'd told them he would be OK. I went straight to the producer and said, "You can't make Trevor work now." They said, "Sorry, Sarah, but we have to do the scene. Afterwards he can go and rest." I said, "But . . .", and they said, "Sarah, we have to do the scene now. That's all there is to it !" So, I got nowhere with them.'

The scene in question was a crowd shot, involving dozens of extras, at Nairobi Station, where Soames welcomes Broughton and his glamorous new bride on their arrival. To be fair to the producer, Simon Perry, because of the numbers involved a postponement would have been costly. The sun blazed down relentlessly throughout the day. Howard had been awoken at six in the morning and given nothing to do but sit and wait for hour after hour in a sweltering tent while preparations were made for the shot. By the time his call eventually came, he was in a distressed state. He was practically on his knees.

Williams told me, 'After the business on the plane, from the moment we landed at Nairobi I stopped him drinking. That was a mistake. I hadn't realized that for somebody with his level of dependence on alcohol his intake should be lowered, not cut off completely. No alcohol at all was as bad for him as too much of the stuff. In the tent in which we waited, he was fine to begin with, but after six hours in that stifling heat, with his system starved of alcohol since the previous day, he started to get the shakes. He looked, and he felt, bloody ill.

'They called the location nurse. I said I could sort him out if they'd get me some scotch and lots of ginger ale. They were horrified at this. I said, "Listen, he's not drunk. The guy's got withdrawal symptoms. Fetch me what I've asked for and he'll be fine." They did, and he was able to do the scene.' In the edited film, Howard is glimpsed in long shot muttering an incomprehensible greeting. It was all he was capable of. But valuable time had been lost getting him into shape, and Radford and Perry were furious.

Encountering Williams in the lift at the Serena Hotel in Nairobi, where the leading players were staying – two other hotels were also packed with unit staff – they accused him of failing to do his job. They told him that they had decided to scrap the day's shoot and replace Howard immediately. They then went to find Sarah Miles to inform her of their decision. Perry said to her, 'Sit down, Sarah, I want to talk to you. I'm afraid it's not good news.' Sarah said, 'What do you mean?'

Radford replied, 'Trevor was completely out of it today. I'm sorry, but we can't have this. He has to go!'

Sarah rounded on them. 'Let's get a few things straight,' she said. 'You phone me and ask "Can he work?" I say, "Yes, provided he has Helen with him." He arrives without her. You put him to work straight away, while we've been swanning around for days. Now you want to sack him. After one day you want to fire a man who has the best track record of any actor that I know. You can't do it. It will finish his career, and you can't end the career of a great actor like Trevor in that way. He'll remember for the rest of his days that this was the one and only time he ever got fired. You can't do that to him. Please.'

Perry was sympathetic but refused to give way. He said, 'I'm afraid we've no choice, Sarah. We don't have the money to mess around. It was a mistake bringing him here. You saw him today. He's not up to it. He should be at home.' But Sarah was in no mood for compromise, either. She told them that if Howard was sacked she would leave immediately. They warned her against an over-reaction which might affect her career, but she stood her ground. 'If he goes, I go, too,' she repeated and walked away. She told me, 'Yes, I would have done it. No question. It was a total injustice. And if I see injustice I can't let it pass. I'm a Capricorn. We're like that.'

Alone in his room on the third floor, Howard was resting. He was exhausted from the day's traumas. Sarah banged on his door, determined that if the company carried out its threat the two of them would go down fighting. She told him, 'We're in big trouble, Trevs.' He couldn't understand her agitation. He thought she was affected by the heat.

Glancing out of his window, Sarah noticed the swimming-pool below. Perry and some executives were sipping drinks at a poolside table. Suddenly she had an idea. Eighteen years before, when Howard had been in much better physical shape, during a tour of Hungary to promote *Ryan's Daughter* she had been impressed by a beautiful swallow dive he had executed from a high board in their Belgrade hotel pool. It had been graceful and eye-catching, a remarkable feat for a man whom Sarah described to me as lacking coordination at the best of times.

Sarah told Howard to put on his swimming trunks straight away and meet her downstairs at the poolside. He stared at her, mystified. She said, 'Get a move on, Trevs. We're both in trouble here.' Sarah had not told him he was being sacked, but Howard had already guessed what was coming. 'They're dumping me, aren't they?' Sarah pulled a wry face and nodded. The light of battle glowed in Howard's eyes. The fatigue left his body as if he had been hit by high-voltage electricity. 'Bastards,' he roared. He dug out a bright, almost obscenely garish pair of Bermuda shorts. Sarah changed into less flamboyant swimming attire and waited beside the pool for him. When he appeared, she pointed at the diving board and said, 'Let's see one of your swallow dives.'

The executives remained huddled together at the edge of the pool, still unaware of Howard or his flamboyant shorts. But that changed when he shouted to Sarah and began limbering up on the board. He waited for their eyes to settle on him, the way a trapeze artist waits for the end of the drum roll. When the moment was right he did his dive. It wasn't quite as spectacular as the one in Budapest but good enough to draw gasps of surprise from everyone watching.

Standing near the shallow end, Sarah called to him when he surfaced, 'Come on, Trevs. Through my legs.' He disappeared from sight again, but there was no mistaking his location. Those shorts glowed underwater like a miner's lamp. Back and forth he propelled himself between Sarah's legs like a giant luminous squid.

The executives who had called for Howard's blood earlier that evening were speechless. Sarah climbed out of the pool and said to them, 'Too drunk to work today, was he? It seems a bit odd to me when he can do this.' The decision to sack him was revoked, but Sarah had to promise to keep a close eye on him for the remainder of the filming. She agreed to become an additional minder and, with Williams rationing his drinks and making sure that he had plenty of early nights, Howard got through the assignment without further trouble. But, on screen, his expression was lifeless. He was nearing the end of the road.

The original title of Howard's last movie, made for British television, was *The Old Jest*. Based on a novel of that title by Jennifer Johnson, and directed by Robert Knights, the film was eventually retitled *The Dawning* (1988) and was set in Ireland during the troubled 1920s. It was basically the story of Nancy Gulliver, an eighteen-year-old orphan girl, played by Rebecca Pidgeon, who lives with her grandfather, who was played by Trevor Howard. All her life she has wondered who her father might be. When a stranger named Cassius, played by Anthony Hopkins, arrives in the village, she day-dreams that it might be him.

It was a slim story, but the sensitive acting of Rebecca Pidgeon and

Hopkins, then on the threshold of international stardom, was sufficient to carry it. Jean Simmons played the girl's Aunt Mary and unwittingly she topped, middled and tailed Howard's film career rather neatly, having made a brief appearance in *The Way to the Stars* at the beginning of his career, co-starred with him in *The Clouded Yellow* during the height of his success and been with him, at the very end, in *The Dawning*. By the time it was ready for screening, in mid January 1988, Howard was dead.

Rebecca Pidgeon failed to achieve stardom, but two young supporting actors in the film did go on to greater things – Hugh Grant and Adrian Dunbar. For the six-week shooting schedule, the main members of the unit stayed at Ballymaloe House, one of the better-known gourmet hotels in Ireland. Cookery expert Jane Grigson once described it as 'well-appointed, gentle, fine, mirthful house'. It was certainly mirthful, and noisy, too, while occupied by the leading members of the cast. Howard was back in Ireland, and for someone whose iron constitution had been worn to the point of collapse he was still capable of joining in a party and enjoying himself.

Mike Johnson, a pensions consultant with several former test cricketers among his clients, was holidaying in Cork when he heard that his friend Graham Benson was co-producing (with Sarah Lawson) *The Dawning* not many miles away. They got together and celebrated. Johnson had played rugby with David Williams, which was another reason to celebrate. Adrian Dunbar also knew Mike Johnson, so he, too, joined in the revelry. These were serious drinkers and, although Howard wanted to keep up with them, at the Ballycotton pub where they got together Williams called 'time' early every night just as he had done in Kenya, to limit the damage to Howard's internal organs and to ensure that he got plenty of rest.

Johnson told me, 'It was a shoestring budget, no spare cash at all, and since I had a large car they could all squeeze into I was the chauffeur. We had some adorable Sunday lunchtime sessions.'

Williams added, 'It was interesting to see how Trevor and Adrian hit it off. Old Booze and Young Booze. The burnt-out old basket who'd done it all and the new guy with it all ahead of him. Adrian had immense respect for him, both as an actor and as a man. If only they could have been the same age, Adrian's age, when they met, then we'd have seen something.'

The morning the unit was due to leave Ballymaloe House, after Joe the barman had served everyone a farewell drink, Howard remained seated at his usual table, leisurely sipping what Mike Johnson described as a 'half-pint glass containing raw eggs, scotch and dry ginger'. Cars pulled up outside, people said their goodbyes and were driven off, still Howard sat hunched over the table, ignoring everything around him, silently sipping the deadly yellow mixture in front of him.

At around quarter to eleven the car arrived that would take him and Williams to the airport. Williams helped the driver load their suitcases into the car boot, while a member of staff made his way to Howard's table to tell him the car was ready. The news brought no response. Howard sipped his glass and continued to stare at it, submerged in his own thoughts. Williams then came in the dining-room and repeated the message. Again the great man took no notice. He could have been auditioning for the role of Buddha. Seeing the difficulty they were having, Mike Johnson decided to have a try. He said to Howard, 'Helen will be upset if you miss the plane. Shall we go?' Howard glanced up and said, innocently, 'You wouldn't want me to hurry my breakfast, would you?'

Back home in Arkley, after a brief rest, he was excited to get a phone call from Peter Bloore, who had grown up in the village and who was working on a *son et lumière* to be performed inside Bristol Cathedral. Bloore's parents, George and Michelle, were friends of the Howards. Bloore told me, 'I was aware of Trevor's connection with Bristol through Clifton College. I thought his voice would be perfect for the narration. I could just imagine it booming up and down the aisles.'

The presentation, which Bloore wrote, produced and directed, involved three screens erected inside the cathedral, on to which various images were projected. Everything was computer-synchronized, giving an impressive high-tech counterpoint to Howard's distinctly old-world presentation. As Bloore wrote in the programme notes, 'The eye flits from object to object, absorbing some things and skimming over others . . . No one is expected to absorb everything on all three screens simultaneously. What we aim to create is an effect, an impression. And all the while, the Cathedral itself, the reality, is all around us.'

The recording was made at Elstree Film Studios in late October 1987. For those of us who knew him, it remains to this day a deeply moving experience to listen to that magnificent, resonant voice accompanied by a beautiful chorale. Bloore told me, 'He was the consummate professional and a delight to work with. He didn't say much between takes, but I gather he was a man who never volunteered opinions, so I wasn't surprised. He was quite ill at that stage and, astonishingly, still drinking. He had vodka because, apparently, his doctor couldn't smell it on his breath.'

The drinking, in the end, killed him. When he shook hands with Bloore and returned home, he was only weeks away from death. He paid several visits to hospital to be patched up after falling and hitting his head or gashing his leg on something he had staggered into while under the influence. Helen told me of one incident where Howard fell over in their bedroom in a drunken state and knocked himself out. She called an ambulance and, although he had regained consciousness by the time the crew arrived, he was too unsteady on his feet to attempt the stairs.

A stretcher was brought into the room and Howard, grumbling about the unnecessary fuss, was lifted on to it and tightly strapped in. As the ambulance men negotiated the stairway, Helen heard him call out, 'I want . . . I want . . .' She said, 'I'm here, darling. What is it you want?' He looked up at her and growled, 'I want another gin and tonic!' The stretcher-bearers almost dropped him, so great was their surprise.

Although the laughs were few and far between as his condition worsened, he had good days as well as bad ones, and on his good days he was well enough to continue working. His name was enough to keep the job offers coming in, although towards the end of November 1987 his sickly appearance and health complications dictated what he could – or, more to the point, what he couldn't – do. He was signed to play a Catholic priest in *Silent Night Holy Night*, which was scheduled begin filming at Cinecittà in Rome in January 1988. Meanwhile Howard and Helen planned a quiet Christmas at home. He and David Williams were booked to fly to Italy at the start of the New Year. Set in the early nineteenth century in Austria, the film told how the world-famous Christmas carol of the title came to be co-written by Father Joseph Mohr, a young Austrian priest who wrote the words, and Franz Gruber, the Oberndorff schoolmaster who composed the music.

Howard was to play Father Holies, the senior but ailing priest whom Mohr assists. Gruber was the church choirmaster and organist, and Holies was the man who brought them together, so his role would have a greater impact on the narrative than its size might suggest. For Howard, still making a fight of it and with more work in the pipeline – he was due to fly to Greece after another rest – these were unexpectedly joyful times. Although he probably guessed that he was nearing the end, he was determined to keep going for as long as he possibly could. However, the plans to fly to Italy had to be shelved when, in mid-December, he developed symptoms of acute liver failure.

The district nurse who visited him each Friday for a routine check-up and to supervise his bath noticed that the whites of his eyes had turned yellowish. Williams, who was downstairs, immediately alerted Howard's doctor, Guy Eglinton, who arranged for him to be taken into the BUPA Hospital in nearby Bushey for further examination. But the only thing they could do for him was to make him more comfortable. After a lifetime of overwork Howard's liver could take no more. He was dying.

Helen was due to travel to Birmingham immediately after the New Year to make a television film with Phyllis Calvert. She felt torn between being at Howard's bedside and fulfilling her contractual obligations, but Howard resolved her dilemma by telling her that she should go. Tearfully she headed off to Birmingham. As she said goodbye to Williams she said, 'David, listen. If Trevor should die while I'm away, please promise me that you won't ring me. I couldn't bear to hear about it over the phone. Please drive up and wait for me outside the studio.'

However, while Helen was rehearsing, the evening before he died, the ward sister phoned her to say that Howard's condition was critical and that he was slipping in and out of consciousness. She left the studio immediately and was met at Arkley by Williams, who drove her to the hospital. Helen told me, 'Trevor was alive, lying on his side sleeping when we arrived. He roused a bit, recognized me, but he was terribly weak. He didn't say anything. I sat there holding his hand. It was the end of forty-three incredible years. Suddenly David said, "Helen, I think he's stopped breathing." We called a nurse, and she confirmed that he had died. He didn't suffer at all. He was just lying there. I held his hand and he drifted off.'

The date was Thursday 7 January 1988. According to his death certificate, Howard died of 'hepatic failure and acute cirrhosis of the liver'. He had been unable to say anything to Helen on that final visit, but on the previous occasion when she saw him, just a couple of days before, they had held hands and he had said to her, 'I've had enough. I'm ready to go.' Helen believes that those were the last words he ever spoke.

As soon as she heard the news Sarah Miles wrote to Helen, 'What can I say, except that I know they have stopped making Rolls-Royces like Trevor any more. In fact, this deteriorating planet is losing all its rare jewels. I feel that Larry [Laurence Olivier] will follow fairly shortly, and then Sir John Gielgud and then what, I pray? No more greatness, at least, none of that quality ever again. I am off to India for the film festival there because I have both *White Mischief* and *Hope and Glory* there . . . in so doing I'll miss the funeral, but then I don't need to be at funerals. I do my loving and remembering in my prayers. Trevor will forever be in them; his spirit is so powerful it will be hovering over you and helping you through the rest of your life.'

Sarah's husband, Robert Bolt, also sent a brief note to Helen, saying that Howard 'was a gentleman among actors, such power and truth. More, he was a gentleman whom one was always delighted to meet, with so much charm and wit.'

At the funeral service in Golders Green David Williams told the congregation, 'The kindness and affection that he showed to me I will cherish for ever.' He added, 'Part of the schoolboy in Trevor never left him. He would do anything for a joke or a few laughs.' He talked briefly about their journeys together to Kenya and to Ireland, mentioned the trip they never made – to Rome – and concluded by saying, 'Trevor told me that he only once acted in a Turgenev play, while he was at RADA in the thirties. The original title of his last film, *The Old Jest*, was taken from a quotation by Turgenev: "Death is an old jest, but it comes to everyone."'

After the funeral Howard's family and friends returned to Arkley for a private reception at the Gate pub. At three in the afternoon the proprietor, and Howard's close friend, Harry Poole closed the place and handed it over to Helen and her guests, who included Adrian Dunbar and Mike Johnson, from *The Dawning* drinking sessions in Ballycotton.

At five o'clock Johnson nudged Dunbar and said, 'Adrian, there's only one place where we can continue this farewell. You know where I'm talking about, don't you?'

Dunbar replied, 'Sure I do. I was thinking of it myself.' A phone call to Luton Airport confirmed that two seats were available on the 6.45 p.m. flight to Cork Airport.

The tickets were promptly booked, a taxi summoned and off they went. They flew to Cork, hopped on another taxi to Ballycotton – a distance of around twenty-five miles along winding roads in the dark – but by nine thirty the two of them were propping up the bar in the harbour pub, to hearty applause from the locals who thought it the most magnificent salute to a departed friend that anyone could possibly dream up. After a night of drinking and singing they were driven to Ballymaloe House for a couple of hours' sleep before heading back to Cork Airport. David Williams told me, 'It was a crazy, impulsive, wonderful thing to do. But Trevor got you thinking like that. He was an inspiration to those guys.'

Years before his death Howard had asked Lieutenant-Colonel John Stephenson, who was Secretary of the MCC until 1993, for permission to have his ashes sprinkled over the grass at Lord's cricket ground in front of his beloved Warner's Stand. This provoked a lengthy debate within the Committee, who understandably wished to discourage members from disposing of their remains in this fashion. Perhaps they realized that, given the age of most of them, the pitch could end up looking like the upper slopes of Vesuvius.

Only in exceptional circumstances, according to Stephenson, as in the case of a regular England test player, is such a request considered. However, denying permission does not always prevent it happening. Stephenson told me about a club made up exclusively of wartime pilots who, having been shot out of the skies by the Germans, had successfully returned to their squadrons to resume the battle. These wily, craggy survivors held their annual reunion dinners at Lord's. Their president was a cricketing fanatic, and when he died his RAF chums asked for his ashes to be sprinkled over Lord's.

Stephenson sent his customary apologetic response, and that, he thought, was the end of the matter. But it wasn't. At their next reunion dinner the crafty veterans revealed that their president's remains had, in fact, been sprinkled where he wanted them. Stephenson told me, 'They just did it. One of them said to me afterwards, with a huge grin on his face, "If the Jerries couldn't stop us, did you seriously think you could?" It was a bit impertinent, really. But the deed was done. What could I say except, "You win. Bloody good show!"

'Even though Trevor attended regularly, and we all loved him, I felt we had to turn him down, and he understood why. It was discussed again shortly after he died, and one or two members of the Committee thought we might have been hasty. He was such a well-known figure, such an enthusiast, it was felt maybe the rules ought to be stretched on this one occasion.'

But in Howard's case there was a snag. While Helen had been happy for him to disappear there for days on end while he was alive, having his ashes deposited there was a different matter. And she had the final say. When Stephenson telephoned her with the news that their original decision had been overturned, Helen replied, 'My goodness, I'm awfully sorry, but it's too late. His ashes have been interred at St Peter's Church in Arkley.'

Stephenson told me, 'Trevor was Arkley's best-known resident for nearly forty years. It was only right that the village should be his final resting-place.' Later, checking through their records, the MCC made a startling discovery. Howard's membership of the club had lapsed. He had not paid his fees for several years. He was never asked to show his pass, because his face was instantly recognizable. Had his ashes been sprinkled at Lord's and the discrepancy over his membership come to light afterwards, the Committee would have ended up with egg on their faces. One almost wishes it had happened that way. Howard loved Lord's but objected to the off-putting formality of the place and to many of the regulations imposed by the men in charge. If he could have left behind a small problem for them, one suspects that he would have enjoyed that.

Howard's assets came to about £3 million, which went to Helen apart for a bequest of £100,000 for Clifton College. Through Helen, his connection with his old college continued each year. From his death in 1988 until 1997 she made the journey to Bristol every summer to present the Trevor Howard trophy to whichever house team won the cricket tournament. At the age of eighty-two, and with health problems of her own, she was forced to give up what had been since its inauguration an important date in her diary. Helen had not had much to do with Clifton before Howard's death, but she had developed a fondness for the college from his stories about the place. And it was in the chapel at Clifton where she held his memorial service.

Following the interment of Howard's ashes at St Peter's in Arkley, at a service attended by their closest friends, Helen turned her thoughts to organizing a memorial service for him. During David Niven's showbizzy send-off at St Paul's in Covent Garden, the church in London traditionally used for actors' memorials, Howard had whispered to her, 'What a bloody farce! Please, don't *ever* do this to me!' The more she thought about it, the less suitable a London venue seemed. Howard had never been a 'luvvie' actor. His friends were mostly from outside the profession. A service at Covent Garden would be inevitably have been high key and inappropriate for a man who hated glittering occasions in honour of either the living or the dead.

One evening, at dinner, after she had voiced her uncertainties to Norris McWhirter, he came up with the idea of Clifton College. 'Why not there?' he asked. Helen thought about it for a moment, and everything fell neatly into place. It was the perfect solution. The service was arranged for 14 May 1988. Explaining her decision to a television reporter in Bristol, Helen said, 'Trevor was so happy here. He never stopped talking about it all his life. He loved the time he spent here.' She used the occasion to announce the setting up of the £100,000 scholarship in his memory.

The memorial service at Clifton Chapel began at noon with the organist playing Sir William Walton's 'Crown Imperial'. This was followed by the Hubert Parry hymn, 'O Praise Ye the Lord', after which David Williams stepped up to the pulpit to read the lesson, taken from the Book of Ecclesiasticus, Chapter 44, Verses 1 to 15, which begins, 'Let us now praise famous men, and our fathers that begat us. The Lord hath wrought great glory by them through his great power from the beginning', and included the lines, 'their glory shall not be blotted out. Their bodies are buried in peace; but their name liveth for evermore.'

The service included two more hymns, 'Immortal Invisible' and 'Thou Whose Almighty Word', and readings by the Reverend Geoffrey Stratton, Vicar of St Peter's Church in Arkley, Norris McWhirter and Sir Geraint Evans, who gave an emotional reading of the Reverend Eli Jenkins's prayer from *Under Milk Wood* by Dylan Thomas, which ends, 'and Thou, I know will be the first, to see our best side not our worst . . . and to the sun we all will bow, and say goodbye but just for now'. Perhaps the most stirring moments of the service came with the playing of the tape of Howard's narration of the *son et lumière* at Bristol Cathedral, which he had recorded only weeks before he died.

Peter Bloore told me, 'Helen asked us to play it, because she found it very moving, particularly with the music behind him from a group of Belgian singers whose voices provided the perfect counterpoint to his own. We played it towards the end of the service, while everyone was still seated. It's one thing to talk about somebody after they've gone, but to hear their voice, to hear Trevor's magnificent voice, echo through the church at that service was extraordinary. What made it all the more moving was the fact that it closed the circle – his last recorded words ringing through Clifton College, where the Trevor Howard story had begun all those years before.'

THEATRE NOTES

Below, in chronological order, is a list of the plays in which Trevor Howard appeared.

1934

Revolt in a Reformatory. By Peter Martin Lampel. Gate Theatre, London. Produced by Peter Godfrey. The play provided an early stage role for Alastair Sim, who would star with Howard in the film *Green for Danger* in 1946.

The Drums Begin. By Howard Irving Young. Embassy Theatre, London. Produced by John Fernald.

Androcles and the Lion. By George Bernard Shaw. Open Air Theatre, Regent's Park, London. Produced by Robert Atkins. Anna Neagle, Jack Hawkins, Greer Garson, Martita Hunt and Hubert Gregg also took part in the 1933 season.

The Faithful. By John Masefield. Westminster Theatre, London. Produced by Norman Page.

Alien Corn. Westminster Theatre, London. Produced by Beatrice Wilson.

1935

The Rivals. By Richard Brinsley Sheridan. Q Theatre, London. Produced by Dennis Roberts.

Crime and Punishment. By Gaston Baty. Embassy Theatre, London. Produced by John Fernald.

Aren't We All? By Frederick Lonsdale. Royal Court Theatre, London. Produced by Harrison Culff.

Justice. By John Galsworthy. Playhouse Theatre, London. Produced by Leon M. Lion.

The Skin Game. By John Galsworthy. Playhouse Theatre, London. Produced by Leon M. Lion.

A Family Man. By John Galsworthy. Playhouse Theatre, London. Produced by Leon M. Lion. Leon M. Lion produced three John Galsworthy plays at the Playhouse Theatre between April and June 1935. *Justice* was premièred on 11 April. Lion appeared in it as Hector Frome; Howard played Walter How. On 2 May the second play of the trio, *The Skin Game*, had its first performance. Howard played Charles Hornblower. In *A Family Man*, which opened on 30 May, Howard played an unnamed newspaper reporter.

Lady Patricia. Based on *Mrs Patrick Campbell*. Westminster Theatre, London. Produced by John Wyse. Howard played opposite Phyllis Neilson Terry.

Legend of Yesterday. Aldwych Theatre, London.

Timon of Athens. By William Shakespeare. Westminster Theatre, London. Produced by John Wyse. This production had its première on 19 November 1935. Ernest Milton played Timon; Howard had a minor role, as Lucillus, a slave.

1936

Shakespeare Season, Shakespeare Memorial Theatre, Stratford-upon-Avon. The season included the following plays:

Romeo and Juliet. Produced and scenery designed by Randle Ayrton. Cast included Peter Glenville (Romeo), Pamela Brown (Juliet), Barbara Couper (Lady Capulet), Rosamund John (Lady Montague), Norman Wooland (Tybalt), Trevor Howard (Benvolio).

The Taming of the Shrew. Produced by B. Iden Payne. Cast included Peter Glenville (Petruchio), Barbara Couper (Katharina), Donald Wolfit (Tranio), Raymond Raikes (Lucentio), Norman Wooland (Hortensio), Rosamund John (Bianca), Trevor Howard (a Lord)

Hamlet. Produced by B. Iden Payne. Cast included Donald Wolfit (Hamlet), Eric Maxon (Polonius), Valerie Tudor (Ophelia), Raymond Raikes (Laertes), Donald Eccles (Horatio), Trevor Howard (Fontinbras), Norman Wooland (Claudius).

Troilus and Cressida. Produced by B. Iden Payne. Cast included Donald Eccles (Troilus), Pamela Brown (Cressida), Eric Maxon (Priam), Peter Glenville (Hector), Trevor Howard (Paris), Donald Wolfit (Ulysses).

King Lear. Produced by Theodore Komisarjevsky. Cast included Randle Ayrton (King Lear), Barbara Couper (Goneril), Buena Bent (Regan), Rosalind Iden (Cordelia), Raymond Raikes (King of France), Norman Wooland (Duke of Burgundy), Stanley Howlett (Duke of Cornwall), Donald Wolfit (Earl of Kent), Donald Eccles (Duke of Albany), Trevor Howard (Attendant to the Duke of Cornwall).

Julius Caesar. Produced by John Wyse. Cast included Donald Eccles (Julius Caesar), Peter Glenville (Marcus Antonius), Donald Wolfit (Cassius), James Dale (Brutus), Barbara Couper (Portia), Valerie Hall (Calpurnia), Trevor Howard (Octavius Caesar).

Much Ado About Nothing. Produced by B. Iden Payne. Cast included Donald Wolfit (Don Pedro), Norman Wooland (Don John), Peter Glenville (Claudio), James Dale (Benedick), Gerald Kay Souper (Leonato), Stanley Howlett (Antonio), Valerie Tudor (Hero).

The Merchant of Venice. Produced by B. Iden Payne. Cast included James Dale (Antonio), Raymond Raikes (Bassanio), Valerie Tudor (Portia), Pamela Brown (Jessica), Randle Ayrton (Shylock), Donald Wolfit (Gratiano), Trevor Howard (Salanio).

Twelfth Night. Produced by B. Iden Payne. Cast included Donald Wolfit (Orsino), Basil Langton (Sebastian), Barbara Couper (Olivia), Roy Byford (Sir Toby Belch), Geoffrey Wilkinson (Sir Andrew Aguecheek), James Dale (Malvolio), Trevor Howard (Fabian).

1936–7

French Without Tears. By Terence Rattigan. Criterion Theatre, London. Produced by Harold French. A then unknown cast included Rex Harrison, Jessica Tandy, Roland Culver, Kay Hammond, Robert Flemyng and Trevor Howard. The play, a new one, was premièred on 6 November 1936 and ran for 1,039 performances at the Criterion Theatre. Its transfer to New York was less successful. *French Without Tears*, again produced by Harold French, opened at the Henry Miller Theater, New York on 28 September 1937, starring Frank Lawton, Penelope Dudley Ward, Cyril Raymond and Guy Middleton (the only member of the original London cast to appear in the New York production). It ran for 111 performances.

Waters Of Jordan. Arts Theatre, London.

1938

A Star Comes Home. Arts Theatre, London.

1939

Shakespeare Season, Shakespeare Memorial Theatre, Stratford-upon-Avon. The season included the following plays:

Twelfth Night. Produced by Irene Hentschel. Cast included Michael Goodliffe (Orsino), Geoffrey Keen (Sebastian), Stanley Howlett (Antonio), Lesley Brook (Olivia), Joyce Bland (Viola), John Laurie (Malvolio), Jay Laurier (Sir Toby Belch), Alec Clunes (Sir Andrew Aguecheek), Dennis Roberts (Fabian).

The Taming of the Shrew. Produced by Theodore Komisarjevsky. Cast included Alec Clunes (Petruchio), Vivienne Bennett (Katharina), Geoffrey Keen (Lucentio), Trevor Howard (Tranio), Lesley Brook (Bianca), George Hagan (Hortensio), James Dale (Gremio).

Richard III. Produced by B. Iden Payne. Cast included John Laurie (Richard, Duke of Gloucester), James Dale (Duke of Buckingham), Alec Clunes (Henry, Earl of Richmond), Joyce Bland (Lady Anne), Geoffrey Keen (Duke of Clarence), Trevor Howard (Lord Hastings).

Othello. Produced by Robert Atkins. Cast included John Laurie (Othello), Joyce Bland (Desdemona), Alec Clunes (Iago), James Dale (Brabantio), John McCallum (Gratiano), Geoffrey Keen (Cassio), Michael Goodliffe (Lodovico), Betty Hardy (Emilia), Trevor Howard (Montano).

Much Ado About Nothing. Produced by B. Iden Payne. Cast included James Dale (Don Pedro), George Hagan (Don John), Alec Clunes (Benedick), Vivienne Bennett (Beatrice), Lesley Brook (Hero), Michael Goodliffe (Leonato), Stanley Howlett (Antonio), Trevor Howard (Borachio).

Coriolanus. Produced by B. Iden Payne. Cast included Alec Clunes (Coriolanus), Lesley Brook (Virgilia), Geoffrey Keen (Cominius), John Laurie (Sicinius Velutus), Dorothy Green (Volumnia), James Dale (Tullus Aufidius), Betty Hardy (Valeria).

The Comedy of Errors. Produced by Theodore Komisarjevsky. Cast included Michael Goodliffe (Solinus, Duke of Ephesus), Trevor Howard (Aegeon), G. Sheldon Bishop (Antipholus of Ephesus), James Dale (Antipholus of Syracuse), Joan Sanderson (Aemilia), Vivienne Bennett (Adriana), Andrew Leigh (Dronio of Ephesius), Dennis Roberts (Dromio of Syracuse), G. Kay Souper (Balthazar).

As You Like It. Produced by Baliol Holloway. Cast included James Dale (the Banished Duke), Sheldon Bishop (Duke Frederick), Geoffrey Keen

(Orlando), Vivienne Bennett (Rosalind), Lesley Brook (Celia), Jay Laurier (Touchstone), John Laurie (Jaques), Michael Goodliffe (Oliver), Trevor Howard (Charles, a Wrestler).

1939–40

Private Lives. By Noel Coward. Colchester Repertory Company, Colchester.

Cinderella. Colchester Repertory Company, Colchester. Trevor Howard played the Demon King, a role specially created for him by Bob Digsby. Derek Bond, who became a star of British films during the 1940s and 1950s, made his professional stage début in this pantomime as the Principal Boy.

1940

The Importance of Being Earnest. By Oscar Wilde. The White Rose Players, Harrogate, Yorkshire. Trevor Howard played Algernon opposite Dulcie Gray as Gwendolen.

Desire Under the Elms. By Eugene O'Neill. The White Rose Players, Harrogate, Yorkshire.

1941

Rope. By Patrick Hamilton. Dunbar, Scotland. Howard produced and appeared in this well-known thriller in an amateur production at the army camp while undertaking Officer Cadet training at Dunbar.

1943

The Recruiting Officer. By George Farquhar. Arts Theatre, London. Produced by Alec Clunes. A popular Restoration comedy by the Irish-born playwright perhaps best known for *The Beaux' Stratagem*, which he wrote shortly before his death at the age of twenty-nine. This production introduced Howard, as Captain Plume, to Helen Cherry, who played Sophie.

1944

A Soldier for Christmas. By Reginald Beckwith. Produced by Judith Furse. This play by Reginald Beckwith, who was also well known as an actor, was staged twice during 1944. Produced first at the Wyndham's Theatre, London, starring the Canadian actor Robert Beatty as the soldier, it was premièred on 3 February 1944 and had a continuous run of twenty-two weeks. It transferred to the Playhouse, London, on 6 September 1944 with a change of cast. Trevor Howard took over the part originally played by Beatty.

Anna Christie. By Eugene O'Neill. Arts Theatre, London. Produced by Judith Furse.

1947

The Taming of the Shrew. By William Shakespeare. New Theatre, London. Produced by John Burrell. This was a play from the Old Vic season in London. The Old Vic's premises was still damaged from wartime bombing, so the play transferred to the New Theatre. Howard starred as Petruchio, Patricia Burke was Katharina. It was a personal triumph for Howard. *The Times* review stated, 'We can remember no better Petruchio.'

1953

The Devil's General. By Carl Zuckmayer. Savoy Theatre, London. Produced by John Fernald. The German play was adapted by Robert Gore Browne and Christopher Hassell and received its première on 23 September 1953. Howard, as the Luftwaffe general Harras, was warmly praised. His batman, Korrianke, was played by Wilfrid Lawson, whom Howard had expressly requested be given the role. The play ran for seventy-seven performances.

1954

The Cherry Orchard. By Anton Chekhov. Lyric Theatre, , London. Produced by John Gielgud. Chekhov's play has enjoyed many revivals. This production, which opened on 21 May 1954, had Howard as Lopahin; Gwen Frangçon-Davies and Pauline Jameson were also in the cast. Among the theatre luminaries who warmly applauded Howard's performance were Michael Meyer, who thought it was the best Lopahin he had ever seen. Noel Coward noted in his diary: 'a magical evening in the theatre . . . every part perfectly played; we came away prancing on the tips of our toes'.

Two Stars for Comfort. By John Mortimer. Garrick Theatre, London. Produced by Michael Elliott. Mortimer wrote this play with Howard in mind to play Sam Turner, a riverside hotel proprietor with a wandering eye and a long-suffering wife. W.A. Darlington, the drama critic of the *Daily Telegraph*, wrote, 'I have never seen Trevor Howard do anything better or with more understanding.' The play ran for six months.

1964

The Father. By August Strindberg. Piccadilly Theatre, London. Produced by Caspar Wrede. Translated for the British stage by Michael Meyer, this version opened at the Piccadilly Theatre on 14 January 1964 after a short run at the Theatre Royal, Brighton. Later it transferred to the Queen's Theatre, London. Howard played the Captain; Joyce Redman played Laura. The *Guardian*'s theatre critic, Philip Hope-Wallace, wrote, 'Howard's study of pathological dissolution, so strongly and naturally conveyed that it seems inevitable, is what makes the evening memorable.' It had a run of sixty-three performances.

1971

Separate Tables. By Terence Rattigan. Excerpt, for a charity performance, to celebrate the knighthood of the playwright in the Queen's Honours List, published in June 1971, for 'services to the theatre'. Rattigan was the third playwright of the twentieth century to receive this honour. The others were Sir Arthur Pinero (1909) and Sir Noel Coward (1970).

1974

Waltz of the Toreadors. By Jean Anouilh. Haymarket Theatre, London. Produced by Peter Dews. Howard played General St Pé. His co-star was Carol Browne. The play was premièred on 14 February 1974.

1976

The Scenario. By Jean Anouilh. Royal Alexandra Theatre, Toronto. Produced by Stuart Burge. Howard played d'Anthac.

FILMOGRAPHY

The dates quoted denote the first year of general release. Howard's role is bracketed after his name.

1944

The Way Ahead (US title: *The Immortal Battalion*). GFD/Two Cities. Director: Carol Reed. Cast: David Niven, Stanley Holloway, Raymond Huntley, William Hartnell, James Donald, John Laurie, Leslie Dwyer, Hugh Burden, Jimmy Hanley, Renée Asherson, Penelope Dudley Ward, Reginald Tate, Leo Genn, Mary Jerrold, A.E. Matthews, Peter Ustinov, Tessie O'Shea (Trevor Howard played a naval officer, uncredited).

1945

The Way to the Stars (US title: *Johnny in the Clouds*). Two Cities. Director: Anthony Asquith. Cast: John Mills, Rosamund John, Michael Redgrave, Douglass Montgomery, Basil Radford, Stanley Holloway, Joyce Carey, Renée Asherson, Felix Aylmer, Bonar Colleano, Trevor Howard (Squadron Leader Carter), David Tomlinson, Jean Simmons.

Brief Encounter. Cineguild. Director: David Lean. Cast: Celia Johnson, Trevor Howard (Doctor Alec Harvey), Stanley Holloway, Joyce Carey, Cyril Raymond, Evelyn Gregg, Valentine Dyall, Irene Handl.

1946

I See a Dark Stranger (US title: *The Adventuress*). GFD/Individual. Director: Frank Launder. Cast: Deborah Kerr, Trevor Howard (Lieutenant David Baynes), Raymond Huntley, Norman Shelley, Michael Howard, Brenda Bruce, Liam Redmond, Brefni O'Rorke, James Harcourt, George Woodbridge, Garry Marsh.

Green for Danger. Rank/Individual. Director: Sidney Gilliat. Cast: Alastair Sim, Sally Gray, Rosamund John, Trevor Howard (Doctor Barnes), Leo Genn, Megs Jenkins, Judy Campbell, Moore Marriott, Ronald Adam, George Woodbridge, Henry Edwards.

1947

So Well Remembered. RKO/Alliance. Director: Edward Dymtryk. Cast: John Mills, Martha Scott, Trevor Howard (Doctor Whiteside), Patricia Roc, Richard Carlson, Reginald Tate, Beatrice Varley, Frederick Leister, Ivor Barnard.

They Made Me a Fugitive (US title: *I Became A Criminal*). Warner/Alliance. Director: Alberto Cavalcanti. Cast: Trevor Howard (Clem Morgan), Sally Gray, Griffith Jones, René Ray, Mary Merrall, Vida Hope, Ballard Berkeley, Phyllis Robins, Eve Ashley, Charles Farrell.

1949

The Passionate Friends (US title: *One Woman's Story*). GFD/Cineguild.

Director: David Lean. Cast: Ann Todd, Trevor Howard (Steven Stratton), Claude Rains, Betty Ann Davies, Isabel Dean, Arthur Howard, Wilfrid Hyde White, Guido Lorraine.

The Third Man. British Lion/London Films/David O. Selznick/Alexander Korda. Director: Carol Reed. Cast: Joseph Cotten, Alida Valli, Trevor Howard (Major Calloway), Orson Welles, Bernard Lee, Wilfrid Hyde White, Ernst Deutsch, Erich Ponto, Siegfried Brever.

1950

The Clouded Yellow. Sydney and Betty Box. Director: Ralph Thomas. Cast: Trevor Howard (David Somers), Jean Simmons, Barry Jones, Sonia Dresdel, Maxwell Reed, Kenneth More, André Morell, Geoffrey Keen, Michael Brennan, Gerard Heinz.

1951

The Golden Salamander. GFD/Pinewood. Director: Ronald Neame. Cast: Trevor Howard (David Redfern), Anouk Aimée, Herbert Lom, Miles Malleson, Walter Rilla, Jacques Sernas, Wilfrid Hyde White, Peter Copley.

Odette. Herbert Wilcox. Director: Herbert Wilcox. Cast: Anna Neagle, Trevor Howard (Captain Peter Churchill; codename Raoul), Peter Ustinov, Marius Goring, Bernard Lee, Maurice Buckmaster (as himself), Alfred Shieske, Gilles Queant.

Lady Godiva Rides Again. London Films/BLPA. Director: Frank Launder. Cast: Dennis Price, John McCallum, Stanley Holloway, Pauline Stroud, Gladys Henson, George Cole, Diana Dors, Bernardette O'Farrell, Eddie Byrne, Kay Kendall, Renée Houston, Dora Bryan, Sidney James (Trevor Howard made a brief guest appearance).

1952

An Outcast of the Islands. London Films. Director: Carol Reed. Cast: Trevor Howard (Peter Willems), Ralph Richardson, Kerima, Robert Morley, Wendy Hiller, George Coulouris, Frederick Valk, Wilfrid Hyde White, Betty Ann Davies, Peter Illing, James Kenney.

The Gift Horse (US title: *Glory at Sea*). British Lion/Molton. Director: Compton Bennett. Cast: Trevor Howard (Lieutenant-Commander Hugh Fraser), Richard Attenborough, Sonny Tufts, James Donald, Joan Rice, Bernard Lee, Dora Bryan, Hugh Williams, Robin Bailey, Meredith Edwards, John Forrest, Patric Doonan, James Kenney, Sidney James.

The Stranger's Hand (Italian title: *Mano del Straniero*). British Lion. Director: Mario Soldati. Trevor Howard (Major Court), Alida Valli, Richard Baseheart, Eduardo Cianelli, Stephen Murray, Richard O'Sullivan, Francis L. Sullivan, Giorgio Constantini.

1954

The Heart of the Matter. British Lion/London Films. Director: George More O'Ferrall. Cast: Trevor Howard (Harry Scobie), Maria Schell, Elizabeth Allan, Denholm Elliott, Peter Finch, Gerard Oury, George Coulouris, Earl

Cameron, Michael Hordern, Colin Gordon, Cyril Raymond, Orlando Martins, Evelyn Roberts, Gillian Lind.

The Lovers of Lisbon (French title: *Les Amants du Tage*) ECG/Fides. Director: Henri Verneuil. Cast: Daniel Gélin, Françoise Arnoul, Trevor Howard (Inspector Lewis), Ginette Leclerc, Marcel Dalio.

1955

Cockleshell Heroes. Columbia/Warwick. Director: José Ferrer. Cast: José Ferrer, Trevor Howard (Captain Thompson), Dora Bryan, Victor Maddern, Anthony Newley, Peter Arne, David Lodge, Walter Fitzgerald, Beatrice Campbell.

April in Portugal. Columbia/Warwick. Writer/director: Euan Lloyd. Travelogue about Portugal. Trevor Howard did the narration.

1956

Run for the Sun. United Artists/Russ-Field. Director: Roy Boulting. Cast: Richard Widmark, Jane Greer, Trevor Howard (Browne), Peter Van Eyck, Carlos Henning.

Around the World in Eighty Days. United Artists/Michael Todd. Directors: Michael Anderson, Kevin McClory. Cast: David Niven, Cantinflas, Robert Newton, Shirley Maclaine and a huge international cast including Trevor Howard (Fallentin).

1957

Manuela (US title: *Stowaway Girl*). British Lion. Director: Guy Hamilton. Cast: Trevor Howard (James Prothero), Elsa Martinelli, Pedro Armendariz, Donald Pleasence, Peter Illing, Leslie Weston, Jack MacGowran, Roger Delgado, Warren Mitchell.

Interpol (US title: *Pickup Alley*). Columbia/Warwick. Director: John Gilling. Cast: Victor Mature, Anita Ekberg, Trevor Howard (Frank McNally), Bonar Colleano, Dorothy Alison, André Morell, Martin Benson, Eric Pohlmann, Peter Illing, Sydney Tafler, Lionel Murton, Danny Green, Sidney James, Yana.

1958

The Key. Columbia/Open Road. Director: Carol Reed. Cast: William Holden, Sophia Loren, Trevor Howard (Chris Ford), Oscar Homolka, Kieron Moore, Bernard Lee, Beatrix Lehmann, Noel Purcell, Bryan Forbes, Russell Waters, James Hayter, Irene Handl.

The Roots of Heaven. Twentieth Century Fox. Director: John Huston. Trevor Howard (Morell), Juliette Greco, Errol Flynn, Eddie Albert, Orson Welles, Paul Lukas, Herbert Lom.

1960

Sons and Lovers. Twentieth Century Fox. Director: Jack Cardiff. Cast: Trevor Howard (Walter Morel), Wendy Hiller, Dean Stockwell, Mary Ure, Heather Sears, William Lucas, Donald Pleasence, Conrad Phillips, Ernest Thesiger, Rosalie Crutchley, Elizabeth Begley.

Moment of Danger (US title: *Malaga*) ABPC/Cavalcade. Director: Laslo Benedek. Cast: Trevor Howard (John Bain), Dorothy Dandridge, Edmund Purdom, Michael Hordern, Paul Stassino, John Bailey, Alfred Burke, Peter Illing, Barry Keegan.

1962

Mutiny on the Bounty. MGM/Arcola. Director: Lewis Milestone. Cast: Marlon Brando, Trevor Howard (Captain William Bligh), Richard Harris, Hugh Griffith, Tarita, Richard Haydn, Percy Herbert, Duncan Lamont, Gordon Jackson, Chips Rafferty, Tim Seely, Noel Purcell, Eddie Byrne.

The Lion. Twentieth Century Fox. Director: Jack Cardiff. Cast: William Holden, Trevor Howard (John Bullitt), Capucine, Pamela Franklin, Samuel Romboh, Christopher Agunda, Paul Oduor, Makara Kwaiha Ramadhani.

1964

Man in the Middle. Twentieth Century Fox/Pennebaker-Belmont. Director: Guy Hamilton. Cast: Robert Mitchum, Trevor Howard (Major Kensington), Keenan Wynn, Barry Sullivan, France Nuyen, Alexander Knox, Sam Wanamaker, Gary Cockrell, Robert Nicholls, Michael Goodliffe, Errol John, Paul Maxwell, Lionel Murton, Russell Napier, Edward Underdown, Howard Marion Crawford.

Father Goose. Universal-International/Granox. Director: Ralph Nelson. Cast: Cary Grant, Leslie Caron, Trevor Howard (Commander Frank Houghton), Jack Good, Nicole Felsette.

1965

Operation Crossbow (US title: *The Great Spy Mission*). MGM/Carlo Ponti. Director: Michael Anderson. Cast: George Peppard, Jeremy Kemp, Tom Courtenay, Richard Johnson, John Mills, Sophia Loren, Lilli Palmer, Anthony Quayle, Patrick Wymark, Trevor Howard (Professor Lindemann), Sylvia Sims, Richard Todd, Paul Henried, John Fraser.

Von Ryan's Express. Twentieth Century Fox. Director: Mark Robson. Cast: Frank Sinatra, Trevor Howard (Major Eric Fincham), Sergio Fantoni, Edward Mulhare, Brad Dexter, John Leyton, Wolfgang Preiss, James Brolin, John Van Dreelen, Adolfo Celli, Vito Scotti, Richard Bakalyan, Michael Goodliffe.

The Saboteur: Code Name Morituri. (US title: *Morituri*). Twentieth Century Fox. Director: Bernhard Wicki. Cast: Marlon Brando, Yul Brynner, Trevor Howard (Colonel Statler), Janet Margolin, Wally Cox, William Redfield, Carl Esmond.

The Liquidator. MGM. Director: Jack Cardiff. Cast: Rod Taylor, Trevor Howard (Colonel Mostyn), Jill St John, David Tomlinson, Wilfrid Hyde White, Derek Nimmo, Eric Sykes, Akim Tamiroff, Gabriella Licudi, John Le Mesurier, Jeremy Lloyd, Jennifer Jayne, Betty McDowell, Colin Gordon.

1966

The Poppy Is Also a Flower (General cinema release in UK. TV film only in USA; US title: *Danger Grows Wild.*). Director: Terence Young. Cast: Trevor Howard (Sam Lincoln), E.G. Marshall, Stephen Boyd, Eli Wallach, Marcello Mastroianni, Angie Dickinson, Yul Brynner, Rita Hayworth, Gilbert Roland.

1967

Triple Cross. Warner/Cineurop. Director: Terence Young. Cast: Christopher Plummer, Yul Brynner, Trevor Howard (as a civilian), Romy Schneider, Gert Fröbe, Claudine Auger.

The Long Duel. Rank Organisation. Director: Ken Annakin. Cast: Yul Brynner, Trevor Howard (Freddy Young), Charlotte Rampling, Harry Andrews, Virginia North, Andrew Keir, Laurence Naismith, Maurice Denham, Imogen Hassall, Zorah Segal, Paul Hardwick, Norman Florence.

Pretty Polly (US title: *A Matter Of Innocence*). Universal. Director: Guy Green. Cast: Trevor Howard (Robert Hook), Hayley Mills, Brenda de Banzie, Shashi Kapoor, Dick Patterson, Kalen Liu, Peter Bayliss, Patricia Routledge, Dorothy Alison.

1968

The Charge of the Light Brigade. United Artists/Woodfall. Director: Tony Richardson. Cast: Trevor Howard (Lord Cardigan), David Hemmings, Vanessa Redgrave, John Gielgud, Jill Bennett, Harry Andrews, Peter Bowles, Mark Dignum, Mark Burns, Alan Dobie, T.P. McKenna, Corin Redgrave, Norman Rossington, Howard Marion Crawford, Helen Cherry.

1969

The Battle of Britain. United Artists. Director: Guy Hamilton. Cast: Michael Caine, Christopher Plummer, Susannah York, Laurence Olivier, Ralph Richardson, Trevor Howard (Air Vice-Marshal Keith Park), Kenneth More, Robert Shaw, Patrick Wymark, Ian McShane, Curt Jurgens, Harry Andrews, Michael Redgrave, Nigel Patrick.

Twinky (US title: *Lola*). Rank Organisation. Director: Richard Donner. Cast: Charles Bronson, Susan George, Trevor Howard (the grandfather), Michael Craig, Honor Blackman, Lionel Jeffries, Elspeth March, Robert Morley, Jack Hawkins.

1970

Ryan's Daughter. MGM/EMI. Director: David Lean. Cast: Sarah Miles, Robert Mitchum, Trevor Howard (Father Hugh Collins), John Mills, Christopher Jones, Leo McKern, Barry Foster, Marie Keen, Evin Crowley, Archie O'Sullivan, Philip O'Flynn, Gerald Sim.

1971

Catch Me a Spy (US title: *To Catch a Spy*; French title: *Les Doigts Croises*).

Ludgate/Capitole/Bryna. Director: Dick Clement. Cast: Kirk Douglas, Trevor Howard (Sir Trevor Dawson), Tom Courtenay, Marlène Jobert, Patrick Mower.

The Night Visitor (US Title: *Salem Comes to Dinner*). Director: Laslo Benedek. Cast: Max von Sydow, Liv Ullmann, Trevor Howard (Police Inspector), Per Oscarsson, Rupert Davies.

Mary Queen of Scots. Universal. Director: Charles Jarrott. Cast: Vanessa Redgrave, Glenda Jackson, Trevor Howard (William Cecil, Lord Burghley), Patrick McGoohan, Nigel Davenport, Timothy Dalton, Daniel Massey, Ian Holm, Maria Aitken.

1972

The Offence (US title: *Something Like the Truth*). United Artists. Director: Sidney Lumet. Cast: Sean Connery, Trevor Howard (Lieutenant Cartwright), Ian Bannen, Vivien Merchant, Derek Newark, Peter Bowles, John Hallam.

Ludwig (French title: *Le Crépuscule des Dieux*). Studio. Director: Luchino Visconti. Cast: Helmut Berger, Romy Schneider, Trevor Howard (Richard Wagner), Silvana Mangano, Helmut Griem, Nora Ricci, Gert Fröbe, John Moulder Brown.

Pope Joan (US title: *The Devil's Imposter*). Big City Productions/Kurt Unger. Director: Michael Anderson. Cast: Liv Ullmann, Trevor Howard (Pope Leo), Olivia de Havilland, Maximilian Schell, Keir Dullea.

1973

A Doll's House. World Film Services/Les Filmes de la Boetie. Director: Joseph Losey. Cast: Jane Fonda, David Warner, Trevor Howard (Doctor Rank), Edward Fox, Delphine Seyrig, Anna Wing.

Craze. EMI. Director: Freddie Francis. Cast: Jack Palance, Diana Dors, Julie Ege, Edith Evans, Hugh Griffith, Trevor Howard (Superintendent Bellamy), Michael Jayston, Suzie Kendall, Martin Potter, Percy Herbert, Kathleen Byron.

1974

Eleven Harrowhouse (US title: *Anything for Love*). Twentieth Century Fox. Director: Aram Avakian. Cast: Charles Grodin, James Mason, Trevor Howard (Clyde Massey), John Gielgud, Candice Bergen, Peter Vaughan, Helen Cherry, Jack Watson, Jack Watling.

Persecution (US title: *The Terror of Sheba*). Tyburn. Director: Don Chaffey. Cast: Lana Turner, Ralph Bates, Olga Georges-Picot, Trevor Howard (Paul Bellamy), Suzan Farmer, Ronald Howard, Patrick Allen, Mark Weavers.

Who? (US Title: *Robo Man*). Director: Jack Gold. Cast: Elliott Gould, Trevor Howard (Colonel Azarin), Lyndon Brook, Joseph Bova, Ed Grover, James Noble.

1975

Conduct Unbecoming. British Lion. Director: Michael Anderson. Cast: Michael York, Stacy Keach, Trevor Howard (Colonel Benjamin Strang),

Christopher Plummer, Richard Attenborough, Susannah York, James Faulkner, James Donald.

Hennessy. AIP/Marseilles. Director: Don Sharp. Cast: Rod Steiger, Richard Johnson, Lee Remick, Trevor Howard (Commander Rice), Eric Porter, Peter Egan, Stanley Lebor, Ian Hogg.

1976

The Bawdy Adventures of Tom Jones. Universal. Director: Cliff Owen. Cast: Nicky Henson, Trevor Howard (Squire Western), Terry-Thomas, Arthur Lowe, Georgia Brown. Joan Collins, William Mervyn.

Aces High. EMI. Director: Jack Gold. Cast: Malcolm McDowell, Christopher Plummer, Simon Ward, Peter Firth, Trevor Howard (Colonel Silkin), John Gielgud, Richard Johnson, Ray Milland.

Slavers (German title: *Die Sklavenjäger*). Director: Jürgen Goslar. Cast: Trevor Howard (Alec Mackenzie), Ron Ely, Britt Ekland, Jürgen Goslar, Ray Milland.

Eliza Frazer (US title: *The Adventures of Eliza Frazer*). Director: Tim Burstall. Cast: Susannah York, Trevor Howard (Captain Foster Fyans).

1977

The Last Remake of Beau Geste. Universal. Director: Marty Feldman. Cast: Marty Feldman, Michael York, Ann-Margret, Peter Ustinov, Trevor Howard (Sir Hector Geste), James Earl Jones, Henry Gibson, Terry-Thomas, Roy Kinnear, Spike Milligan, Hugh Griffith, Irene Handl.

1978

Superman – The Movie. Warner Brothers/Alexander Salkind. Director: Richard Donner. Cast: Christopher Reeve, Margot Kidder, Jackie Cooper, Marlon Brando, Gene Hackman, Ned Beatty, Susannah York, Trevor Howard (First Elder), Valerie Perrine, Glenn Ford, Phyllis Thaxter, Harry Andrews, Maria Schell, Terence Stamp, Larry Hagman.

Stevie. First Artists/Grand Metropolitan. Director: Robert Enders. Cast: Glenda Jackson, Mona Washbourne, Trevor Howard (the Man), Alec McGowan, Emma Louise Fox.

1979

Meteor. Movielab. Director: Ronald Neame. Cast: Sean Connery, Natalie Wood, Karl Malden, Brian Keith, Martin Landau, Trevor Howard (Sir Michael Hughes), Henry Fonda.

Hurricane (US title: *Forbidden Paradise*). Dino De Laurentiis/Famous Films. Director: Jan Troell. Cast: Jason Robards Jr, Mia Farrow, Trevor Howard (Father Malone), Max von Sydow, Dayton Kane, Timothy Bottoms, James Keach.

1980

The Sea Wolves. Euan Lloyd. Director: Andrew V. McLaglen. Cast: Gregory Peck, David Niven, Roger Moore, Trevor Howard (Jack Cartwright), Barbara Kellerman, Patrick Macnee, Patrick Allen, Bernard Archard,

Faith Brook, Kenneth Griffith, Donald Houston.

Windwalker. Pacific International Enterprises. Director: Kieth Merrill. Cast: Trevor Howard (the Windwalker), Nick Ramus, James Remar, Serene Hedin, Dusty 'Iron Wing' McCrea.

Sir Henry at Rawlinson End. Charisma. Director: Steve Roberts. Cast: Trevor Howard (Sir Henry Rawlinson), Patrick Magee, Denise Coffey, J.G. Devlin, Harry Fowler, Sheila Reid.

1981

Light Years Away (French title: *Les Années Lumière*). Director: Alain Tanner. Cast: Trevor Howard (Yoshka Poliakoff), Mick Ford, Bernice Stegers, Henri Vorogeux.

1982

Gandhi. Columbia/Goldcrest. Director: Richard Attenborough. Cast: Ben Kingsley, Candice Bergen, Martin Sheen, Edward Fox, John Mills, John Gielgud, Trevor Howard (Judge Bloomfield), Ian Charleston.

Sword of the Valiant. Director: Stephen Weeks. Cast: Miles O'Keefe, Cyrielle Claire, Leigh Lawson, Sean Connery, Trevor Howard (King Arthur), Peter Cushing, Ronald Lacey, Douglas Wilmer, Lila Kedrova.

The Missionary. Handmade. Director: Richard Loncraine. Cast: Michael Palin, Maggie Smith, Denholm Elliott, Phoebe Nichols, Trevor Howard (Lord Ames), Michael Hordern, Rosamund Greenwood, David Suchet, Roland Culver, Graham Crowden.

1985

Dust. Daska Films/Flach Films. Director: Marion Hansel. Cast: Jane Birkin, Trevor Howard (Le Père), John Matshikiza, Nadine Uwampa, Lourdes Christina Sayo, René Diaz, Tom Vrebus.

1986

Foreign Body. Director: Ronald Neame. Cast: Victor Banerjee, Warren Mitchell, Trevor Howard (Doctor Stirry), Geraldine McEwan, Amanda Donohoe, Denis Quilley, Eve Ferret, Anna Massey, Stratford Johns.

1988

White Mischief. Director: Michael Radford. Cast: Charles Dance, Joss Ackland, Greta Scacchi, Sarah Miles, John Hurt, Geraldine Chaplin, Murray Head, Susan Fleetwood, Alan Dobie, Ray McAnally, Jacqueline Pearce, Trevor Howard (Jack Soames).

TELEVISION PRODUCTIONS

1954

Tonight at Eight/Still Life (US). Director: Otto Preminger. Cast: Trevor Howard (as Alec Harvey), Ginger Rogers.

The Flower of Pride (US). Director: Franklin Schaffner. Cast: Trevor Howard (role unknown), Geraldine Fitzgerald.

1962

Hedda Gabler (UK/US). Director: Alex Segal. Cast: Ingrid Bergman, Trevor Howard (Lovberg), Michael Redgrave, Ralph Richardson.

1963

The Invincible Mr Disraeli (US). Director: George Schaefer. Cast: Trevor Howard (Benjamin Disraeli), Greer Garson, Kate Reid, Hurd Hatfield, Denholm Elliott, Geoffrey Keen.

1965

The Poppy Is Also a Flower (released for the cinema as *Danger Grows Wild*) (see Films) (US).

Eagle in a Cage (US). Director: George Schäefer. Cast: Trevor Howard (Napoleon Bonaparte), Pamela Franklin.

1973

Catholics (UK/US). Director: Jack Gold. Cast: Martin Sheen, Trevor Howard (the Abbot), Cyril Cusack, Raf Vallone, Andrew Kier, Michael Gambon, Leon Vitale.

1975

The Count of Monte Cristo (US TV; released for the cinema in the UK). Director: David Greene. Cast: Richard Chamberlain, Tony Curtis, Louis Jourdan, Trevor Howard (Abbé Faria), Donald Pleasence, Taryn Power.

1978

Easterman (UK – *Scorpion Tales*). Director: David Reid. Cast: Trevor Howard (CID Inspector), Don Henderson, Patrick Allen.

1979

Night Flight (US). Director: Desmond Davies. Cast: Bo Svenson, Trevor Howard (Rivière), Celine Lomez.

The Shillingbury Blowers (UK). Director: Val Guest. Cast: Trevor Howard (Dan 'Saltie' Wicklow), Robin Nedwell, Diane Keen, Jack Douglas, Sam Kydd, John Le Mesurier.

1980

Staying On (UK). Director: Silvio Narizzano. Cast: Trevor Howard ('Tusker' Smalley), Celia Johnson.

1981

No Country for Old Men (UK). Director: Tristram Powell. Cast: Trevor Howard (Jonathan Swift), Cyril Cusack.

1983

Inside the Third Reich (US). Director: Marvin J. Chomsky. Cast: Rutger Hauer, Trevor Howard (Professor Heinrich Tessnow), John Gielgud, Maria Schell, Derek Jacobi, Randy Quaid, Stephen Collins, Ian Holm, Elke Sommer, Robert Vaughn.

The Deadly Game (US). Director: George Schaefer. Cast: George Segal, Trevor Howard (prosecuting counsel), Robert Morley, Emlyn Williams, Alan Webb.

George Washington (US). Director: Buz Pulick. Cast: Trevor Howard (Lord Thomas Fairfax).

1984

God Rot Tunbridge Wells (UK). Director: Tony Palmer. Cast: Trevor Howard (George Frederic Handel).

1985

Time After Time (UK). Director: Bill Hayes. Cast: John Gielgud, Googie Withers, Helen Cherry, Ursula Howells, Brenda Bruce, Trevor Howard (Brigadier 'Hippo' Croshawe).

This Lightning Always Strikes Twice (UK). Director: David Carson. Cast: Charles Dance, Trevor Howard (Sir Daniel Penwarden).

1986

Peter the Great (US). Director: Marvin J. Chomsky. Cast: Maximilian Schell, Vanessa Redgrave, Omar Sharif, Laurence Olivier, Mel Ferrer, Trevor Howard (Sir Isaac Newton), Hanna Schygulla, Lilli Palmer.

Sharka Zulu (South Africa). Director: Bill Faure. Cast: Christopher Lee, Edward Fox, John Carson, Roy Dotrice, Fiona Fullerton, Kenneth Griffith, Trevor Howard (Lord Somerset), Gordon Jackson, Robert Powell.

Christmas Eve (US). Director: Stuart Cooper. Cast: Loretta Young, Trevor Howard (Maitland), Ron Liebman, Arthur Hill, Patrick Cassidy, Season Hubley, Kate Reid.

1988

The Unholy (US). Director: Camilo Vila. Cast: Ruben Rabass, Nicole Fortier, Ned Beatty, Hal Holbrook, Trevor Howard (Father Silva).

The Dawning (UK). Director: Robert Knights. Cast: Anthony Hopkins, Rebecca Pidgeon, Jean Simmons, Trevor Howard (the Grandfather), Tara MacGowran, Hugh Grant, Adrian Dunbar.

Baines, Jocelyn, *Joseph Conrad*, Weidenfeld and Nicholson, London, 1959

Bogarde, Dirk, *Snakes and Ladders*, Chatto and Windus, London, 1978

Callan, Michael Feeney, *Richard Harris: A Sporting Life*, Sidgwick and Jackson, London, 1996

SELECT BIBLIOGRAPHY

Chapman, Caroline, *Russell of the Times*, Bell and Hyman, London, 1994

Downing, David, *Robert Mitchum*, W.H. Allen/Comet Books, 1985

Raymond, Durgnat, *A Mirror for England*, Faber and Faber, London, 1970

Eells, George, *Robert Mitchum*, Robson Books, London, 1984

Everson, William K., *Love in the Film*, Citadel Press, Secaucus, NJ, 1979

Falk, Quentin, *The Golden Gong*, Columbus Books, London, 1987

Fleming, Kate, *Celia Johnson*, Orion Books, London, 1991

James, Fox, *White Mischief*, Jonathan Cape, London, 1982

Gielgud, John, *An Actor and His Time*, Sidgwick and Jackson, London, 1979

Denis, Gifford, *The British Film Catalogue*, David and Charles, Newton Abbot, 1973

Godfrey, Lionel, *Cary Grant: The Light Touch*, Robert Hale, London, 1981

Grobel, Lawrence, *Conversations with Marlon Brando*, Bloomsbury, London, 1991

Hawkins, Jack, *Anything for a Quiet Life*, Elm Tree Books, London, 1973

Higham, Charles, *Brando*, Sidgwick and Jackson, London, 1987

Kaminsky, Stuart, *John Huston: Maker of Magic*, Angus and Robertson, London, 1978

Ephraim, Katz, *The International Film Encyclopedia*, Macmillan, London, 1982

Johnson, Jennifer, *The Old Jest*, Hamish Hamilton, London, 1979

Kelley, Kitty, *His Way*, Bantam Books, New York, 1987

Lejeune, Anthony (ed.), *The C.A. Lejeune Film Reader*, Carcanet, Manchester, 1991

Manso, Peter, *Brando*, Weidenfeld and Nicholson, London, 1994

Mason, James, *Before I Forget*, Sphere Books, London, 1992

McKern, Leo, *Just Resting*, Methuen Books, London, 1983

Meyer, Michael, *Not Prince Hamlet*, Secker and Warburg, London, 1989

Miles, Sarah, *Bolt from the Blue*, Orion Books, London, 1996

Miles, Sarah, *Serves Me Right*, Macmillan, London, 1994

Mills, John, *Up in the Clouds, Gentlemen Please*, Penguin Books, Harmondsworth, 1980

Milne, Tom, *Time Out Film Guide* (third edition), Penguin Books, Harmondsworth, 1993

More, Kenneth, *More or Less*, Hodder and Stoughton, London, 1978

Moss, Robert F., *The Films of Carol Reed*, Columbia University Press, New York, 1987

Munn, Michael, *Kirk Douglas: A Biography*, Robson Books, London, 1985

Perry, George, *Movies from the Mansion*, Pavilion Books, London, 1976

Perry, George, *The Great British Picture Show*, Paladin, St Albans, 1975

Redgrave, Michael, *In My Mind's Eye*, Weidenfeld and Nicholson, London, 1983

Richardson, Tony, *A Long Distance Runner*, Faber and Faber, London, 1993

Rotha, Paul, *Rotha on the Film*, Faber and Faber, London, 1958

Scott, Paul, *Staying On*, William Heinemann, London, 1977

Sellar, Maurice, *Best of British*, Sphere Books, London, 1987

Sherry, Norman, *The Life of Graham Greene*, Penguin Books, Harmondsworth, 1996

Shipman, David, *Marlon Brando*, Sphere Books, London, 1989

Silverman, Steven M., *David Lean*, André Deutsch, London, 1989

Thomas, Bob, *Brando*, W.H. Allen, London, 1973

Tookey, Christopher, *The Critics' Film Guide*, Boxtree Books, London, 1994

Walker, Alexander, *It's Only A Movie, Ingrid*, Headline Books, London, 1988

Wansell, Geoffrey, *Terence Rattigan*, Fourth Estate, London, 1995

Wapshott, Nicholas, *The Man Between*, Chatto and Windus, London, 1998

Woodham-Smith, Cecil, *The Reason Why*, Constable, London, 1953

Woodward, Ian, *Glenda Jackson*, Weidenfeld and Nicholson, London, 1985

INDEX